IS THIS THE END?

People are asking . . .

IS THIS THE END?

Signs of God's Providence in a Disturbing New World

DR. DAVID JEREMIAH

W PUBLISHING GROUP

AN IMPRINT OF THOMAS NELSON

Is This the End?
© 2016 David P. Jeremiah

Published in Nashville, Tennessee, by W Publishing Group, an imprint of Thomas Nelson.

Published in association with Yates & Yates, LLP, www.yates2.com.

Thomas Nelson titles may be purchased in bulk for educational, business, fund-raising, or sales promotional use. For information, please e-mail SpecialMarkets@ ThomasNelson.com.

ISBN 978-0-7180-9043-2 (ITPE)

Library of Congress Control Number: 2016946695

ISBN 978-0-7180-7986-4

Printed in the United States of America

16 17 18 19 20 RRD 10 9 8 7 6 5 4 3

CONTENTS

INTRODUCTION

In 2011, I wrote a book titled *I Never Thought I'd See the Day*. In that book I discussed the changes occurring in America that, in my younger days, I never dreamed possible. Throughout the first half or more of my life, the principles of Christianity provided the underpinnings of our culture. That foundation was laid two centuries earlier, and most of us thought it was too solid and enduring ever to crack.

But crack it did. As I wrote in that book, I never thought I'd see the day when marriage would be obsolete, morality would be in free fall, and the church would become irrelevant to society.

But now, only five years later, I almost think I wrote that book too soon. The changes that shocked me then were soon to grow even more appalling. In the ensuing half-decade since that book, those cracks that riddled America's foundation have spread into gaping fissures, and many more have appeared. Morality in the United States is no longer in free fall; it has hit bottom. In today's America, anything goes. Christianity is no longer merely pushed aside; American Christians are now experiencing overt repression and even persecution. Civility in politics and tolerance of opposing ideas has disappeared. Corruption and dishonesty in government is rampant and open. Race relations are deteriorating, earnings are declining, civic disorder is accelerating, and the national debt is beyond control.

We no longer feel safe in our world. Our national borders are being overrun. We have turned our back on our greatest ally; our other allies no longer trust us; our enemies no longer fear us; and the world no longer respects us. Our national leaders seem impotent in the face of a reconstituted, ambitious Russia; nuclear proliferation in rogue states; and the rise of militant terrorism.

Instability now plagues our world both nationally and internationally in ways we have not before witnessed in our lifetimes, creating a nationwide wave of anxiety and insecurity. According to Brookings Institution polls, 49 percent of Americans think our country's best days are in the past.[1]

So as you can see, many in our nation share my perception that our culture, security, morality, religion, economics, and civility are in the process of serious deterioration. In my conversations with people of all ages, races, and professions, I find deepening anxiety and even fear that things cannot go on as they are for long. It is clear to many people that ominous clouds are darkening our future and events are coming to a head. Many are asking, "Is this the end?"

Christians and secularists alike are asking this question. Christians wonder whether the end times prophesied in the book of Revelation are upon us. Is the rising disorder we are experiencing a precursor of the approaching Rapture of the church and the final return of Christ? Secularists wonder whether the nation is on the verge of collapse into economic, racial, and political anarchy; or whether a hostile nation such as Russia, China, or Iran might unleash its atomic fury on our cities; or whether militant Islamic terrorists flooding through our porous borders might inflict enough damage to bring us to our knees.

Our current anxiety reminds me of a story that came out of the Nazi blitz on London that began in late 1940. Londoners quickly set up an emergency system of air-raid sirens and bomb shelters. Children were later sent away to safety in other towns. But before this evacuation could be organized, children and adults alike had to endure the terrifying screams of falling bombs, the roar of planes overhead, the staccato bursts of antiaircraft gunfire, and the booming explosions of bombs destroying London targets.

One little girl was returning home from school when the sirens suddenly sounded. She knew what to do, for she had done it several times before. She dropped her books and ran headlong toward her home. Nazi planes buzzed low over the city. Royal Air Force gunfire shattered the air. A bomb exploded a block away. When she arrived home, her frantic father scooped her up and rushed the family to the nearest shelter. There they huddled in the darkness with other families as the terrifying cacophony of war raged outside.

The little girl clung to her father and said, "Daddy, can we please go somewhere where there isn't any sky?"

Perhaps you are wishing the same thing. The sky seems ready to fall, and you wonder whether there is any place left where you can feel safe. The sky fell on the Puritans of England when the authorities stifled their freedom to worship. They came to America and found the religious liberty they were looking for. Now it seems the sky may be falling in America, and when we look at the state of the world as a whole, we wonder if there is any place of refuge.

To most of us, it is clear that things cannot go on as they are, and we wonder, is everything we have known coming to an end? Is it too late to save our nation? Our world? Where can we go to find a realistic reason for hope?

These are questions I will address in this book. But to avoid the possible accusation that I am promising more than I can deliver, let me be quick to say that some of the answers we seek are hidden in the mind of God. Only He knows whether the flickering ember of

America's flame can be fanned back to life. And only He knows the timetable for Christ's return.

But the question "Is there hope?" I can answer with an unqualified and resounding yes! You must, however, take care that your hope is accurately placed.

America has been written off before. In the Revolution of 1776, many—possibly the majority—thought the patched-together citizen army of the Colonies was no match for the seasoned British troops. When the British captured Washington, DC, in 1814, many thought the fledgling nation had died an early death. In the dark days of the Civil War, many doubted whether the United States would survive intact. The same sense of doom marked the Great Depression of the 1930s. Even in the first years of World War II, the outcome was far from certain. But each time, the nation survived the crisis and surged forward with renewed strength.

Will America revive again? Will we reverse our descent and regain our respect, strength, and stability? Maybe, maybe not. But those are not the questions we really should be asking. If the survival of America and the stability of the world are the sources of your hope, then your hope is sadly misplaced. The question you must address is not whether America and the world will regain their footing, but how you will respond whether they do or not. That is what this book is about.

In my current interactions with people, I see four common responses to the growing fears about the future—three wrong and one right. The first wrong response is denial. Many people are burying their heads in the sand. They live in the illusion that nothing will change materially, refusing to heed the clouds gathering on the horizon. The second wrong response is despair. Collapse is inevitable. All is hopeless. Nothing can be done, and we are doomed. The clouds on the horizon have seeped into their souls, allowing their fear of tomorrow to darken their today. The third wrong response is one that Solomon warned us against. Death is knocking at the door, so let's pack into the time remaining all the pleasure we can "because a man has nothing better under the sun than to eat, drink, and be merry" (Ecclesiastes 8:15). None of these responses is productive. Not one of them offers hope.

The one right response is to look beyond the gathering storm to the one solid and certain source of hope—to God Himself. Hope in the future of America and the stability of the world is little more than wishful thinking. It is not reliable. The hope God offers is the only realistic, absolute hope that carries the promise of a certain outcome.

We do not know whether America will soon fall. We do not know when the Lord will return. But we do know that whatever our circumstances, God's desire for us is to live without anxiety and with hope. He offers you "thoughts of peace and not of evil," and He wants "to give you a future and a hope" (Jeremiah 29:11).

In this book I will show you how to find that hope. It is a hope that is not dependent on whether America falls or recovers or whether world order stabilizes or disintegrates. It is a hope that rises above trouble and chaos, enabling you to keep your focus on your future reward and endure whatever comes, whether good or evil, with grace and equanimity.

The added benefit of this hope is that those who exercise it before others set an example that may just make a difference in the outcome. Enough Christians exhibiting faith in God just might be the salt that saves America.

—Dr. David Jeremiah
San Diego, California
June 2016

PART I

IS THIS THE END FOR AMERICA?

CHAPTER 1

THE AGE OF ANYTHING GOES

On May 8, 2011, Tony Bennett walked across the stage of the Jacob Javits Center to sing a couple of ballads and open the program for a famous New York City charity. The full crowd before him was a glittering cosmos of New York's brightest celebrities. Bennett's timeless voice thrilled the house, and everyone marveled at the eighty-five-year-old crooner's enduring ability to charm an audience.

But later in the evening, it was Bennett himself who was charmed as he listened to a singer exactly sixty years his junior. He was swept off his feet by the clarion voice of Lady Gaga. Bennett later confessed to getting goose bumps listening to the power and clarity of her songs, and he became an instant fan. Meeting her backstage, Bennett regaled her with stories of his favorite songwriter, Cole Porter, and impulsively asked her to collaborate with him on a recording project.[1] The album, *Cheek to Cheek*, was released in 2014, and the opening song was Porter's "Anything Goes."[2]

It was an apt choice. "Anything Goes" is a bouncy, toe-tapping number—you can't help but smile as you hum the melody—but its words, written in 1934, celebrated the moral free fall of the American twentieth century. The song boasts of how times have changed and claims the Puritans are in for a shock. The lyrics brag that profanity and nudity are in vogue. For all its toe-tapping trendiness, "Anything Goes" represents the moral relativism that has infected our culture, leaving the West on the brink of spiritual collapse.

Ironically, it is a philosophy that ruined Porter's own life. The famous composer grew up on an Indiana farm. His mother went to church, but her young son was not impressed. "I never felt religion was serious to her," he recalled. "It was of no importance. She went to show off her new hats."[3]

Porter learned to play the violin at age six and the piano at age eight. With his mother's help, he published his first song at age ten. While attending Yale, he immersed himself in New York's glitzy nightlife and fell in love with the theater. He wrote his first Broadway show tune in 1915 and went on to provide crooners, such as Tony Bennett and Frank Sinatra, with dozens of hits—"I've Got You Under My Skin," "Night and Day," "Just One of Those Things," "Don't Fence Me In," and "I Get a Kick out of You."

His fans did not realize that his love songs were written for his boyfriends, that his marriage was a sham, or that his earnings financed an endless series of "anything goes" parties. "His life was a kind of theatre," recalls actor Kevin Kline. "He had an enormous appetite for pleasure, gastronomical and sexual. He was endlessly curious."[4]

Porter enjoyed popular acclaim, deep pockets, and four beautiful homes, each well-staffed and kept in perpetual readiness for his visits. His apartment in Paris was clad in platinum wallpaper with chairs upholstered in zebra skins. His nine-room suite at New York's Waldorf Towers was a virtual museum of his memorabilia and awards. He also kept an estate in Massachusetts and a home in California.[5]

Porter lived as he sang—"anything goes." But after being injured in an equestrian accident, he never regained his health or happiness.

He became reclusive and spent his last years depressed, diseased, drinking, and drugging. When his health declined to the point that he could no longer anesthetize himself with alcohol, he kept a cache of cigarettes nearby, saying, "It's all I have left."[6]

In 1964, Porter was wheeled into a California hospital for the last time. The nurse studied the patient, perhaps wondering how anyone so famous could look so cheerless. Clicking off the items on the questionnaire, the nurse came to the issue of the patient's religion.

"Put down none," replied Porter.

The nurse said, "Protestant?"

"Put down—none."

"Why not list Protestant?" asked a friend who knew Porter's mother had attended Baptist churches. But at Porter's insistence, the answer was a definite *none*. Shortly after being wheeled to his room, he sent someone to destroy his pornographic photographs. With that done, he died.

"He was terribly alone at the end," said a friend. "He really didn't have anything or anyone he was close to."[7]

His secretary lamented that her boss never found the strength that came from faith in God. "Without faith, one is like a stained glass window in the dark," she said. "How to reach his particular darkness," she added, "is an enigma."[8]

A similar darkness has descended on our world, and American culture now resembles that stained glass window through which no light is shining. We are living in a world where anything goes, but nothing satisfies. No matter how America's moral relativism is celebrated by songwriters and social pundits, it leaves people terribly alone at the end. That is why I grieve as I survey today's popular culture and why it is vital for Christ-followers to resist the siren calls of our increasingly decadent age.

THE EXPRESSION OF OUR MORAL DECLINE

The Bible anticipated that decadent times like our present age would come. In speaking of His second coming, the Lord Jesus said, "But as the days of Noah were, so also will the coming of the Son of Man be" (Matthew 24:37).

What were those "days of Noah" like? Genesis 6:5 tells us: "Then the Lord saw that the wickedness of man was great in the earth, and that every intent of the thoughts of his heart was only evil continually." This is a description of the society swept away by the Flood.

In his book about the days of Noah, Jeff Kinley wrote:

> If the Bible is correct in stating that earth's entire population was thinking only about evil 24/7, certainly those evil thoughts would have included sexual promiscuity, adultery, and perversion, as well as rape, prostitution, homosexuality and lesbianism, and pedophilia. Does that sound extreme or far-fetched? Considering that most of these aberrations and perversions have been prevalent among us since Noah's day, it's not a stretch to imagine how prominent they would have been in a world without any moral compass or restraint.[9]

Perhaps America has not yet sunk to the lows of Noah's day. But as I say in my book *I Never Thought I'd See the Day*, "Our moral compass seems no longer to have a 'true north.' The needle spins crazily, looking for a direction on which to settle."[10]

Second Timothy 3:1–5 says,

> But know this, that in the last days perilous times will come: For men will be lovers of themselves, lovers of money, boasters, proud,

blasphemers, disobedient to parents, unthankful, unholy, unloving, unforgiving, slanderers, without self-control, brutal, despisers of good, traitors, headstrong, haughty, lovers of pleasure rather than lovers of God, having a form of godliness but denying its power.

The description of Noah's generation and Paul's prediction of the generation that will introduce the last days summarize the depravity of man—yes, even the total depravity of man. I know that *total depravity* is a controversial term and certainly one that is often misunderstood.

Total depravity does not mean, as most people think, that human beings are as depraved as they could possibly be. This would, by necessity, mean that there is no good in humans at all. But we know this is not the case. Not all human beings are drunkards, felons, adulterers, or murderers. Many are noble, generous, self-sacrificing, highly moral, and loving. Total depravity defines the extent, not the degree, of our sinfulness. In other words, while our depravity does not make us as bad as we could be, it does affect us in every area of our being, corrupting every part of our humanness at varying degrees.

Charles Swindoll wrote:

If depravity were blue, we'd be blue all over. Cut us anywhere and we'll bleed blue. Cut into our minds and you'll find blue thoughts. Cut into our vision and there are blue images full of greed and lust. Cut into our hearts and there are blue emotions of hatred, revenge, and blame. Cut into our wills and you'll find deep blue decisions and responses.[11]

Further, J. Dwight Pentecost explained:

The doctrine of depravity has to do, not with man's estimation of man, but rather with God's estimation of man. We are the heirs of generations of the teaching of evolution which sees man in an ever-ascending spiral, rising higher and higher from the depth from which he has sprung, until finally he will reach the stars. So widely accepted is that concept that we have come somehow to feel that there is so much good in the worst of us that man is not so bad off after all. When we measure men by man, we can always find someone who is lower that we are on the moral or ethical scale, and the comparison gives us a feeling of self-satisfaction. But the Scriptures do not measure men by man; they measure men by God who has created them. The creature is measured by the Creator and is found to be wanting.[12]

Human depravity is a symptom of our isolation from God, which occurred at the fall when man and woman rejected God's Spirit and chose to follow their own desires. Without God at the wheel of the human heart, we are like a driverless car careening down the freeway. A crash is inevitable.

This depravity, or godlessness, is the root cause of America's moral decline. We grasp for what feels good instead of what *is* good. Our depravity manifests itself in several ways. Let's look at a few examples.

Depravity in Our Minds

In January 2016, the Internet's largest online pornography site released its annual statistics. On just this one website in just one year—2015—consumers watched 4,392,486,580 hours of pornography. Convert those hours into years, and it means those people collectively spent more than 500,000 years watching porn.

On this particular site in 2015 alone, people watched 87,849,731,608 X-rated videos. Over 87 billion! That's twelve videos for every man, woman, boy, and girl on the planet.

In reporting these statistics, Jonathon van Maren warns that much of this pornography was "rough-stuff" and "driven by the market." He says, "People wanted to watch women humiliated. Beaten. Violated. Millions and millions of them. . . . We need to take this seriously, or our churches will drown in a sea of filth right along with the rest of the culture."[13]

It gets even worse. It is estimated that over a quarter of Internet pornography is child-related.[14] I was sickened when I read about the prevalence of child pornography in our nation. According to a CNN article, the United States is home to more commercial child porn websites than anywhere else on earth.[15] Every day, 116,000 Internet queries are related to child pornography, and each year 300,000 or more children in the United States are forced into the commercial sex trade. Some 68 percent of children trafficked into the sex trade have been in the care of social services or foster care; and one out of every ten children will be the victim of sexual abuse in our country.[16]

The emotional scars from such abuse last a lifetime. A recent Australian study found that "young people who had experienced child sexual abuse had a suicide rate that was 10.7 to 13.0 times the national Australian rate. . . . Thirty-two percent of abused children had attempted suicide."[17]

The other side of the child pornography issue has to do with innocent children inadvertently stumbling onto lurid material on their home or school computers. Many children grow up with constant exposure to porn, which blinds them to its dangers. A Barna study found that most teenagers are so acclimated to the culture that they believe not recycling is more immoral than pornography.[18]

Pornography and child abuse are not the only symptoms of our sex-laden society. There is sexting, the practice of sending explicit pictures of oneself over mobile phones. It has become a phenomenon among teenagers and young adults, with surveys showing 62 percent of teens and young adults have received a sexually explicit image, and 41 percent have sent one.[19]

The young Jewish writer and political commentator Ben Shapiro wrote in his book *Porn Generation*, "I am a member of a lost generation. We have lost our values. . . . In a world where all values are equal, where everything is simply a matter of choice, narcissism rules the day. . . . The mainstream acceptance of pornography has become a social fact."[20]

I do not have space to describe the sex, violence, and addictive nature of some of today's video games and interactive digital entertainment. And look at what is on television—not just on the cable stations, but also on the major networks. On second thought, don't look! Every season gets worse. Sometimes I just shake my head in near despair and say, "What's next?"

In Noah's day, every thought and intent of the heart was evil continuously, and now we have the technology to take the most lurid fantasies of the human mind and project them onto a screen a child can hold in his or her hand. All this has led to the coarsening of Western culture. We have become a profane people, with fewer and fewer restraints on behavior and language and with a diminishing respect for human life.

Depravity in Our Marriages

In the 2015 case of *Obergefell v. Hodges*, the Supreme Court of the United States, in a 5-to-4 vote, took it upon itself to "redefine" marriage to include committed relationships between same-sex couples. I put "redefine" in quotation marks because the inherent definition of marriage cannot be altered by any human agency.

God Himself defined the marriage covenant in Genesis 2, in the garden of Eden, long before human governments were established. He originated the ordinance of marriage before the Mosaic law was given, before the State of Israel existed, before the church was founded, and before any church council ever met. The Lord established the formula for marriage before any of these institutions came into existence, and it is every bit as inviolable as the law of gravity or the axioms of physics.

Jesus described marriage like this: "From the beginning of the creation, God 'made them male and female. For this reason a man shall leave his father and mother and be joined to his wife, and the two shall become one flesh'; so then they are no longer two, but one flesh" (Mark 10:6-8). In other words, marriage is marriage only when it involves the merging of two beings with complementary attributes designed specifically for the purpose of oneness. God ordained marriage as a lifelong covenant between these two beings—one man and one woman—and this is the only proper, God-given arena for the exercise of sexual relations.

We cannot control what a secular society does, but as Christians we can demonstrate a better way and let the Word of God govern our own convictions and conduct. Nevertheless, the Court's ruling on *Obergefell v. Hodges* undeniably puts Bible believers in a tough spot. Justice Samuel A. Alito Jr., in his dissent to the majority opinion, predicted this decision would become a basis for aggressive legal discrimination against those who hold a biblical view of marriage:

> It will be used to vilify Americans who are unwilling to assent to the new orthodoxy. In the course of its opinion, the majority compares traditional marriage laws to laws that denied equal treatment for African-Americans and women. The implications of this analogy will be exploited by those who are determined to stamp out every vestige of dissent.[21]

As you will see in the third chapter of this book, titled "The Increase of Intolerance," Justice Alito's warning was dead-on prophetic.

Depravity in Our Military

As I was writing this chapter, I read about a POW/MIA display at a Veteran's Administration clinic in Akron, Ohio. Among the displayed items was a Bible, which is historically appropriate, for I have read many testimonies telling how POWs endured their captivity only because the Word of God sustained them. Yet the VA removed the Bible because of protests from secularists. The space on the display table is now empty, a silent witness to the intolerance of those determined to rid American society of scriptural influence.[22]

Bible-believing members of our armed forces face new restrictions on expressing their religion, and our military chaplains are on the front lines of intense politically correct pressure. While there is no official policy banning voluntary prayer, religious services, or pastoral counseling at this point, there have been several instances where Christian chaplains have run into politically correct buzz saws for praying in Jesus' name, counseling from a Christian perspective, and expressing biblical standards for sexuality.

As John J. Murray, a minister with the Free Church of Scotland, wrote, "We are back to the situation as it was in the days of the early church. . . . The Roman Empire, under which so many Christians were martyred, was pluralistic and supremely tolerant of religion. The only people they could not tolerate were the Christians."[23]

Depravity in Medicine

Dr. Paul Church is one of Boston's most-loved physicians, a urologist who invested twenty-eight years practicing medicine at Beth Israel Deaconess Medical Center and teaching at Harvard University.

Recently hospital officials noticed that on the hospital's online portal Dr. Church had posted his concern about the very real and well-documented health dangers of same-gender sexual activity. Hospital administrators instructed him to discontinue expressing his views, a demand he viewed as a gag order and a violation of his public and private rights under the Massachusetts Civil Rights Act. "Celebrating sexual perversions is highly inappropriate," he wrote in response, "especially in the context of a medical center that should be aware of the negative health consequences of high risk behaviors."

In September 2014, the hospital launched a formal investigation into Dr. Church's views, the beginning of a long and losing battle for him. He has now been expelled from the hospital.[24]

Perhaps the most glaring example of depravity in medicine is what is called the "abortion industry." Since the Supreme Court legalized abortion in 1973, well over 58 million babies have been legally murdered. According to research by the Guttmacher Institute, the rate of US abortions since 1975 has been consistently over one million per year.[25]

Space will not permit me to survey many other areas of societal moral decay—the loss of ethics in business; the breakdown of family life and the out-of-wedlock birthrate; the loss of the concept of fatherhood in our society; the rampant materialism that is driving us ever deeper into debt; substance abuse, alcoholism, and runaway addictive disorders; the lack of civility in public discourse; racial tensions; the doping scandals in sports; gambling and gaming; cheating and bullying; and our crime rates and prison populations. Even our comic book superheroes have become grittier, grimmer, and darker as the lines between good and evil have blurred and broken.

In his book *Vanishing Grace*, Philip Yancey summarized the moral free fall of our nation:

In my own lifetime the divorce rate has doubled, the rates of teen suicide and violent crime have both tripled, and births out of wedlock have sextupled. With less than 5 percent of the world's population, the US has almost a quarter of the world's prisoners (about the same number as Russia and China combined). We have become accustomed to homeless people sleeping in parks and under bridges, something virtually unknown in my childhood. The leading causes of death are self-inflicted, the side-effects of tobacco, obesity, alcohol, sexually transmitted diseases, drugs, and violence.[26]

THE EXPLANATION FOR OUR MORAL DECLINE

It's time to ask the question: How did Western morality stray onto such a slippery slope? What happened to us? I can explain it in two ways: historically and biblically.

The Explanation from History

The historical explanation dates back to the eighteenth-century Enlightenment. Throughout the Middle Ages, the Western world, for all its darkness and depravity, at least had an understanding of objective truth. The existence of God was taken for granted, which provided a basis for belief in absolute values of right and wrong. The Reformation of the 1500s set this truth on fire. But hard on the heels of the Reformation, the secular thinking of the Enlightenment (or the Age of Reason) radiated from France like a force field across Europe and to the New World.

Many of the Enlightenment thinkers could not totally shake off belief in the existence of God, but they dispatched Him to insignificance by promoting a religion of deism, the teaching that the Creator, if He exists, is disinterested and uninvolved with the world. They believed humans were the true moral force in the universe and, as Voltaire's friend Marie-Jean-Antoine-Nicolas de Caritat wrote, in "the idea of the limitless perfectibility of the human species."[27] He believed this new doctrine would deliver the final blow to religion.

As philosophy detached itself from religion, morality was liberated from divine authority. This newfound "freedom" and doctrine of the perfectibility of humanity set the stage for all kinds of mischief—the Communist movement of Karl Marx, the theological liberalism of Julius Wellhausen, and the evolutionary hypotheses of Charles Darwin. The unifying belief, which laid the foundation for the philosophy of secularism, is this: God, if He exists, is irrelevant. Humanity is calling the shots, and humans are evolving biologically, socially, governmentally, and morally. Forget about answering to a holy Creator. We are responsible for ourselves, and we can now govern our morality by societal consensus.

Darwin's evolutionary ideas spread to all other areas of thought, including non-scientific philosophical arenas. We are constantly changing and forever evolving, said the "enlightened" thinkers, and that includes our values. Darwinian morality—the dog-eat-dog philosophy of survival of the fittest—replaced biblical codes of conduct and character.

Dave Breese, in his book *Seven Men Who Rule the World from the Grave*, wrote:

> The early 1900s was the first era in which Darwin and his ideas had come to full flower. By that time, evolution was well on its way to capturing the world of academia and the thought processes of the average man. Virtually everyone believed that history was moving up from the gross and the animalistic into the sublime and even

the angelic. . . . Social Darwinism was fast persuading society . . . that no problem was unsolvable, no difficulty unresolvable. Given enough time, all would be well. Humanity had within it a potential that would not be denied.[28]

The rising tide of humanistic secularism was shoehorned into America's educational system by John Dewey, a shy, bookish educator who hailed from Vermont. Dewey's core principle was the rejection of absolute, unchangeable truth. Final truth, he believed, was illusionary.[29] Breese explained, "This humanism, of which Dewey was a fountainhead . . . became pervasive in our American schools, especially on the graduate level. From that point on, the ruling point of view in American education was that there was no ruling point of view."[30]

About that time the American judicial system entered the picture and began mandating secularism almost as though it were the nation's new official religion. The famous *Scopes* trial in Dayton, Tennessee, in 1925 galvanized sympathy for teaching evolution in schools. In 1963, the US Supreme Court prohibited school officials from organizing or leading Bible reading or prayer exercises in schools. Two subsequent generations have shown us how well that has worked out.

Against this backdrop, moral relativism entered pop culture with a vengeance between the 1920s and 1960s, setting the stage for the sexual revolution of the 1960s through the 1980s. Hollywood jumped on the bandwagon, and America's moral values turned downward like the economic charts of the Great Depression.

In the meantime, secularism—the removal of theism or God-consciousness from public life—has become America's *de facto* religion. "A secular world-view," writes my friend, Ravi Zacharias, "is admittedly and designedly the underlying impetus that presently propels Western culture."[31]

As Os Guinness puts it, secularization is "the process by which religious ideas, institutions, and interpretations have lost their social significance."[32]

Albert Mohler helpfully summarizes how we got where we are today. In the premodern age of antiquity and the medieval period, it was *impossible not to believe*. There was no intellectual alternative to belief in God. In the modern age, it became *possible not to believe* as philosophers began to posit alternatives. Nowadays secularists are asserting it is *impossible to believe*. The alternatives to God have become dominant. Christians have become "intellectual outlaws" in the secular world, says Mohler. "Secularism in America has been attended by a moral revolution without precedent and without endgame. . . . The story of the rise of secularism is a stunning intellectual and moral revolution."[33]

There are more causes for the collapse of Western morality, of course—many more names and many more movements. While I have given only an abbreviated outline of the collapse, it is not a simplistic one. It is a history of ideas, and ideas matter; each follows the other like dominoes falling in a successive line through the decades from the Enlightenment to today. One thinker put it this way:

> Our society, once rightly called a Christian civilization, has become secular to a greater degree than the solons of Western civilization would have thought possible. Education, government, business, the media, and, in many cases, religion, have moved through progressive stages of secularization from Christianity to atheism. As a result, God is not merely ignored but rather is resented, opposed, and vilified at every opportunity. With unimaginable arrogance, our society has declared Jesus Christ to be *persona non grata* in the culture. Concomitantly, the Bible has lost its final authority, the

Christian religion has been pluralized, the family is fast disappearing, and morals are at low ebb.[34]

In short, there is no telling where a society will end up when "anything goes." Or rather, we *do* know where such a culture ends up. Sooner or later it circles around to the days of Noah.

The Explanation from the Bible

There is another way of understanding the destruction of our national morality. We need to view our times not just through the lens of history, but also through the lens of Scripture. Although history traces the philosophical decline of our moral foundations from medievalism to postmodernism, the true explanation is found in humanity's rebellion against the holy character of God as explained in His Word. If you really want to understand what is happening to Western morality today, trace the theological chain from the rejection of the Creator to total moral collapse as Paul described it in Romans 1:18–32.

This passage presents the clearest domino theory in the Bible—except it is no theory. It is an infallible analysis of how a society spirals into the sewers like bathwater draining from the tub. Paul's explanation sets the stage for his classic presentation of the doctrine of justification by grace through faith, which is the theme of the book of Romans and the only hope for the human heart.

A culture begins to collapse, Paul said, when it rejects the reality of creationism and of a Creator:

> For the wrath of God is revealed from heaven against all ungodliness and unrighteousness of men, who suppress the truth in unrighteousness, because what may be known of God is manifest in them, for

God has shown it to them. For since the creation of the world His invisible attributes are clearly seen, being understood by the things that are made, even His eternal power and Godhead, so that they are without excuse. (Romans 1:18–20)

The existence of a Creator is obvious when we study creation itself. Its very existence and its intricate design shout the necessity of an intelligent source. How intricate is creation? Consider this: You are probably sitting down right now while reading this book, perhaps in an easy chair or in a coffee shop. Or maybe you are standing in line, waiting to board a flight, or stretched out in bed with this book propped on your chest. You may think you are still and stationary, but you are actually hurtling through space at a fantastic speed.

Our Milky Way galaxy is rotating at almost 140 miles per second while speeding through the universe at nearly 190 miles a second like a roller coaster spinning while plunging down its tracks. In the minute it has taken to read this paragraph, you have actually traveled thousands of miles. What's more, you are spinning on a globe that is revolving on its axis at the speed of nearly 1,000 miles an hour and orbiting the sun at a speed of 66,000 miles per hour. If you had a plane capable of that speed, you would travel across the United States in three minutes.[35] Yet God has so fine-tuned the ride that you feel no movement at all. One slight miscalculation in these intricately inter-related movements would doom everything to a gigantic cosmic train wreck, yet everything moves with the precision of a vast machine designed by a master engineer.[36]

Whether looking through a telescope or a microscope, I am amazed at the symmetry, the scope, and the systematic order of creation. As Psalm 19:1 tells us, the universe itself makes the existence of God too obvious to deny: "The heavens proclaim the glory of God.

The skies display his craftsmanship" (NLT). This glory and complexity confirm the Bible's assertion in Psalm 14:1: "The fool has said in his heart, 'There is no God.'"

The bottom-line reason for humanity's rejection of this obvious evidence is that the existence of a Creator implies His authority over all His creation. If we are subject to a Maker, we are not autonomous, for morality is intrinsically rooted in His holy character. We cannot live however we would like, nor should we. God's personal purity supplies a moral baseline for the universe and provides the guidelines by which we live healthy and holy lives.

To escape these implications, our society has chosen to believe the unbelievable—that everything came from nothing in an unexplainable explosion of dense matter with an inexplicable origin; that primordial sludge was jolted from death to life; that molecules developed from randomness into complexity; and that human beings are the resulting accidents—mere pieces of carbon destined to die as quickly as we arose, living in a universe without purpose and facing a future without ultimate hope. That is the foundation of secularism, and it leads downward in belief and behavior. Here are the downward steps as the apostle Paul described them.

Ingratitude

Paul wrote, "Although they knew God, they did not glorify Him as God, nor were *thankful*, but became futile in their thoughts, and their foolish hearts were darkened" (Romans 1:21).

Idolatry

Paul went on to say in Romans 1:22–23, "Professing to be wise, they became fools, and changed the glory of the incorruptible God into an image made like corruptible man—and birds and four-footed animals and creeping things."

God created the human heart with a vacuum that can only be filled by the love of God. That hole demands to be filled with something, and when we reject the true God, we inevitably form other gods to fill it. That is called idolatry.

In antiquity—even today, in some societies—idolatry meant worshipping statues, images, and fetishes. But you do not have to bow down to a stone statue to be an idolater. An idol is whatever comes first in your life. Anything that comes before Jesus Christ in your affections or priorities—that is your idol. In Colossians 3:5, the apostle Paul told his readers, "Therefore put to death your members which are on the earth: fornication, uncleanness, passion, evil desire, and covetousness, which is idolatry." In our materialistic age, millions of people are serving the god of money, possessions, and the accumulation of wealth. When our desire for financial success overshadows our love for God, it becomes just as idolatrous as bowing before a man-made image. Our goals, ambitions, dreams, obsessions, addictions, pleasures, or opinions can become our gods.

Even our families, children, or loved ones can become our idols. Jesus said, "He who loves father or mother more than Me is not worthy of Me. And he who loves son or daughter more than Me is not worthy of Me. And he who does not take his cross and follow after Me is not worthy of Me. He who finds his life will lose it, and he who loses his life for My sake will find it" (Matthew 10:37–39).

Make no mistake—when we reject the Creator-God of Scripture, we must find a substitute. When we reject God, we turn away from His love and provision and become our own god.

Donald Baillie helps us visualize what happens when we turn

away from God's love. He pictured humanity standing in a circle facing God at the center:

> In that circle we ought all to be standing, linked together with lovingly joined hands, facing towards the Light in the centre, which is God; seeing our fellow creatures all around the circle in the light of that central Love, which shines on them and beautifies their faces; and joining with them in the dance of God's great game, the rhythm of love universal. But instead of that, we have, each one, turned our backs upon God and the circle of our fellows, and faced the other way, so that we can see neither the Light at the centre nor the faces on the circumference. And indeed in that position it is difficult even to join hands with our fellows! Therefore instead of playing God's game we play, each one, our own selfish little game. . . . Each one of us wishes to be the centre, and there is blind confusion, and not even any true knowledge of God or of our neighbors. That is what is wrong.[37]

Immorality

Paul continued in Romans 1:24–25 with this: "Therefore God also gave them up to uncleanness, in the lusts of their hearts, to dishonor their bodies among themselves, who exchanged the truth of God for the lie, and worshiped and served the creature rather than the Creator, who is blessed forever. Amen."

When we give up the true God of heaven, all other gods lead to an erosion of morality, to sensuality, to sexual sins, and to lust-driven lives. In fact, this passage says that God gives people up to this kind of depravity. How can a loving God give people up to the evils they choose? As I say in *The Jeremiah Study Bible*, "He gives them up only after an adequate revelation of His being (Romans 1:20). He does not cause anyone's demise; the natural law of consequences does. He cannot abide in the presence of sin, which is why He abandoned His own Son at Calvary as Christ bore the sins of the world."[38]

How sad to follow this downward course when God offers us an upward path. But when we step off of His path, the steps keep descending toward the days of Noah.

Iniquity

When a culture denies its Creator, worships its own gods, and succumbs to a lust-driven existence, it inevitably becomes overly sexualized. Paul put it plainly: "For this reason God gave them up to vile passions. For even their women exchanged the natural use for what is against nature. Likewise also the men, leaving the natural use of the woman, burned in their lust for one another, men with men committing what is shameful, and receiving in themselves the penalty of their error which was due" (Romans 1:26–27).

The headlines of recent years are simply our society's commentary on this passage. This downward spiral of indecency leads finally to the cesspit of debauchery—total moral collapse. Dr. Donald Grey Barnhouse weighed in on these verses, marking the downward steps to their inevitable end:

The last nine verses in the first chapter of Romans are the most terrible in the Bible. This is the description of mankind abandoned by God and the scene is a frightful one. The cause of the abandonment was the successive departure from God by the human soul in the successive steps of desertion that began with a failure to acknowledge God in worship and thanksgiving, and continued through the various stages of the deification of human reason to the ultimate folly of man in the most corrupt form of idolatrous practices. Having departed from God, man made a god in his own image.[39]

As if verses 26–27 were not bad enough, look at Romans 1:28–31—especially Paul's conclusion, which I have put in list form for emphasis:

And even as they did not like to retain God in their knowledge, God gave them over to a debased mind, to do those things which are not fitting; being filled with all

- unrighteousness,
- sexual immorality,
- wickedness,
- covetousness,
- maliciousness;
- full of envy,
- murder,
- strife,
- deceit,
- evil-mindedness.

Paul went on to label this generation with the following terms:

- whisperers
- backbiters
- haters of God
- violent
- proud
- boasters
- inventors of evil things
- disobedient to parents
- undiscerning
- untrustworthy

- unloving
- unforgiving
- unmerciful

As appalling as this passage is, Dr. Martyn Lloyd-Jones says it is merely a preview of something even worse:

Hell is just what is described here exaggerated and going on to all eternity. That is hell! Hell is a condition in which life is lived away from God and all the restraints of God's holiness. All that is described in this passage, exaggerated still more, and going on endlessly! In other words, hell is people living in all eternity the kind of life they are living now, only much worse! That is hell![40]

I know that some of you are thinking, *do we really have to deal with all this? Why can't we just focus on the grace of God and get away from all this sin stuff?* Obviously, that is what so many churches have done in our generation. Romans 1 would never appear on the preaching schedule of most modern churches. But before we ignore sin and bask in the grace of God, we need to hear these words from theologian Cornelius Plantinga:

To speak of grace without sin is . . . to trivialize the cross of Jesus Christ, to skate past all the struggling by good people down through the ages to forgive, accept, and rehabilitate sinners, including themselves, and therefore to cheapen the grace of God that always comes to us with blood on it. What had we thought the ripping and the writhing on Golgotha were all about? To speak of grace without looking squarely at these realities, without painfully honest acknowledgment of our own sin and its effects, is to shrink grace to a mere embellishment of the music of creation, to shrink it down to a mere grace note. In short, for the Christian church (even in its recently popular seeker services) to ignore, euphemize or otherwise mute the lethal reality of sin is to cut the nerve of the gospel. For the sober truth is that without full disclosure on sin, the gospel of grace becomes impertinent, unnecessary, and finally uninteresting.[41]

One of my most memorable moments as a teacher of the Word of God took place on Sunday night, April 28, 1995. I was just beginning to teach the book of Romans in our evening service, and my scheduled passage was Romans 1:29–32.

On this particular night, we were planning to observe the Lord's Table at the beginning of our service. But after studying these verses from Romans, I decided to teach first and observe Communion afterward.

I waded through the words Paul used to describe the corruption and depravity of man, and then we celebrated Communion. In that service something beautiful occurred in my heart, and I sensed that it was happening in the hearts of many of our people as well. I saw tears. I fought back my own!

On Monday morning, still somewhat mystified by what had happened the night before, I read these words in a book called *Not the Way It's Supposed to Be: A Breviary of Sin*:

> Self-deception about our sin is a narcotic, a tranquilizing and disorienting suppression of our spiritual central nervous system. What's devastating about it is that when we lack an ear for wrong notes in our lives, we cannot play right ones or even recognize them in the performances of others. Eventually we make ourselves religiously so unmusical that we miss both the exposition and the recapitulation of the main themes God plays in human life. The

music of creation and the still greater music of grace whistle right through our skulls, causing no catch of breath and leaving no residue. Moral beauty begins to bore us. The idea that the human race needs a Savior sounds quaint.[42]

I thought, *how many times has the "music of grace whistled right through our skulls" during our celebration of the Lord's Table?* But that Sunday night we all caught a fresh glimpse of our sinfulness and realized just how badly we needed a Savior. And then we were caught up in the fact that Jesus came, and through His death He washed all that ugliness and filthiness away from our souls. I don't ever remember being more thankful for grace and forgiveness than I was that night. Maybe for the first time I understood what Martyn Lloyd-Jones said about grace: "There is no more wonderful word than 'grace.' It means unmerited favor or kindness shown to one who is utterly undeserving. . . . It is not merely a free gift, but a free gift to those who deserve the exact opposite, and it is given to us while we are 'without hope and without God in the world.'"[43]

THE END OF OUR MORAL DECLINE

One of the most vivid and overlooked pictures in the Bible is the scene of the glory of the Lord departing the temple shortly before the Babylonians invaded Jerusalem and destroyed the house of God. This scene graphically illustrates what is happening to our nation today.

The presence of the glory of God had descended and filled the temple in the days of Solomon: "When Solomon had finished praying, fire came down from heaven and consumed the burnt offering and the sacrifices; and the glory of the LORD filled the temple. And the priests could not enter the house of the LORD, because the glory of the LORD had filled the LORD's house" (2 Chronicles 7:1–2).

The Lord's glory dwelt in His temple for the next four hundred years. By the time of King Zedekiah, however, it was a different place. It had been desecrated by the invading Babylonians and emptied of its treasures and its worship. This was God's judgment against the nation of Judah because they had followed step-by-step the sequence of sin described in Romans 1: the rejection of the Creator, the proliferation of idols, lust-driven hearts, a sexually saturated age, and, finally, a total moral collapse.

One of the early victims of the Babylonian assault was Ezekiel, a young priest who was seized and force-marched to Babylon. There he ministered to his fellow exiles while receiving visions and messages from God. In chapters 8 through 11 of his book, Ezekiel described how he was given the awful privilege of watching the glory depart from Judah.

Ezekiel 8:3 would be comical were it not so serious: "He . . . took me by a lock of my hair; and the Spirit lifted me up between earth and heaven, and brought me in visions of God to Jerusalem, to the door of the north gate of the inner court." Verse 4 continues: "And behold, the glory of the God of Israel was there."

In the remainder of chapter 8, Ezekiel made a visual tour of the temple, seeing on every side visions of Israel's debauchery, all reminiscent of Paul's descriptions in Romans 1. Then as Ezekiel watched, the glory of the Lord began to move out of the Holy of Holies, the temple's central chamber. "Now the glory of the God of Israel had gone up from the cherub, where it had been, to the threshold of the temple" (Ezekiel 9:3).

Before leaving the temple, the glory "paused over the threshold of the temple; and the house was filled with the cloud, and the court was full of the brightness of the LORD's glory" (10:4). Finally, in verse

18 the departure is complete. "Then the glory of the LORD departed from the threshold of the temple and stood over the cherubim." After leaving the temple, "the glory of the LORD went up from the midst of the city and stood on the mountain, which is on the east side of the city" (11:23).

The meaning of Ezekiel's vision is clear. The holy God could no longer live with a nation that had descended into depravity. The dramatic clouds of God's glory, which had filled the temple from Solomon's reign, now moved from the Holy of Holies, to the threshold, to the rafters, and on out of the building. The last time Ezekiel saw the glory, it was disappearing over the Judean hills, returning to the heaven of God.

The biblical word for what you just read is *Ichabod*, which means "the glory has departed."[44] Where is the hope for a nation over which the word *Ichabod* has been written? All hope for Israel was gone— decimated by the Babylonians. But before you despair that *Ichabod* may now be indelibly inscribed on America, let me offer some hope:

> G. K. Chesterton named five moments in history, such as the fall of the Roman Empire and the period of Islamic conquest, when Christianity faced apparent doom. Each time, a fresh spirit of renewal emerged from the crisis and the faith revived. As Chesterton put it, when "the Faith has to all appearance gone to the dogs . . . it was the dog that died. . . . Christianity has died many times and risen again; for it had a God who knew the way out of the grave."[45]

In chapter 5, I will tell the story of the resurrections and revivals that have saved our nation in the past. It has happened before, and I believe it will happen again.

CHAPTER 2

THE BLEEDING OF OUR BORDERS

In October 2015, our radio and television ministry, *Turning Point*, held an arena event in Denver, Colorado. It was our first ever event in that city, and we were overwhelmed with a crowd of more than fifteen thousand people. After the event, I found that one of the reasons for our robust attendance was the tremendous support we had received from the Hispanic community.

A few days later one of the candidates for the United States presidency asked me, along with several other pastors, to come to his office so we could meet him, hear his heart, and pray with him. I was told this was to be a private meeting and no photography, videography, or recording would be allowed. But some enterprising person filmed my prayer for this candidate, and it went viral on the Internet.

My Hispanic friends were very upset with me. They assumed that my prayer for this man was an endorsement. Because he had made some statements about deporting all undocumented immigrants, they assumed I agreed with him.

I was quickly inundated with e-mails and phone calls asking me to come back to Denver and get this issue straightened out. I felt terrible that I had offended my brothers, but I knew in my heart that I had not meant to do so. The purpose of my prayer had been misinterpreted. It was not meant to imply endorsement. I will pray for anyone who asks for prayer or needs it, regardless of his politics or whether I agree or disagree with him.

We finally decided to set up a conference call so I could answer the questions of a coalition of Hispanic pastors and leaders in Denver. I began my part of the conversation by expressing my love for the Hispanic people. I told them that the church I led had a thriving Hispanic ministry with an average attendance of more than seven hundred and that these Christians were as much a part of our congregation as other members. I told them that most of the books I had written had been translated into Spanish and that we were on the radio in Spanish in almost every Spanish-speaking country in the world. I concluded my opening statement by telling them that my youngest daughter was married to Emmanuel Sanchez.

The conference call was a good experience for me, and throughout most of the conversation, I accepted the admonitions of my brothers. Just before the call ended, I asked the question that had been burning in my heart since this conflict had arisen.

I said something like this: "During our conversation, we have been talking about *undocumented* immigrants, but should we not be using the term *illegal* immigrants?" I asked what I should say to those who look to me for leadership when they ask me about illegal immigrants. Can I, with good conscience as a man of God, support that which is illegal?

It was this experience that drove me to investigate the controversial issue of American immigration and write this chapter. I believe that immigration is one of the most important and, at the same time, most difficult cultural issues of our day. I am not naïve enough to think that I can resolve this controversy in one short chapter. But I hope that I might bring to the issue some biblical clarity that will help us, as followers of Christ, choose a godly course.

In order to frame our discussion, I will begin by drawing from the personal experiences of a noted California writer to show two sides of the immigration controversy.

Selma, California, about six hours north of the Mexican border, is the hometown of well-known author and journalist Victor Davis Hanson. Selma is 70 percent Hispanic. How many of these are US citizens is not known. Most of the cars in Selma display a Mexican flag decal. Hit-and-run accidents, armed robberies, auto theft, drug manufacturing and sale, murders, rapes, and armed robberies are common events.

One night at 3:00 a.m. Hanson chased away at gunpoint three Hispanics who were forcing their way into his house. On another occasion policemen chased drug dealers through his driveway. He failed to stop a carload of thieves stealing oranges from his orchard, finding himself outmanned and outgunned.

Intoxicated illegal immigrants have crashed their cars into his vineyard four times, causing thousands of dollars in damage. The drivers limp away and disappear. When the police investigate, they parrot the usual response, "No license, no insurance, no registration," and tow the cars away.

Yet Hanson admits that this is not the whole story. "I also walk through vineyards" he said, "at 7:00 a.m. in the fog and see whole families from Mexico, hard at work in the cold while the native-born unemployed of all races will not—and cannot—prune a single vine. By natural selection, we are getting some of the most intelligent and industrious people in the world, people who have the courage to cross the border, the tenacity to stay." But he adds, if these people are not assimilated, they have "the potential to cost the state far, far more than they can contribute."[1]

Immigration has become a hot political and social issue, creating sharp division in the United States. But historically, immigration has been part of our national DNA. Our country was largely built on it. America is often called a "melting pot" of diverse peoples from many lands who work together to build, preserve, and protect a nation characterized by freedom, optimism, and opportunity. Our nation's attitude toward immigrants is eloquently expressed in the words engraved on the pedestal of the Statue of Liberty:

> Give me your tired, your poor,
> Your huddled masses yearning to breathe free,
> The wretched refuse of your teeming shore.
> Send these, the homeless, tempest-tost, to me,
> I lift my lamp beside the golden door![2]

American immigration began in the Colonial era when settlers flocked to the New World mostly from Europe, particularly Germany, England, and France, seeking economic opportunity or a new start in life. Some came in search of religious freedom, as did the Pilgrims of the early 1600s. From the seventeenth to nineteenth centuries, hundreds of thousands of Africans were brought to America as slaves.

From 1820 through 2010, the United States attracted eighty million newcomers with almost fourteen million arriving between 2001 and 2010.[3]

Within the past few decades, the immigration pattern has shifted. Most no longer come from Europe, but from Asia and Latin America, with a growing number from Middle Eastern countries. The disturbing fact buried within these statistics is the number of undocumented immigrants presently living in our country. The current estimate is a little more than eleven million.[4]

Some immigrants are refugees driven here by circumstances such as political oppression, war, or natural disaster. Others come of their own volition. They may be driven by poverty or drawn by the opportunity to increase their education or to take advantage of generous social programs within the United States.

America has historically been proud of this openness to outsiders, but today many factors have triggered a change in thinking and a growing concern. So, as we can see, immigration is a complex, two-sided issue with many positives and many negatives. The national media and our prominent political figures have made us well aware of the negative side, but before we draw any conclusions, let's look fairly and squarely at the other side of the story. It is this part of the discussion that is too often left unaddressed.

THE POTENTIAL OF IMMIGRATION

Immigrants enhance American culture by bringing into it new perspectives and experiences. Multiculturalism, according to some, increases tolerance for differences and adds variety to our cultural experience. We love our choices between Mexican, Italian, German, Chinese, or Thai cuisines. Americans celebrate Saint Patrick's Day, Cinco de Mayo, Yom Kippur, Ramadan, the Chinese New Year, and other observances brought here by immigrants. We owe Irish dance, African-American spirituals, German Oktoberfests, and fascinating oddities such as sitar and bagpipe music to the immigrants among us.

We see the universe differently because of the Jewish refugee Albert Einstein. Our entertainment history would be duller without the talents of English-born Cary Grant, Sicilian Frank Capra (director of *It's a Wonderful Life*), and the Danish comedian-musician Victor Borge.

According to 2013 data, "Immigrants make up 61 percent of all gas station owners, 58 percent of dry cleaners owners, 53 percent of grocery store owners, 45 percent of nail salon owners, . . . 38 percent of restaurant owners, and 32 percent of both jewelry and clothing store owners."[5]

In 2004, the film *A Day Without a Mexican* asked us to imagine what would happen to the Californian economy if every Mexican were to suddenly disappear for a day.[6] According to one movie critic,

> The mockumentary postulates that the lack of Latino gardeners, nannies, cooks, policeman, maids, teachers, farm workers, construction crews, entertainers, athletes, and the world's largest growing consumer market would create a social, political, and economic disaster, leaving the concept of the "California Dream" in shambles.[7]

One of the important books I read during my research for this chapter was *The New Pilgrims* by Joseph Castleberry, an Assembly of God pastor who spent twenty years on the mission field in Latin America. On the back cover of his book are written these words:

> In the midst of an apparent religious decline in the United States, many are looking for spiritual solutions to this dilemma. . . . As the "new pilgrims" settle into their lives here, they are taking the American church by storm and helping rebuild America's conservative foundations.[8]

Within the text of the book, Castleberry fleshes out this thought and adds another positive benefit these Christian immigrants may bring to America:

> The New Pilgrims have come to America *to help us*—to renew our faith, strengthen our families, transform our churches, and fill

our schools and universities with hope in the form of ambitious learners who dream of a better future. As more and more American Christians are feeling like foreigners in our own land in the face of opposition to the Church and the attack on biblical morality, isn't it ironic that these Evangelical immigrants may very well tip the scale back to a conservative America at some point?[9]

It is estimated that 75 percent of immigrants profess to be Christians when they come to this country. That's 5 percent higher than the number of American residents who claim to be Christians. And the faith of these immigrants "reveals an amazing intensity and sincerity that will compound their effect on America's faith."[10]

Former presidential candidate Marco Rubio is the son of an immigrant from Cuba. In a speech at the end of his 2016 campaign, he acknowledged the debt Americans owe to their immigrant forebears:

We are all the descendants of someone who made our future the purpose of their lives. We are the descendants of pilgrims. We are the descendants of settlers. We are the descendants of men and women that headed westward in the Great Plains not knowing what awaited them. We are the descendants of slaves who overcame that horrible institution to stake their claim in the American Dream. We are the descendants of immigrants and exiles who knew and believed that they were destined for more, and that there was only one place on earth where that was possible.[11]

Despite the turmoil over immigration today, it is clear that America owes much of its past and potentially much of its future to the industry, determination, courage, and Christian values of its immigrants.

THE PROBLEMS WITH IMMIGRATION

Working against the immigration advantages are several growing and unsolved problems arising from both legal and illegal immigration.

Problems with Legal Immigration

The flood of immigration in the past few decades is a major contributor to increasingly high unemployment in the United States. According to the Bureau of Labor Statistics, in May 2016, the real unemployment rate, which includes discouraged workers no longer looking for jobs, was 9.7 percent.[12] Businesses naturally gravitate toward workers willing to take lower wages, which often results in immigrants being hired over natural citizens. According to Hanson, "The Labor Department attributes 50 percent of real wage declines to the influx of cheap immigrant labor."[13]

High immigration rates can also hurt the nation from which workers emigrate. One result is "brain drain," as highly skilled or educated workers leave developing countries to take more financially rewarding jobs in the United States. Many come here "temporarily" for education but find American life and opportunities so attractive that they never return.

For as long as I can remember, this has been a challenge for world missions. Many come to the United States from other countries with the expressed purpose of getting educated and trained in their chosen discipline in order to return to their countries and carry the gospel to their people. But far too many of these well-intentioned immigrants fall in love with America and never return to their country of origin.

Another problem is the failure of some ethnic groups to integrate into American life. Throughout most of our nation's history, immigrants adopted the language, laws, and common customs of the host country. The term "melting pot" was a descriptive metaphor, indicating that the potentially divisive attitudes and customs of the old country would be left behind as the newcomers blended into a new commonality of purpose. But today it seems that the pot is no longer melting. Some incoming groups defy cultural assimilation. They cluster into enclaves and demand special concessions for their ethnic customs, beliefs, languages, and, in some cases, even their laws. According to Samuel Huntington, author of the bestselling *Clash of Civilizations*, "New arrivals today are not assimilating at the same rate or with the same conviction to leave behind their original national identity. In fact, they seem reluctant to do so. . . . Evidence of this lack of assimilation . . . is found in declining levels of English language acquisition, less educational achievement, and poorer socioeconomic success."[14]

Hispanic students far outnumber all other ethnicities in most United States public schools in the lower parts of states bordering Mexico. Some of these schools display the Mexican flag in classrooms on an equal basis with the American flag. On the flagpole of one Californian school, the Mexican flag was actually flown above the American flag.

It is natural for immigrants from a given country to cluster together within a city. They need a support system as they learn the new language and make the transition into a new culture. But today big cities such as Houston deal with numerous Hispanic enclaves that speak nothing but Spanish. Learning English is less necessary than in the past because major businesses, schools, and government offices take steps to accommodate those who do not speak English. This failure to learn English creates a domino effect of continuing poverty as immigrant children grow up unable to compete in society for lack of language skills.[15]

Many Muslim immigrants choose not to assimilate in order to retain closer adherence to the tenets of their religion that conflict with

US law and customs. According to one news source, "Islamist groups are, as we speak, hard at work creating Muslim states-within-states in the U.S. Indeed, this process has been unfolding for a long time across the Western world, through the creation of isolated Muslim enclaves in both rural and urban areas."[16] Many of these enclaves are sponsored and partially supported by the Muslim Brotherhood and are breeding grounds for terrorists and centers for proselyting new members of groups such as ISIS.

The Center for Immigration Studies shows that immigrants from the Middle East are now the fastest growing immigration demographic in the United States. In just three years, more immigrants came from the Middle East than from Mexico and Central America combined.[17] According to the *National Review*,

> There is no official estimate of Muslims in the U.S.; religious affiliation is not tracked by the Census Bureau. However, Pew's estimate of 2.75 million seems to be on the lower end. The Council on American-Islamic Relations says there are approximately 7 million Muslims in the country. Whatever the exact level, it can hardly be considered surprising that as the Muslim population in the country has expanded, so has the incidence of radicalism.[18]

While many Muslims are peaceful, we cannot deny the fact that some are not. European countries have become victims of increased radical terrorism. In November 2015, an ISIS attack in Paris left 130 dead and 368 injured.[19] In a 2015 New Year's Eve riot in Cologne, Germany, Middle Eastern men molested at least ninety women.[20] In March 2016, Muslim terrorist bombings in a Brussels subway and airport killed 34 and injured over 106.[21] Islamic extremists have committed virtually all acts of terrorism in the United States, and many experts warn that if Muslim immigration is not controlled and Muslim applicants are not vetted, we can expect more attacks, rioting, and lawless acts similar to those occurring in Europe.

According to former House Intelligence Committee chairman Rep. Pete Hoekstra, assimilation is an essential component to immigration:

> What we need to do is make sure everyone coming into the United States understands who we are and that we are founded on Judeo-Christian values, that there is one rule of law and that's what's on the books and it's not Sharia and we need to make sure we don't engage in the same kind of mistakes in Europe where they did not engage in assimilation.[22]

Problems with Illegal Immigration

According to a combined study conducted by three US government departments, immigrants entering the United States illegally are responsible for an extremely high number of crimes. The study was based on a sample of 55,322 illegal immigrants incarcerated in US prisons. Members of this group were arrested 459,614 times—an average of eight arrests per person. About 45 percent of the arrests were for drug or immigration offenses. Another 15 percent were property related—burglary, larceny-theft, motor vehicle theft, and property damage. About 12 percent were for violent crimes, including murder, robbery, assault, and sex offenses. The balance of the arrests were for fraud, forgery, counterfeiting, weapons violations, obstruction of justice, and traffic violations, including DUI.[23]

Another rising problem with illegal immigration is its effect on social and government services, which include medical care, education, welfare, policing, and incarceration. Hospital emergency rooms have become the primary care facility for those here illegally. By law, hospital ERs cannot turn away anyone in need. Yet the sheer number of immigrants often clog ER waiting rooms in metropolitan hospitals. When ER beds are filled, ambulance patients are often diverted to more distant hospitals, which sometimes results in worsening conditions or death.

Dallas' Parkland Hospital offers the second-largest maternity service in the United States. In one recent year, sixteen thousand babies were born at Parkland, and 70 percent of them were to illegal immigrants at a cost of $70.7 million. Because few of these patients speak English, the hospital now offers premium pay to medical employees who speak Spanish. This need has forced the University of Texas Southwestern Medical School to add a Spanish language requirement to its curriculum.[24]

The cost of educating the children of illegal immigrants in the United States was estimated at $52 billion in 2010, while the overall cost of all services combined was estimated at $113 billion. This says nothing about the cost in educational quality and efficiency when schools must make special accommodations for significant numbers of students who speak no English.[25]

Many US cities, counties, and states are facing severe financial shortfalls—even to the point of looming bankruptcy—brought on by the cost of providing free social services to illegal immigrants. This drain on resources may well reach the point that we no longer have the means to provide the blessings that immigrants come here to find.

One of the most disturbing aspects of illegal immigration is simply that it is *illegal*. The apostle Paul was quite emphatic in commanding Christians to obey governmental laws (Romans 13:1–7). He explained that God ordained governments to keep order and protect citizens. Our national, state, and local governments all have on the books laws that prohibit non-citizens from crossing our borders and living in our communities without proper qualifications and legal documentation. Today those laws are often ignored, usually in the name of compassion. The fact that so many in the United States not only tolerate but also encourage and defend a practice that works outside of the framework of the law should be troublesome.

We see this tolerance even in our government. Sanctuary cities offer havens to illegal immigrants to protect them from deportation. The national government deliberately refuses to enforce immigration laws and threatens states that attempt to enforce them. The government even provides publications that tell illegal immigrants how to secure available social services.

The danger of encouraging violations to immigration laws goes far beyond the fiscal and societal costs of illegal immigration. It leads to a disrespect of law in general. It fosters the attitude that each individual can decide for himself what laws are just or unjust, which he will obey and which he will ignore.

Among government accommodations to immigration lawlessness is the number of states that are having their voter ID laws struck down by federal courts. With no official proof of citizenship—or even of one's residence—all it takes for non-citizens to vote is a sworn affidavit of eligibility.

Illegal immigrant voting creates a dangerous political imbalance, as those living here illegally are certain to favor the political party that offers them the greatest benefits and least restrictions. This imbalance dilutes and can even override the will of the majority of legal citizens that, according to statistics, lean heavily toward enforcement of US immigration laws in every category.[26]

These are merely samplings of the factors that have generated our current national controversy over immigration. Many fear that uncontrolled immigration is among the destructive forces undermining our nation today, and if it is not addressed, the America we have known faces an uncertain future. One often-expressed fear is that we may be nearing the end of the great experiment in democracy and freedom brought to this continent by our ancestors.

THE PAST OF IMMIGRATION

God's original ideal for humanity was for all of mankind to be one unified family speaking one common language throughout all the earth. This kind of unity would have been no problem if our primeval parents had not rebelled against God in Eden. But sin brought separation, not only separation from God and separation of body and spirit in death but also the need for separation of peoples. This need for separation arose because the prideful nature of fallen man has always led him to usurp the place of God, elevate self as supreme, and grasp for power over others. Separation would create limiting barriers to this persistent tendency toward unlimited tyranny.

This tendency arose in all its rawness several generations after the Flood when all people still spoke a common language. Nimrod, ruler of the Mesopotamian city of Babel, moved to gain power over all the people of the earth by building a massive tower that would draw everyone to a central location under his control. It was man's first attempt at one-world government, which, devoid of God, would have brought about almost unlimited tyranny.

God brought a stop to Nimrod's rebellion simply by dividing the world's single language into many. Workers could no longer communicate with one another, which abruptly ended tower construction. People scattered throughout the earth, grouping according to their new languages (Genesis 11:1–9).

While worldwide unity was God's original intent, the national separateness we experience today is a God-ordained protection against one of the worst effects of Adam's fall—man's prideful craving for power.

The apostle Paul wrote:

> He has made from one blood every nation of men to dwell on all the face of the earth, and has determined their preappointed times and the boundaries of their dwellings, so that they should seek the Lord, in the hope that they might grope for Him and find Him, though He is not far from each one of us. (Acts 17:26–27)

As Paul explained, God scattered men and set "the boundaries of their dwellings" so they would seek after God. Prophecy theologian Dave Breese has written:

> I think we need to understand that political internationalism is not the will of God. Nationalism is God's will. God has ordained individual nations and not a complex of nations. . . . When men try in their own unregenerate power to put together a complex of nations and make them cohere without God, then you have built into the complex the seeds of its own destruction.[27]

We must be ever wary of the current move toward globalism and calls for one-world government. The amassing of nations under a single human authority is not God's will. To the contrary, it is the sure road to unprecedented tyranny.

What attitude should Christian citizens adopt in the face of the immigration controversy? To find answers, we can do no better than to look to the Bible for principles and examples of how God has had His people deal with the biblical equivalency of immigration—how to respond to the presence of outsiders (strangers and sojourners) in one's homeland.

THE PRINCIPLES OF IMMIGRATION

The concept of nationalism was never meant to separate people absolutely. Throughout human history, various circumstances such as famine, poverty, and the need for refuge have caused people to cross national borders. Therefore, God provided specific rules for how His people should treat the foreigners residing among them.

God's People Are to Assist the Stranger

God charged the people of Israel to care for the strangers and sojourners who came among them, invoking their national history to induce empathy: "You shall not oppress a stranger, for you know the heart of a stranger, because you were strangers in the land of Egypt" (Exodus 23:9).

Hospitality to strangers was critical in ancient times because travel was treacherous. Roads were often mere trails, and travelers were vulnerable to weather, wild animals, and violent thieves. Food and shelter were vital necessities, and hospitality was expected. Hosts were enjoined to be generous, and guests were not to take advantage or overstay their welcome.

Many Old Testament scriptures show how deeply hospitality was embedded into the Jewish psyche. Jeremiah instructed Judah's King Zedekiah, "Do no wrong and do no violence to the stranger, the fatherless, or the widow" (Jeremiah 22:3). God promised the Israelites that they would dwell long in their land "if [they did] not oppress the stranger, the fatherless, and the widow, and [did] not shed innocent blood in this place, or walk after other gods to [their] hurt" (7:6).

The prophets came down hard on those who failed to extend hospitality. Ezekiel foretold the fall of Jerusalem and explained part of the reason for it: "The people of the land have used oppressions, committed robbery, and mistreated the poor and needy; and they wrongfully oppress the stranger" (Ezekiel 22:29). Malachi warned that God would render harsh judgment against those who "deprive the foreigners among you of justice" (Malachi 3:5 NIV). Zechariah told the people of Israel that they suffered captivity because they failed to heed God's commands to "not oppress the widow or the fatherless, the foreigner or the poor" (Zechariah 7:10 NIV).

God's People Are to Accept the Stranger

God commanded acceptance of foreigners who were willing to adopt His laws: "You shall therefore keep My statutes and My judgments, and shall not commit any of these abominations, either any of your own nation or any stranger who dwells among you" (Leviticus 18:26; see also 24:16; Exodus 20:10; Numbers 15:30).

The Old Testament gives us many examples of foreign-born men and women who were accepted as productive citizens of Israel. Rahab, the Jericho prostitute who saved the lives of the Israelite spies, became a believer, married an Israelite, and lived among the Israelites for the rest of her life (Joshua 6:25). Ruth, another foreign-born woman, was the widow of an Israelite who lived in her home country, Moab. After her husband's death, she accompanied her Jewish mother-in-law to Israel, married a prominent Israelite landowner, and became the grandmother of the great King David (Ruth 4). These two immigrants were among the most highly honored women in Israel's history as mothers listed in the New Testament ancestry of Christ (Matthew 1:5–6).

We are all familiar with the Hittite immigrant Uriah, one of King David's finest warriors whose fierce loyalty was rewarded with treachery (2 Samuel 11:1–17). Ittai the Gittite was another immigrant soldier who was staunchly loyal to David (15:19–22). Doeg the Edomite was the chief of King Saul's herdsmen (1 Samuel 21:7).

The New Testament does not address immigration directly, but we find Christ demonstrating attitudes of love and acceptance toward non-Israelites throughout His earthly ministry. In His famous encounter with the Samaritan woman at the well, He ignored the deep disdain Jews projected toward Samaritans and defied long-standing custom by speaking to her. Not only did He speak to her, but He engaged her in earnest conversation, which eventually led to many of her Samaritan friends coming to belief (John 4:1–26).

In another incident, Jesus was traveling north to the Phoenician area of Tyre and Sidon. A Canaanite woman came to Him and begged Him to heal her demon-possessed daughter. After a brief conversation designed to test her, Jesus said, "O woman, great is your faith! Let it be to you as you desire" (Matthew 15:28).

In His well-known parable of the good Samaritan, Jesus again did the unthinkable. He made a Samaritan the hero of a story that stressed the necessity of meeting the needs of others no matter who they are or where you find them (Luke 10:25–37).

Jesus made no distinction among races. All were created in God's image, and in these incidents He demonstrated that we are to love all persons equally, regardless of ethnicity. Peter summed up God's attitude toward all people, insiders and outsiders alike, when he said, "In truth I perceive that God shows no partiality. But in every nation whoever fears Him and works righteousness is accepted by Him" (Acts 10:34–35).

God's People Are to Assimilate the Stranger

The Scriptures make it clear that outsiders living in Israel were to be treated well. But there was a flip side to the coin. Strangers and sojourners living among them—immigrants, if you please—did not have *carte blanche* to live any way they wanted in their host country. God gave His people explicit limits to their acceptance of strangers. Since religion was at the center of Israel's life, most of these limits concerned worship and religious activities. The restrictions were sometimes severe and exclusionary, but they were necessary to protect Israel from destructive outside influences, especially the idolatry that was common in neighboring countries. Idolatry would lead Israel to apostasy and alienation from God and ultimately would cause the disintegration of the nation.

The overarching principle was that strangers who desired to live in Israel were to be subject to the same laws as the native Israelites.

"You shall therefore keep My statutes and My judgments, and shall not commit any of these abominations, either any of your own nation or any stranger who dwells among you." (Leviticus 18:26)

"And whoever blasphemes the name of the LORD shall surely be put to death. All the congregation shall certainly stone him, the stranger as well as him who is born in the land." (24:16)

"The seventh day is the Sabbath of the LORD your God. In it you shall do no work: you, nor your son, nor your daughter, nor your male servant, nor your female servant, nor your cattle, nor your stranger who is within your gates." (Exodus 20:10)

"The person who does anything presumptuously, whether he is native-born or a stranger, that one brings reproach on the LORD, and he shall be cut off from among his people." (Numbers 15:30)

Foreigners in Israel were expected to "earn their keep"—to work and be active contributors to the overall success of the nation. We have already noted that Saul employed an Edomite as head of his herdsmen. Several foreigners were among David's best warriors. Other foreigners worked as laborers and hired servants (Deuteronomy 24:14). When King Solomon began constructing the temple, he conducted a census and determined there were 153,600 foreigners residing in Israel. He drafted them to work as carriers, stonecutters, and supervisors (2 Chronicles 2:17–18).

The message of the Bible concerning strangers in the land is clear: If they accept the national culture and work as participants in the national economy, they are welcomed and allowed full participation in the life of the nation. If they refuse to assimilate and cling to their old laws, beliefs, and customs, their activities must be restricted for the good of the nation.

THE PERFECTION OF IMMIGRATION

Satan's successful temptation in Eden dealt a terrible blow to God's creation, bringing not only death, blight, and pain but also enmity between peoples. But God will not allow Satan a victory over what He pronounced to be good. As Castleberry tells us, "The book of Revelation envisions the endgame of the biblical description of God's mission. In John the Revelator's vision of the end of time, he describes a great heavenly multitude 'that no one could count, from every nation, tribe, people and language, standing before the throne and before the Lamb . . . And they cried out in a loud voice, "Salvation belongs to our God, who sits on the throne, and to the Lamb"'" (Revelation 7:9–10).[28]

In heaven the enmity between people that began with man's fall in Eden will end. All nations will be one—unified in the presence of God. But even before this great gathering in heaven, God intends to put things on this earth back as He originally created them to be. Many scriptures tell of a coming time when enmity between peoples will be healed. The apostle Peter spoke of the "restoration of all things, which God has spoken by the mouth of all His holy prophets since the world began" (Acts 3:20–21).

Just as Peter said, the prophetic books of the Bible fairly bulge with predictions of the coming time when God will restore earthly conditions as He intended them in the beginning. One of the most striking prophecies as it pertains to our present topic is found in Isaiah 19:

> In that day there will be a highway from Egypt to Assyria, and the Assyrian will come into Egypt and the Egyptian into Assyria, and the Egyptians will serve with the Assyrians. In that day Israel will be one of three with Egypt and Assyria—a blessing in the midst of the land, whom the LORD of hosts shall bless, saying, "Blessed is Egypt My people, and Assyria the work of My hands, and Israel My inheritance." (vv. 23–25).

What a day it will be when this prophecy is fulfilled! The deadly animosity between the Israelites and their Arab neighbors has existed since the days of their progenitors Isaac and Ishmael. When the Middle Eastern Islamic nations claim brotherhood with their ancient enemy Israel, we can be sure that an era of brotherhood between all the nations has finally come to the earth.

Isaiah spoke of a time of unity not only between Israel and the Arab nations, but among all peoples. He said that those who had been previously excluded from the temple would be welcomed in the land and invited to participate in worship of God.

Their burnt offerings and their sacrifices

Will be accepted on My altar;

For My house shall be called a house of prayer for all nations.

The Lord GOD, who gathers the outcasts of Israel, says,

"Yet I will gather to him

Others besides those who are gathered to him." (Isaiah 56:7–8)

In the New Millennium, there will no longer be such a thing as strangers, sojourners, or immigrants. All will be one under the loving and benevolent rule of Jesus Christ. As Dr. John F. Walvoord summed it up, "Taken as a whole, the social and economic conditions of the millennium indicate a golden age in which the dreams of social reformists through the centuries will be realized, not through human effort but by the immediate presence and power of God and the righteous government of Christ."[29]

The unity of all people for the thousand years of the New Millennium is good news to a world continually torn apart by strife between nations and distrust of ethnic differences. God's perfected kingdom on earth has not yet come, but in this chapter we have studied His ideal for relationships between races, especially with people of other races who live among us. His relational ideal is grounded in the fact that He created every person of every race in His own image. And He loves each of us so dearly that He would rather die than live throughout all eternity without any one of us—a love He has proved by the cross.

As God's people, we are enjoined to love others as He loves us (1 John 4:11). This means we are to think of the foreigners among us as highly valued people created in God's image, whom He loves as dearly as He loves us. We will share eternity with many of them. The tension we face before we reach eternity is how to express that love within the controversy over immigration. As one theologian has written:

This is not about "issues" or "culture wars" but about persons made in the image of God. Our churches must be the presence of Christ to all persons, regardless of country of origin or legal status. . . . Our commitment to a multinational kingdom of God's reconciliation in Christ must be evident in the verbal witness of our gospel and in the visible makeup of our congregations. . . . We might be natural-born Americans, but we're all immigrants to the kingdom of God.[30]

As I write this chapter, we are in the midst of an election year, and immigration is at the center of much of the controversy between candidates. But as one writer has eloquently put it, "at the end of the day, immigration reform does not stem from the agenda of the donkey or the elephant; rather, welcoming the stranger is a conviction that flows from the agenda of the Lamb."[31]

James Kesler, in the weekly magazine of the Assemblies of God church, asks, "How should Christians respond to the overwhelming tide of immigration?" Then he answers his own question: "It is imperative that we take a new, long look at Christ's command and develop a responsible attitude toward Home Missions. America has become a mission field in the truest sense."[32]

Immigration into our own community has opened up for our church an enormous opportunity for just this kind of mission. In 2015, our little city of El Cajon in San Diego County became the home of the largest number of Iraqi immigrants in the United States. It is estimated that one-quarter of our city's one hundred thousand people are Iraqi. Most of these immigrants are Chaldeans.

One of the great and unexpected blessings we have experienced at Shadow Mountain Community Church is our ministry not only to this immigrant group but also to the other ethnic communities in our immediate area. During the last ten years, we have helped more than 2,500 immigrants learn the English language through our English language courses taught by volunteers from our church. We have done this with no expectations on our part. We have simply tried to help them adapt to and flourish in our city.

We also have four international congregations currently. Each Sunday morning finds our campus buzzing with people from every corner of the world as our Arabic, Filipino, and Iranian congregations gather for worship.

Under the direction of Pastor Robert Helou, our Arabic congregation has grown steadily. For Easter 2016, more than seven hundred worshippers attended the weekend services.

Pastor Sohrab Ramtin leads about thirty Iranian believers, and Pastor Henry Amarila oversees nearly 100 Filipino Christians.

On Sunday afternoon our Hispanic congregation, led by Pastor Erick Zaldaña, meets in the main worship center of our church with more than seven hundred in regular attendance. But that does not tell the whole story of the Hispanic ministry at Shadow Mountain. Our congregation was recently given a church property in Encinitas, California, and we have an English video venue in that facility on Sunday mornings. But on Sunday afternoons, we deliver Pastor Zaldaña's message by our satellite system to another 150 Hispanic believers in the same facility. When we add together all the numbers of our Hispanic worshippers, we are ministering to approximately 900 Hispanics each week.

And there is more. Because Pastor Zaldaña is such an excellent communicator, the two Hispanic television stations in our community have given us two hours of free airtime every Sunday. This enables us to televise the Hispanic service to our community, just as we do our English service.

Almost every week in our English services, we have the opportunity to hear the testimonies of those who are being baptized. On many of these occasions we are blessed by the testimonies of those who have been won to Christ in our ethnic congregations. Often these testimonies require an interpreter, which makes me feel as if I have visited a mission field—which, in fact, I have. Immigration has brought a mission field to us.

On February 20, 2016, we had the opportunity to hear the testimony of a young man who had grown up in a Muslim nation and came to this country as a refugee. His story is just one example of the excitement we all feel because of the Lord's work in our international churches:

My name is Yousef. May the peace of the Lord Jesus be on you, the people of God. I share with you how I left the darkness of Islam and came into the light of Christ.

When I left Iraq and came to America as a refugee, I left the terrible killing Muslims do in the name of religion. I met in America my sponsor and friend Noel, who is a member of Shadow Mountain Arabic church. He took good care of me, and he told me that God loves me and He gave His Son for me. As a Muslim, this sounded very strange to me. So I asked, "Who is this Son?"

Noel said, "This is the Lord Jesus Christ."

I said, "Does God have a Son?"

He answered, "Yes, He is Issa the Son of Mary, and we call Him Jesus." He gave me the Bible. I started reading it and studying it. Because I knew the Quran, I started discerning big differences between the two books—the love in Christianity, and the hatred and killing in Islam.

Then the Lord Jesus Himself appeared to me, and with His light He illuminated my dark way. I believed in Him and asked

Him to save me. After that I started faithfully attending all the church services.

I am getting baptized today in obedience to the Lord's command. I thank God for His daily dealings with me and my family. And I today declare with joy, saying with Joshua, "As for me and my house, we will serve the Lord."

To Him be all glory, amen.

Yousef's testimony was given in broken English, and when it ended, our congregation erupted with joyous applause. And I have it on good authority that applause erupted in heaven as well (Luke 15:7). I am convinced that Yousef's testimony and others like it reveal the real heart of the immigration story. Over and above all its problems and benefits, immigration is to us an opportunity to expand the kingdom of God. We should look at immigration as God's way of bringing to us a world of people who need to know Him so that we can share with them what He has given to us. I believe Samuel Rodríguez was thinking along these lines when he wrote these words:

> Immigration reform is both a vertical and horizontal issue. Vertically, the heart of God stands moved by the plight of immigrants and their suffering. Horizontally, passing immigration reform will serve as a reconciliatory prescription for a nation divided by partisan politics. Accordingly, it is the cross that prompts us to lift our hands toward heaven and to stretch our hands toward our neighbor. It is the cross that compels us to declare that a human being cannot be illegal. It is the cross that drives us to reconcile the rule of law (Romans 13) with treating the immigrant as one of our own (Leviticus 19).[33]

CHAPTER 3

THE INCREASE OF INTOLERANCE

Kelvin Cochran is the fourth of six children raised in extreme poverty by a single mother in Shreveport, Louisiana. He attended church regularly and developed a strong and active faith in God.

From the moment he witnessed a firefighting crew put out a fire in a neighbor's house, young Kelvin knew he wanted to be a firefighter. After graduation he became one of the first African Americans hired by the Shreveport Fire Department. He moved up through the ranks to become Shreveport's first African American fire chief while still in his mid-thirties.

Eight years later, Cochran was invited to head Atlanta's 750-member fire department. He left Atlanta in 2009 when the president appointed him head of the US Fire Administration. But Atlanta's new mayor persuaded Cochran to return and rebuild the city's deteriorating fire department. He did just that, making the Atlanta Fire Department one of only sixty US departments to receive a Class 1 rating.

Although Cochran is a committed Christian, he carefully observed workplace rules in sharing his faith, discussing religion only with those who approached him first. He led Bible studies in his church and formed a study group specifically for men searching for authentic manhood, which led him to write a privately published book on the subject. He gave the book only to people with whom he had worked and shared his faith and, as a courtesy, to Atlanta's mayor and a handful of civic leaders.

Almost a year after the book's publication, Councilmember Alex Wan read the few pages outlining the biblical approach to sexuality—that sex outside of male–female marriage is contrary to God's will. That's when the trouble began. Meetings among Atlanta's top officials followed, and as *National Review* reported, "On January 6, 2015, the City of Atlanta fired Cochran—without providing him the proper process prescribed by city codes and, he claims, without providing him an opportunity to respond to either his suspension or his termination. At no point did any employee of the fire department complain of mistreatment or discrimination."

Councilmember Wan, however, made the reason for Cochran's dismissal clear: "When you're a city employee, and [your] thoughts, beliefs, and opinions are different from the city's, you have to check them at the door."[1]

This incident is merely one of many in which governments, businesses, and organizations have recently repressed Christian beliefs or penalized people for expressing their faith. In 2014, Arizona's governor Jan Brewer vetoed a bill designed to allow "businesses that asserted their religious beliefs the right to deny service to gay and lesbian customers."[2] Dr. Eric Walsh, a district health director in Georgia, was fired when the state learned that he had preached sermons in his church articulating orthodox Christian positions on sexuality and creation.[3] The matchmaking service eHarmony, originally founded on Christian principles, was forced by a 2008 lawsuit to create a new website for gay and lesbian users.[4]

Jesus scolded the Pharisees for their inability to discern the signs of the times (Matthew 16:3). The signs of our times should be clear to us. The incidents related previously are merely a sampling from hundreds of similar ones that reveal the arc of the future. American culture is growing increasingly hostile toward Christianity, which has lost its place as the nation's primary guiding ethic. Laws and societal pressures have begun to encroach seriously on Christian freedom. We are in the first stages of repression of Christian speech and actions, and even stronger measures may well follow.

America was originally founded on Christian principles. The Declaration of Independence explicitly recognizes that God, not government, is the source of human rights and freedom: "We hold these truths to be self-evident, that all men are created equal, that they are endowed *by their Creator* with certain unalienable Rights" (italics added).[5]

This foundational premise began to erode in the mid-twentieth century with the affluence generated by the post–World War II economic boom and the rise of the protest culture of the 1960s. Today the concept of freedom has degenerated into license typified by the elimination of virtually all moral restraints. Christianity is being pushed to the edges because its adherence to biblical morality is at odds with the philosophy of unrestricted freedom that now dominates America's cultural landscape.

As Moody Bible Institute President Dr. Paul Nyquist noted:

For nearly 250 years, Christians in America were able to live in relative freedom from persecution. We escaped because our society historically embraced and promoted biblical values. Our founding fathers penned a Constitution esteeming religious freedom and establishing that rights come from God, not the government.

But we're witnessing an epic change in our culture—a spiritual climate shift threatening to reshape life as we know it. Hostility and intolerance are replacing toleration. Rejection and even hatred are pushing aside acceptance.[6]

It is no secret that Christianity is declining in America. The Pew Research Center reports that in 2014 about 70 percent of Americans identified as Christians.[7] But this figure is misleading. According to a study by sociologists C. Kirk Hadaway and Penny Long Marler published in the *Journal for the Scientific Study of Religion*, less than 20 percent of Americans regularly attend church on a weekly basis.[8] This statistic gives us a better indication of actual Christian commitment.

The downward trend has begun, and momentum is building. The government, the educational system, the entertainment industry, and the media no longer share our values, which means faithful Christians are becoming alienated from the dominant forces in society. Christianity is now a religious subculture, increasingly demonized, ridiculed, and marginalized.

"Get ready," Dr. Nyquist urges. "An exciting, yet terrifying era is beginning for American believers. As cultural changes sweep our country, we'll soon be challenged to live out what the Bible says about confronting and responding to persecution."[9]

THE SUBSTANCE OF CHRISTIAN PERSECUTION

You may wonder whether *persecution* is too strong a word to describe what is happening to Christians in America today. Dr. Nyquist answers, "Because of our relative inexperience, we Americans tend to have a limited view of persecution. We typically think of it in physical terms (imprisonment, martyrdom), and as such, may question whether our experience truly qualifies as persecution. But this definition is too narrow. The biblical term suggests a broader view including aggression, oppression, and violence affecting the body, mind, and emotions."[10]

Theologian Geoffrey Bromiley agrees: "Persecution is the suffering or pressure, mental, moral, or physical, which authorities, individuals, or crowds inflict on others, especially for opinions or beliefs, with a view to their subjection by recantation, silencing, or, as a last resort, execution."[11]

Christianity Today reminds us that "most persecution is not violence. Instead, it's a 'squeeze' of Christians in five spheres of life: private, family, community, national, and church."[12]

As you can see, the term *persecution* covers any kind of stifling or oppression of religious belief or practice. We should not assume, however, that everything bad that happens to us is a form of persecution. Persecution is only trouble that occurs "for righteousness' sake" (Matthew 5:10), the kind that comes from one's identification with Jesus Christ. Sometimes our own stress, sin, or bad choices bring difficulties into our lives. As 1 Peter 4:15 reads, "Let none of you suffer as a murderer, a thief, an evildoer, or as a busybody in other people's matters." Trouble that comes as a result of our own wrongdoing cannot be labeled persecution.

To be persecuted for righteousness' sake means that we are hated or opposed or suffer solely for following Christ and living for God. That is persecution, and that defines the substance of this chapter.

THE STAGES OF CHRISTIAN PERSECUTION

To show the extent of the persecution problem, let's look at five stages of religious suppression now occurring in our nation.

Stage 1: Stereotyping

Today Christians are often stereotyped as ignorant, uneducated, backward, inhibited, homophobic, hateful, and intolerant. Even the president joined in when, in 2008, he said of workers who vote according to their values, "They get bitter, they cling to guns or religion or antipathy to people who aren't like them or anti-immigrant sentiment or anti-trade sentiment as a way to explain their frustrations."[13]

Movies and television often feature a Christian as the evil antagonist, a holier-than-thou bigot who sits on a high horse and judges others harshly. The character is usually either angry and overbearing or stupid and naïve. Or he may be a compromised, emotionally repressed, or fallen Christian. Usually he is portrayed as a hypocrite who doesn't live what he professes to believe, like the prison warden in the movie *The Shawshank Redemption* who recites the Bible but abuses inmates.

A movie that stereotypes Christians in another way is the oft-telecast classic *Inherit the Wind*, an insidious distortion of the 1925 Scopes "Monkey Trial," which pitted evolution against creation. The movie is credited with doing much to mold the public image of Christians as intolerant, willfully ignorant, and anti-science. It also tilted the creation/evolution debate to the point that today secularists do not allow creation even to be discussed in public school and university science courses. Thus, the populace as a whole does not realize that, far from being based on ignorance, the doctrine of creation is built on solid scientific evidence and highly rational applications of scientific method.

While it is true that some professed Christians represent the faith poorly, these stereotypes do not reflect the reality of authentic Christianity; they grow out of the rising cultural prejudice against the Christian faith. Our duty is to live our convictions in a way that shows these slanderous pictures to be gross distortions of the truth.

Stage 2: Marginalizing

What many secularists want is for Christianity to be displaced from the center of American life. If the church must be allowed to exist, they want it confined to the realm of personal privacy and denied any effect on public life. That is why public prayer must be forbidden, Christian influence in public policy eliminated, and Christian holidays secularized. Christians must be excluded from positions of power and influence, which includes politics, academia, entertainment, and the media. As MSNBC personality Chris Matthews tweeted, "If you're a politician and believe in God first, that's all good. Just don't run for government office, run for church office."[14]

More and more, Christian belief and practice are being pushed out of public life. For example, Christian organizations are now barred from many university campuses. The court upheld the ban on Christmas carols with religious content imposed by schools in New Jersey and Philadelphia.[15] A California appeals court upheld the verdict against two doctors who refused to artificially inseminate a lesbian woman. The woman's attorney said, "When [a] doctor is in her church, she can do religion, but not in the medical office."[16]

Stage 3: Threatening

Banning religious expression within academic, institutional, corporate, or public arenas is not enough for many secularists. They are determined to make Christians pay the price even when privately performing actions that conflict with the progressive agenda.

For example, an intern at California State University Long Beach was terminated and threatened with expulsion from the graduate program for discussing her faith with co-workers, even though she did it only in her off hours.[17] A Maryland middle school student was forced to stop reading her Bible, even though she read it only during her lunch hour. She was not, however, forbidden to read Harry Potter or other books.[18] A manager in a national insurance firm was fired solely for expressing his opposition to gay marriage in a post he wrote online from his home computer.[19] In 2014, Brendan Eich, chief executive of Mozilla, was forced to resign when it was discovered he had contributed $1,000 to support California's Proposition 8, which defined marriage as the union of a man and a woman.[20]

Stage 4: Intimidating

In 2005, California parents sued to prevent psychological testing on first, third, and fifth graders because the tests contained explicit sexual questions. They lost. The court's ruling: "Parents have no due process or privacy right to override the determinations of public schools as to the information to which their children will be exposed."[21]

In 2013, the American Civil Liberties Union (ACLU) sued Mercy Health Partners, a Catholic hospital, because it did not offer abortion services to a client experiencing a difficult pregnancy. The ACLU is seeking to use the case to force all Catholic hospitals to perform abortions. As the editors of *National Review* noted, "The issue is not whether those who wish to avail themselves of certain services will be able to, but that those who object to them must be forced to participate."[22]

In October 2014, several Houston pastors encouraged Christians to sign a petition calling for a referendum on a newly passed non-discrimination ordinance that allowed men and women to use one another's restrooms. The Houston city government, under mayor Annise Parker, ordered five of the pastors to turn over all sermons, text messages, and e-mails addressing homosexuality or gender issues. Refusal to comply would mean contempt of court and jail. Mayor Parker later rescinded the subpoenas in the wake of nation-wide negative reaction.[23]

As I write this chapter, a bill is pending before the California State Senate that would prevent Christian universities from requiring from their students a profession of faith, the inclusion of core units of Bible courses in their schedule, or attendance to chapel services. It would prevent these colleges from integrating faith throughout their teaching curriculum or offering spiritual direction or pastoral care. Why these restrictions? To prevent these colleges from denying LGBT students free expression of their gender preferences or sexual orientation. As the conservative California Policy Council wrote, this "means a Baptist school can be sued for refusing to allow a male student who 'identifies' as a woman to live in a women's dormitory, or to use women's restrooms and showers."[24]

Stage 5: Litigating

A growing number of Christians and Christian organizations are being taken to court for refusing to compromise their Christian convictions. At the frontline of the battle are small businesses that provide wedding services, such as bakeries, florists, printers, caterers, and photographers. Several of these cases have made national news, including one with a Christian photographer in New Mexico who refused to photograph a lesbian "commitment ceremony." The couple sued; the photographer lost and was fined more than $6,000.[25] The most outrageous of these incidents to date is the $135,000 fine levied against the Oregon bakery owned by a Christian couple who declined to bake a wedding cake for a lesbian couple.[26] In many of these cases, Christians have paid heavily for standing by their convictions. Some lost their life's savings; others were forced out of business or into bankruptcy; and several even received death threats from activists.

Some of these disturbing stories have inspiring endings. The

ACLU brought criminal contempt charges against Florida's Pace High School principal Frank Lay and Athletic Director Robert Freeman for blessing a meal served to about twenty adult booster club members in a local church. The charge carried penalties of a six-month jail term and fines of $5,000 for each man.[27]

As the Pace High School graduation ceremonies approached, the ACLU became concerned that the controversy might lead to further violations of their agenda. They demanded that school officials prevent students from saying anything religious or offering prayers at the event. To avoid further trouble, the administrators complied.

But the almost four hundred graduating seniors took matters into their own hands. They pre-arranged to rise up *en masse* during the ceremony and recite the Lord's Prayer. Many of them painted crosses on their graduation mortarboards to make a statement of faith and show support for their beleaguered principal and coach. Parents, family, and friends in the audience joined in the recitation and thundered their applause at the end.[28]

Unless there is a major turnaround, we can expect lawsuits and court judgments against Christians who practice their faith to escalate. According to one writer, "Persecution could well accelerate to include Henry VIII–style seizure of church property and monies because of Christian leaders' refusal to bow to the doctrines of the State. . . . Even jail time for Christians is quite possible."[29]

I think America is a long way from the kind of persecution that involves torture and death, as Christians endured in the New Testament and now endure in other countries. But one never knows what may lurk around the corner. In my younger days, I never in my wildest nightmares dreamed that Christianity would be under fire as it now is in the United States.

THE STORY OF CHRISTIAN PERSECUTION

Christianity has suffered severe opposition from its very inception, beginning with Christ Himself. He was vilified, plotted against, arrested, convicted in a rigged trial, scourged, and crucified. He warned that following Him would mean similar persecution. Consider these selected phrases spoken to His disciples in Matthew 10: "Behold, I send you out as sheep in the midst of wolves. . . . Beware of men, for they will deliver you up to councils and scourge you in their synagogues. You will be brought before governors and kings for My sake. . . . Now brother will deliver up brother to death, and a father his child; and children will rise up against parents and cause them to be put to death. And you will be hated by all for My name's sake" (vv. 16, 17–18, 21–22).

In his book *Christ Plays in Ten Thousand Places*, Eugene Peterson wrote:

> Eighteen hundred years or so of Hebrew history capped by a full exposition in Jesus Christ tell us that God's revelation of himself is rejected far more often than it is accepted, is dismissed by far more people than embrace it, and has been either attacked or ignored by every major culture or civilization in which it has given its witness: magnificent Egypt, fierce Assyria, beautiful Babylon, artistic Greece, political Rome, Enlightenment France, Nazi Germany, Renaissance Italy, Marxist Russia, Maoist China, and pursuit-of-happiness America.[30]

Why does the gift of salvation encounter such persistent opposition? In a nutshell, it's because along with salvation comes submission to God. But since humanity's fall in Eden, people have resisted submission to any power outside self. They demand freedom to define right and wrong for themselves and to live life on their own terms. They reject suggestions that any choice they make should bring down criticism or censure. Their credo is that of poet William Ernest Henley: "I am the master of my fate, I am the captain of my soul."[31]

Christian behavior angers non-Christians because it makes them feel judged. It resurrects the embedded truth of moral accountability that God planted firmly in every human heart—a truth they are determined to kill and bury. But as the apostle Paul wrote, the existence of God and the tenets of natural law are too obvious to be suppressed:

> Since the creation of the world His invisible attributes are clearly seen, being understood by the things that are made . . . so that they are without excuse, because, although they knew God, they did not glorify Him as God, nor were thankful, but became futile in their thoughts, and their foolish hearts were darkened. (Romans 1:20–21)

When Christianity in practice arouses the dormant consciences of non-Christians, their response is seldom to accept the message but rather to "kill the messenger." Silencing us allows them to stifle the latent knowledge of truth resurrected by our behavior. This is why persecution has been a persistent counterpoint to Christianity throughout its entire history.

Persecution of Christians in the Bible

Persecution in the New Testament begins shortly after Christ's birth in Bethlehem and does not end until the final chapters of Revelation. Here are a few of the most notable examples:

- The Judean king Herod, fearful of reports that a prophesied king had been born in Bethlehem, tried to protect his dynasty

68

by killing all the male babies born there within the prophetic time frame (Matthew 2:1–16).

- John the Baptist, the first public proclaimer of Christ, was beheaded by Herod's son, Herod Antipas (Mark 6:25–29).
- Several times the Jewish people and their leaders, angered over Jesus' message and His rebukes, tried to seize and kill Him even before their successful crucifixion plot (Luke 4:28–30; 13:31; John 5:16, 18; 7:1, 19, 25, 44; 8:37, 40; 11:53).
- Peter and other apostles were arrested, beaten, and imprisoned several times for preaching Christ (Acts 4:1–3; 5:17–18, 22–40; 12:1–4).
- Stephen was stoned to death by angry Jews for preaching Christ (7:54–60).
- The first Christian converts living in Jerusalem were dispersed to other lands, fleeing persecution by the Jewish leaders (8:1).
- All twelve of the apostles died violent deaths at the hands of their persecutors except John, who was exiled to the penal island of Patmos (Revelation 1:9).
- The apostle Paul suffered almost every kind of persecution that could be inflicted. He was often imprisoned, stoned almost to death, five times beaten with thirty-nine stripes, three times beaten with rods, run out of town, and often hungry, cold, and without adequate clothing (2 Corinthians 11:22–29).

The amazing thing about the early Christians is how they reacted to all the persecution heaped on them. When the Jews began persecuting them soon after Pentecost, many were forced to uproot their lives, leave their homes, and even face possible imprisonment or death. Did this make them bitter, unhappy, or regretful? Did it discourage them or cause second thoughts? Hardly! Instead of bemoaning their fate,

Luke tells us that they formed a community of mutual support and flourished:

> The multitude of those who believed were of one heart and one soul; neither did anyone say that any of the things he possessed was his own, but they had all things in common. And with great power the apostles gave witness to the resurrection of the Lord Jesus. And great grace was upon them all. Nor was there anyone among them who lacked; for all who were possessors of lands or houses sold them, and brought the proceeds of the things that were sold, and laid them at the apostles' feet; and they distributed to each as anyone had need. (Acts 4:32–35)

When Peter and John reported how they had been arrested, jailed, and warned under threat never again to preach about Jesus, these disciples responded with an exuberant prayer of elation: "Now, Lord, look on their threats, and grant to Your servants that with all boldness they may speak Your word, by stretching out Your hand to heal, and that signs and wonders may be done through the name of Your holy Servant Jesus" (Acts 4:29–30).

Persecution only increased their dedication and made them bolder in proclaiming the truth. It is an inspiring example for us today.

Persecution of Christians in History

The empire best known for persecuting Christians is ancient Rome. In the first century, Romans under Nero burned Christians on stakes and fed them alive to lions for arena entertainment. The apostles Peter and Paul were executed under Nero. Later in the century, the Roman emperor Domitian declared himself to be "Lord and God" and executed Christians who refused to worship him.[32] The apostle John was exiled under the reign of Domitian. Romans continued to persecute Christians with varying degrees of intensity until the emperor Constantine declared Christianity legal in AD 313.

Other empires, nations, and religions also have taken up the sword against Christians:

- In the various inquisitions between 1540 and 1685, the Catholic church martyred over 1.7 million Christians accused of heresy throughout Europe.[33] They also persecuted the "Wycliffites," who tried to distribute the first English Bibles.[34]
- In France, the Saint Bartholomew's Day Massacre killed an estimated 3,000 French Protestants in Paris.[35]
- Seventeenth-century Japan made Christianity illegal, expelled missionaries, and executed converts.
- Eighteenth-century China made Christianity illegal and persecuted Christians severely.
- The French Revolution of 1789 outlawed Christianity. Clergy were banished or killed. Churches were desecrated, and all semblances of Christianity were removed.[36]
- The Ottoman Empire has a long history of persecuting Christians. In 1915 alone, the Islamic Turks massacred 2.7 million Christians. Estimates of Christian deaths during the history of the empire run as high as 50 million.[37]
- After the Russian Revolution of 1917, churches, Christian teaching, training, and liturgy were made illegal. The state confiscated all church property. Millions of dissenters were executed.[38]

Many who have suffered for their faith have embraced persecution with joy. One such story comes out of the reign of England's

Queen Mary, known as "Bloody Mary" for her relentless persecution of Protestants. Nicholas Ridley had been a chaplain to King Henry VIII, the founder of the Protestant Church of England. When Mary ascended the throne, she was determined to force English subjects back into Catholicism. Ridley refused to comply and was condemned to burn at the stake in 1555. As he was being tied to the stake, Ridley prayed, "Oh, heavenly Father, I give unto thee most hearty thanks that thou hast called me to be a professor of thee, even unto death."[39]

Persecution of Christians in Today's World

Many believe that worldwide persecution of Christians today is worse than at any time in history. Each month, 322 Christians are killed for their faith, 214 church buildings and Christian properties are destroyed, and 772 forms of violence are committed against individual Christians or Christian groups. Those figures add up to more than fifteen thousand incidents of serious persecution of Christians per year.[40] The top ten persecuting countries are North Korea, Iraq, Eritrea, Afghanistan, Syria, Pakistan, Somalia, Sudan, Iran, and Libya.[41]

Given the history and present state of Christian persecution worldwide, it becomes less surprising that we are beginning to feel the sting of it in the United States. To have a nation established on and aligned with Christian principles has been the exception historically. That alignment is now breaking down, and we are reverting to the historical norm.

THE SIDE EFFECTS OF CHRISTIAN PERSECUTION

How should Christians in the United States react to persecution? The first response might naturally be anger. But the New Testament gives us a more constructive response. The first Christians suffered persecution much more severe than anything we presently face, and we never find them responding in anger. In fact, they found positive benefits in suffering.

Paul told the Philippian church, "For to you it has been granted on behalf of Christ, not only to believe in Him, but also to suffer for His sake" (Philippians 1:29). Note the way he put it: "it has been *granted* to you." He made suffering sound like a gift. Suffering is a gift? Really? The natural impulse is to say we'd like to return it and settle for a necktie or headscarf instead. But to reject suffering is to miss out on enormous blessings. Let's explore just what this means.

Suffering Promotes Character

A man came to his pastor and said, "Pastor, I've come to realize that I'm an extremely impatient man. Would you please pray that God will give me patience?"

Two weeks later, he returned and said, "Good grief, Pastor! What did you pray? Terrible things are happening to me. My life's coming unglued."

"Well," replied the pastor, "You wanted patience. The Bible says, 'Tribulation works patience,' so I prayed for tribulation. God must be answering my prayer."

Suffering is to be borne with patience because it helps to shape Christian character. Although persecution is inflicted by enemies of God, He can use it as a form of discipline to mold us into greater Christlikeness. As Paul told us, "We also glory in tribulations, knowing that tribulation produces perseverance; and perseverance, character; and character, hope. Now hope does not disappoint, because the love of God has been poured out in our hearts by the Holy Spirit who was given to us" (Romans 5:3–5).

Contrary to what we often hear, the call to follow Christ is not a call to an easy life filled with green lights and smooth highways. Such a life would never jar loose the tenacious grip of self-will that has clutched our hearts since the fall of Adam.

As John Ortberg put it, "God isn't at work producing the circumstances I want. God is at work in bad circumstances to produce the me he wants."[42]

C. S. Lewis explained the purpose of suffering like this:

> Now God, who has made us, knows what we are and that our happiness lies in Him. Yet we will not seek it in Him as long as He leaves us any other resort where it can even plausibly be looked for. While what we call "our own life" remains agreeable, we will not surrender it to Him. What then can God do in our interest but make "our own life" less agreeable to us, and take away the plausible sources of false happiness.[43]

When Pierre-Auguste Renoir, the great French impressionist, was afflicted with arthritis, his hands became twisted and deformed. The simple act of holding a brush became excruciating. In time he was confined to his wheelchair, but did he give up his painting? Absolutely not!

One day Renoir's artist friend Henri Matisse visited him and watched the great painter as he painfully grasped a brush using only his fingertips. Every movement was agony, yet he doggedly kept at his painting.

Matisse exclaimed, "How can you paint at the expense of such torture?"

Renoir replied, "The pain passes, but the beauty remains."

So it is with the beauty of the soul that endures the agony of suffering. One of our hymns, "How Firm a Foundation," puts it this way:

When through fiery trials thy pathway shall lie,
My grace, all-sufficient, shall be thy supply;
The flame shall not hurt thee; I only design
Thy dross to consume, and thy gold to refine.

Suffering Provokes Courage

Courage is a hallmark of authentic Christianity because it reflects Christ's character in adverse circumstances. It is the crucial virtue that Christians must deploy when facing cultural demands that conflict with biblical teaching.

The apostles Peter and John faced such a demand when the Jewish leaders hauled them into court for preaching Christ and demanded that they cease immediately. Peter and John replied, "Whether it is right in the sight of God to listen to you more than to God, you judge. For we cannot but speak the things which we have seen and heard" (Acts 4:19–20).

The Jewish leaders released the apostles, thinking their stern warning would cower them. So what did Peter and John do? They went straight back out and kept on preaching. No amount of arrests, jail time, or court edicts could intimidate these courageous apostles.

After the apostle Paul's dramatic conversion, his entire life became a sterling example of this kind of courage. As he wrote to the Philippians, "I eagerly expect and hope that I will in no way be ashamed, but will have sufficient courage so that now as always Christ will be exalted in my body, whether by life or by death. For to me, to live is Christ and to die is gain" (Philippians 1:20–21 NIV).

A young woman and her small daughter were walking through the woods when a sudden rustling in the underbrush caused the little girl to cling to her mother's skirt and cry out, "Mommy, I'm afraid!"

"We're all afraid sometimes," replied the mother. "That's when we need courage."

"What is courage?" asked the daughter.

At that moment they came upon a patch of earth blackened and charred by a recent forest fire. No living thing could be seen except for a single, delicate red flower thrusting up from the ashes. The mother pointed to the flower and said, "Look at that little flower, living and growing where everything around it is lifeless; displaying its color where everything around it is gray; unafraid to bloom alone where there is no other beauty to be seen. That, my dear, is courage."[44]

Suffering Proves Godliness

A. W. Tozer wrote, "To be right with God has often meant to be in trouble with men."[45] As Paul put it, "All who desire to live godly in Christ Jesus will suffer persecution" (2 Timothy 3:12). It's really a matter of simple logic: Why would the enemies of Christianity bother anyone who is not displaying the nature of Christ?

As we noted earlier, God often uses persecution as a means of discipline—a severe but necessary way of producing godliness by rooting out of us everything that is not eternal. The writer of Hebrews said, "For whom the LORD loves He chastens" (Hebrews 12:6). If God did not love us, why would He bother with discipline? Seen from this angle, persecution gives us cause for thanksgiving and praise, for it forms the character of God in us: "But may the God of all grace, who called us to His eternal glory by Christ Jesus, after you have suffered a while, perfect, establish, strengthen, and settle you" (1 Peter 5:10).

D. Martyn Lloyd-Jones wrote, "If you are suffering as a Christian, and because you are a Christian, it is one of the surest proofs you can ever have of the fact that you are a child of God."[46]

Suffering Produces Joy

When we realize the purpose, blessings, and positive results of suffering persecution, it can become a source of real joy, as it was for Paul and Silas when they encountered opposition in the city of Philippi. In Acts 16:22–24, they were mobbed, arrested, beaten severely, and thrown into prison with their feet fastened in stocks. Then we read, "But at midnight Paul and Silas were praying and singing hymns to God, and the prisoners were listening to them" (v. 25).

These two disciples, beaten and imprisoned without a trial, were so joyful they couldn't help but burst into song! This tells us that joy comes not from the absence of suffering or even in spite of suffering; it often comes *because* of suffering. The source of joy is our relationship with God, and that relationship is affirmed when we courageously suffer persecution. This affirmation of God's approval is the source of our joy, and it may never come to us as powerfully as when we are persecuted.

Peter and John exhibited this kind of joy after the Jewish leaders had them beaten for preaching Jesus: "They departed from the presence of the council, rejoicing that they were counted worthy to suffer shame for His name" (Acts 5:41).

Suffering Provides Rewards

The Scriptures abound with promises of lavish rewards for those who endure suffering. Often we allow these future rewards to be obscured by the immediate gratifications found in status, power, pleasure, or social acceptance. Moses could easily have allowed the immediate to obscure the distant. Raised as a prince in the luxury of Egypt's royal palace, he had access to it all—security, riches, pleasure, status, and power. But the Bible tells us that "By faith Moses, when he became of age, refused to be called the son of Pharaoh's daughter, choosing rather to suffer affliction with the people of God than to enjoy the passing pleasures of sin, esteeming the reproach of Christ greater riches than the treasures in Egypt; for he looked to the reward" (Hebrews 11:24–26).

Because Moses saw and realized the high value of the eternal reward, he was willing not only to turn his back on immediate pleasure, position, and power but also to suffer affliction in order to receive the promise of heaven.

What are some of the rewards promised to those who endure persecution?

- They will be avenged (Revelation 6:9–11; 16:5–7; 18:20; 19:2).
- They will be rewarded with white robes, signifying holiness and purity (6:11).
- They will be given perfect and abundant lives free of sorrow (7:14–17).
- Heaven will rejoice over them because they did not shrink from death (12:11–12).
- They will find eternal rest (14:13).
- They will reign with Christ for 1,000 years (20:4, 6).
- They will receive the crown of eternal life (James 1:12).
- They will have no more death to fear (1 Corinthians 15:54; Revelation 20:14).

These are just a few of the uncountable rewards that await those who suffer persecution for Christ's sake. The apostle Paul wrote, "For I consider that the sufferings of this present time are not worthy to be compared with the glory which shall be revealed in us" (Romans 8:18).

John Stott reminds us that suffering is a prerequisite to this glory:

The sufferings and the glory belong together indissolubly. They did in the experience of Christ; they do in the experience of his people also. It is only after we "have suffered a little while" that we will enter God's "eternal glory in Christ," to which he has called us. So the sufferings and the glory are married; they cannot be divorced. They are welded; they cannot be broken apart.[47]

Dr. Nyquist addressed persecution in a way that almost makes it seem exciting. I offer his words as an inspiring wrap-up to this section:

In God's economy, persecution means *we're blessed, not cursed*. Persecution brings blessing because it allows us to know Christ more. Persecution brings blessing because it allows us to become more like Christ.

For years we've sung *God Bless America*, and we've usually associated divine blessing with prosperity and freedom. Certainly that's blessing because every good gift and all freedom comes from God. But there's a significant part of God's blessing we missed in America— the blessing that comes with persecution. Perhaps the cultural change in our country and the arrival of persecution for believers is God's answer to our plea, "God bless America!" Perhaps believers in America will be able to experience divine blessing like never before in our history. Believers in the rest of the world know and experience this blessing. Maybe it's time for us to get in on the party.[48]

THE STRENGTH TO FACE CHRISTIAN PERSECUTION

Many Christians have not yet faced serious opposition for holding to their beliefs. When we are untried and untested, we wonder just how strong we will be when it is our freedom, our job, or our pocketbook that is on the line.

I have a friend who raised three daughters. When the girls reached dating age, he gave them advice on resisting temptation that I think applies to persecution as well:

> If you wait until the moment of temptation to decide how you will handle it, it's too late. You've already lost the battle, because you have not prepared your will to override your feelings. You must put steel into your will by deciding in advance that you will not yield, and you must take positive steps to reinforce that decision. Visualize yourself in the situation. Rehearse in your mind just what you will do and say. Resolve in advance to follow your predetermined program even in the face of pressure. And then when the temptation comes, you will have built a solid wall against it, and resistance becomes merely a matter of acting on your predetermined conviction.

Paul knew the importance of preparing his converts for suffering. He said to the new believers in Thessalonica: "And [we] sent Timothy . . . to establish you and encourage you concerning your faith, that no one should be shaken by these afflictions. . . . For, in fact, we told you before when we were with you that we would suffer tribulation, just as it happened, and you know" (1 Thessalonians 3:2–4).

After their first missionary journey, Paul and Barnabas "returned to Lystra, Iconium, and Antioch, strengthening the souls of the disciples, exhorting them to continue in the faith, and saying, 'We must through many tribulations enter the kingdom of God'" (Acts 14:21–22).

Richard Wurmbrand knew suffering. He "was an evangelical minister who spent fourteen years in Communist imprisonment and torture in his homeland of Romania."[49] His experience led him to help others prepare for suffering:

> I remember my last Confirmation class before I left Romania. I took a group of ten to fifteen boys and girls on a Sunday morning, not to a church, but to the zoo. Before the cage of lions, I told them, "Your forefathers in faith were thrown before such wild beasts for their faith. Know that you also will have to suffer. You will not be thrown before lions, but you will have to do with men who would be much worse than lions. Decide here and now if you wish to pledge allegiance to Christ." They had tears in their eyes when they said yes.
>
> We have to make the preparation now, before we are imprisoned. In prison you lose everything. You are undressed and given a prisoner's suit. No more nice furniture, nice carpets, or nice curtains. You do not have a wife any more and you do not have your children. You do not have your library and you never see a flower. Nothing of what makes life pleasant remains. Nobody resists who has not renounced the pleasures of life beforehand.[50]

There are certain decisions we can make and certain steps we can take in advance to steel ourselves for the moment when persecution comes. Let's look at three things we can do to prepare for that moment.

Determine to Stand for Truth

In his famous Harvard commencement address, Alexandr Solzhenitsyn said, "A decline in courage may be the most striking feature that an outside observer notices in the West in our days."[51]

We as Christians must turn that criticism on its head. It is imperative that fear of rejection, criticism, or loss does not cower us into hiding our light. To live worthy of the gospel is to stand for God's truth without bending. As Paul urged the Corinthians, we are to "watch, stand fast in the faith, be brave, be strong. Let all that you do be done with love" (1 Corinthians 16:13–14).

Two men who recently followed Paul's admonition are the twin brothers David and Jason Benham. The Benhams are successful real estate entrepreneurs who were contracted to host a series on HGTV called "Flip It Forward." After filming a few episodes, activists discovered that the brothers were Christians and that David had made controversial comments about abortion and gay marriage in the past. Although the brothers' beliefs on these subjects had nothing to do with the content of their show, the activists pressured HGTV into canceling the program.[52]

Afterward David Benham said, "I believe that God looks down from Heaven and he sees men and women that will stand in the gap on behalf of the land and will rebuild the wall and get back to the foundations of true biblical Christianity."[53]

Don't think because you are not in a high-profile situation like the Benham brothers that your stand for truth doesn't matter. It can make a big difference, as it did when an unknown man prayed on his knees in the snow outside a Maryland abortion clinic. Inside sat a young woman waiting to have an abortion. She looked out the window and saw the praying man, and his simple piety convicted her. She canceled her appointment and had her baby.[54]

Wherever we are and whatever we do, we are called to be God's agent at that particular time and place. Whatever the situation, our task is really quite simple: Don't think about the cost; don't think about the result; just think about what you decided in advance that you would do when you are tested. God can use your courage in little things to accomplish bigger things.

Sometimes the persecution we experience may be nothing more

than scorn or denunciation. Even so, it can make standing against prevailing opinion very painful. One of our deepest needs is acceptance, which is why we naturally seek the approval of our peer groups. But difficult as it may be, peer acceptance is one of the things we may be called to sacrifice. This means willingness to be labeled a prude for avoiding movies, books, speech, TV shows, and activities that promote immorality, sacrilege, or ungodly values. It means willingness to be labeled stupid for believing in creation, homophobic for rejecting homosexuality, anti-feminist for rejecting abortion, and intolerant for professing the exclusivity of Christ. As Paul put it, we must be willing to be "fools for Christ's sake," or even to be scorned as "the filth of the world" (1 Corinthians 4:10, 13).

John Piper wrote:

> Following Jesus means that wherever obedience requires it, we will accept betrayal and rejection and beating and mockery and crucifixion and death. Jesus gives us the assurance that if we will follow him to Golgotha during all the Good Fridays of this life, we will also rise with him on the last Easter day of the resurrection.[55]

We need more strong examples like the Benham brothers who are unafraid to defend unpopular truths and refuse to be silent when truth is trampled. Or like Hobby Lobby's David Green, who refused to back down when confronted with immoral governmental mandates. We need more leaders like Governor Mike Pence and members of the Indiana legislature who refused to back down under immense pressure after passing a law strictly limiting the basis on which abortions can be performed.[56]

It is our duty to stand up and speak out for biblical truth when it is attacked. But it is also our duty to confront with love, taking care that we do not justify the labels of hate and intolerance that some people slap on us. Paul gave us our rules of engagement: "Being reviled, we bless; being persecuted, we endure; being defamed, we entreat" (1 Corinthians 4:12–13). And Peter added that when faced with persecution, we must be prepared to defend our faith with reason and civility: "Always be ready to give a defense to everyone who asks you a reason for the hope that is in you, with meekness and fear; having a good conscience, that when they defame you as evildoers, those who revile your good conduct in Christ may be ashamed" (1 Peter 3:15–16).

Draw Support from One Another

Even in the best of times, Christians should make the church their primary peer group and social circle. When we are under attack, having a support group of others who share our beliefs and values makes resisting the onslaught of progressivism much easier. This is why regular church attendance is so critical to a healthy Christian lifestyle. By attendance I mean more than just showing up for organized worship on Sunday morning. Attend classes, join service groups, involve yourself in outreach, and participate in social fellowship. In order to sail through today's troubled waters, the church needs all hands on deck. The church needs you, and you need the church. As the writer of Hebrews put it, "Let us consider one another in order to stir up love and good works, not forsaking the assembling of ourselves together, as is the manner of some, but exhorting one another, and so much the more as you see the Day approaching" (Hebrews 10:24–25).

We cannot be Christians alone. We need the company of others like ourselves with whom we can share encouragement, struggles, and victories. It is easy for us to feel alone and discouraged, but in the company of fellow believers, we draw strength, discipline, knowledge, encouragement, support, and love from one another. A courageous example can spur any one of us to say, "If he or she can do it, by God's grace so can I."

Derive Your Security from the Lord

The key to standing firm in the face of persecution is to remember whom we belong to and where we are going. We belong to Christ, and He secures us in His hand. Thus we need not fear danger to our reputations, our jobs, our finances, or even our physical lives. As He said, "For whoever desires to save his life will lose it, but whoever loses his life for My sake will find it" (Matthew 16:25).

All the persecution we experience originates in Satan, the usurper who is temporarily the lord of the earth. That is why C. S. Lewis called this fallen world "enemy-occupied territory." We Christians form a resistance movement fighting to reclaim lost territory under the leadership of our supreme commander, Jesus Christ. We draw courage from knowing who we belong to, where we are going, and the glory that awaits us when we get there: "Our citizenship is in heaven. And we eagerly await a Savior from there, the Lord Jesus Christ, who, by the power that enables him to bring everything under his control, will transform our lowly bodies so that they will be like his glorious body" (Philippians 3:20–21 NIV; see also 4:1).

John Chrysostom, the golden-tongued preacher who was made archbishop of Constantinople, ran afoul of the Byzantine Empress Eudoxia for preaching against the court's misuse of wealth, the neglect of the poor, and immoral indulgences. Trumped-up charges of heresy were brought against Chrysostom, and he was brought before the empress for trial. When he refused to bend, the story is told that the empress threatened to banish him.

"You cannot banish me," Chrysostom replied. "For this world is my Father's house."

"But I will kill you," said Eudoxia.

"No, you cannot, for my life is hidden with Christ in God."

"I will take away your treasures."

"No you cannot, for my treasure is in heaven and my heart is there."

"But I will drive you away from your friends and you will have no one left," said Eudoxia.

"No, you cannot, for I have a Friend in heaven from whom you cannot separate me. I defy you, for there is nothing you can do to harm me."

What do you do with a man like that? Eudoxia finally exiled Chrysostom. He was force-marched through hostile conditions that soon brought about his death.[57]

We, like Chrysostom, must realize that our persecutors can take nothing from us that we don't already have securely fixed in Christ, whether it is home, family, friends, treasure, or life itself. That is the key to standing up to persecution. Our security, our peace, and our joy is ultimately found only in Christ.

It is not likely that Christians in America will soon face martyrdom. But we can draw courage from Christians like Chrysostom, martyrs throughout the centuries, and Christians who are now enduring severe persecution in other countries. If they can stand strong in the face of torture and death, we should be willing to stand strong in the face of the Christian repression that is rising in our nation today.

CHAPTER 4

THE APATHY OF AMERICA

Almost two hundred years ago, Scottish professor Alexander Fraser Tytler wrote the following words about the Athenian Republic, which had fallen more than two thousand years earlier:

> A democracy is always temporary in nature; it simply cannot exist as a permanent form of government. A democracy will continue to exist up until the time that voters discover they can vote themselves generous gifts from the public treasury. From that moment on, the majority always votes for the candidates who promise the most benefits from the public treasury, with the result that every democracy will finally collapse due to loose fiscal policy, which is always followed by a dictatorship.
>
> The average age of the world's greatest civilizations from the beginning of history, has been about 200 years. During those 200 years, these nations always progressed through the following sequence: From bondage to spiritual faith, from spiritual faith to great courage, from courage to liberty, from liberty to abundance, from abundance to complacency, from complacency to apathy, from apathy to dependency, and from dependence back to bondage.[1]

An honest appraisal of our nation strongly indicates that we are moving steadily toward the end of Professor Tytler's list. It is not a stretch to describe the United States as an apathetic nation.

According to Webster, apathy is "the feeling of not having much emotion or interest." The word is composed of the prefix *a*, meaning "without," added to the root word *pathos*, meaning "emotion, feeling."[2] An apathetic nation is a cynical one—a nation whose people simply don't care anymore.

Someone has said, "The nice thing about apathy is you don't have to exert yourself to show you're sincere about it." A story was once circulated during the presidency of Ronald Reagan, saying that as he presided over a cabinet meeting, two factions were locked in a rancorous debate—one side persistently seeking information and the other not wanting to be bothered. A frustrated department secretary finally said, "Mr. President, which is worse: ignorance or apathy?" Always able to diffuse tension with a touch of levity, Reagan replied, "I don't know, and I don't care."

In his article "The United States of Apathy's Motto Is 'We Don't Care,'" Professor Howard Steven Friedman describes the indifferent attitude of our country:

> Americans don't care. We don't care about voting unless we're convinced it's a "once in a lifetime" candidate. We don't care about our outrageously expensive and often ineffective health care unless we are uninsured and sick. We don't care that the economic crisis robbed us and future generations of "untraceable" billions unless we're unemployed. We don't care that tax cuts for the wealthy are provided under the thin guise of "stimulating the economy" unless we are rich. We don't care that the future of the middle class is being choked by declining support for education unless our

children are illiterate. We don't care about the homeless and the poor unless they are dying on our doorstep. We don't care that our crime and incarceration rates are vastly higher than other wealthy countries unless we are a victim. We don't care about America's weak internal security unless we get attacked. We don't care about the lives lost in Iraq and Afghanistan unless we have a relative or close friend there. We don't care about religion unless a mosque is being proposed near Ground Zero. America is truly exceptional in its ability to not care.[3]

To help us understand how we have become a nation marked by indifference, let's go back to the beginning of America's story. Perhaps remembering God's providence and provision for our nation will move our hearts from apathy to thanksgiving.

AMERICA AND THE PROVIDENCE OF GOD

He refused to be called "Your Highness" or "Excellency." When he was unanimously elected the first president of the newly constituted nation called America, George Washington, with typical humility, settled on "Mr. President." He also set other precedents that have remained to this day. He instituted the first cabinet of advisors, initiated the tradition of the inaugural address, and established two terms as the traditional limit for a president to serve.

His rise to leadership was not wholly a surprise. He came from a prominent, wealthy Virginia family; he was tall, distinguished, well-spoken, and a natural leader. The Continental Congress asked him to lead the Continental Army in a winner-take-all struggle to drive the British from American shores. He endured the freezing conditions at

Valley Forge, Pennsylvania, during the 1777–1778 winter. Plagued by limited resources throughout the war, he led the Colonies to victory in 1783—seven years after the Declaration of Independence. Instead of grasping for the power that he could easily have claimed, Washington resigned his military commission and returned to Virginia and the farming life.

He was recalled to service in 1787 to lead the Constitutional Convention—the anvil on which the new democratic republic would be hammered out by conviction and compromise. And then the obvious happened: Washington was elected the first president in 1789. He traveled from Virginia to New York, the seat of American government at that time, to be sworn in as the first president.

On April 30, 1789—inauguration day—Washington took the oath of office on a second floor balcony of Federal Hall on Wall Street in what is now lower Manhattan. A large crowd stood in the street below to watch "the father of his country" be sworn in.

After the ceremony, Washington and the members of Congress gathered in the Senate Chamber of Federal Hall, where the newly minted president revealed his heart to the leaders of the experiment called America. For perhaps the very first time, the stately leader realized the enormity of the new responsibility settled upon him. Senator William Maclay of Pennsylvania recorded this remembrance of Washington standing before the assembled leaders of the nation: "This great man was agitated and embarrassed more than ever he was by the levelled Cannon or pointed Musket."[4]

I doubt it was stage fright that made Washington nervous. I believe he, and probably most of the leaders in that room, were humbled by the sense of destiny that had settled upon that moment. All one has to do is read the well-documented thoughts of our Founding Fathers to know they felt the hand of Providence upon their lives. These men, almost all well-versed in their knowledge of Scripture, understood that all nations are under God regardless of whether they know it or like it. It will serve us well to familiarize ourselves with the same testimony of the Word of God that was so clear in the minds of our nation's founders:

> When the Most High divided their inheritance to the nations,
> When He separated the sons of Adam,
> He set the boundaries of the peoples
> According to the number of the children of Israel.
> (Deuteronomy 32:8)

> Yours is the kingdom, O Lord,
> And You are exalted as head over all.
> Both riches and honor come from You,
> And You reign over all.
> In Your hand is power and might;
> In Your hand it is to make great
> And to give strength to all. (1 Chronicles 29:11–12)

> He makes nations great, and destroys them;
> He enlarges nations, and guides them. (Job 12:23)

> The king's heart is in the hand of the Lord,
> Like the rivers of water;
> He turns it wherever He wishes. (Proverbs 21:1)

> He removes kings and raises up kings;
> He gives wisdom to the wise
> And knowledge to those who have understanding. (Daniel 2:21)

> The Most High rules in the kingdom of men,
> Gives it to whomever He will,
> And sets over it the lowest of men. (4:17)

> His dominion is an everlasting dominion,
> And His kingdom is from generation to generation.
> All the inhabitants of the earth are reputed as nothing;
> He does according to His will in the army of heaven
> And among the inhabitants of the earth.
> No one can restrain His hand
> Or say to Him, "What have You done?" (4:34–35)

> God, who made the world and everything in it, since He is Lord of heaven and earth, does not dwell in temples made with hands. . . . And He has made from one blood every nation of men to dwell on all the face of the earth, and has determined their preappointed times and the boundaries of their dwellings. (Acts 17:24, 26)

One might well wonder, if God is in control of nations, why aren't all of them righteous, just, strong, and enduring? This is not the place to get into the complexities of how God's providence and control can coexist with man's free will, but we know from the history of nations in the Old Testament that God allows governments to descend into evil only to a point before He steps in and brings the nation down. John Phillips has written:

> Governments may be weak or strong, just or oppressive, benevolent or cruel, wise or foolish, but in each case, God has His way and moves His own plans forward. Democracies and dictatorships alike are under His control. . . . Nations come and go, kingdoms rise and

fall, empires wax and wane, but behind them all is God, overruling in the affairs of men. . . . From our viewpoint, the strands may seem tangled, meaningless, hopelessly knotted, unequal and wrong. But the tapestry He is weaving is perfect, and all the pressures of Satanic force and human sin are gloriously overruled by a God who is both omnipotent and omniscient.[5]

Fast-forward from 1789 to 2016 to see how things have changed in America. Our leaders still maintain a surface level of respect for the role of God in our nation—they still say, "God bless America," and "In God We Trust" is still the official motto of the United States. But those phrases often ring hollow on the lips of those who mouth them. Their actions belie the words. It may be just a matter of time before those foundations so firmly set by our forefathers disappear. It is already happening in some mainstream parts of the culture.

Take for example the NBCUniversal news and media organization. During the US Open championship golf tournament in 2011, NBC twice featured a segment showing children reciting the Pledge of Allegiance to America. In the recitation, the words *under God* and *indivisible* were omitted. When Senator Dan Coats of Indiana, in a letter to NBC, expressed his "serious concern" about NBC's editing of the Pledge of Allegiance, the company admitted it was a "bad decision" made by a small group of people.[6]

It later became obvious that NBCUniversal's explanation was disingenuous. If the company leaders really thought those cuts were a bad decision made by rogue employees, why did they make the same cuts again in 2015? In a television promo for an upcoming spy thriller called, ironically, "Allegiance," a chorus of voices can be heard reciting the Pledge of Allegiance—and leaving out, again, the words "under God."[7] When the foundations of devotion are obliterated, it is no wonder that apathy sets in.

AMERICA AND THE PROVISION OF GOD

In 1815, President James Madison proclaimed, "No people ought to feel greater obligations to celebrate the goodness of the Great Disposer of Events of the Destiny of Nations than the people of the United States. . . . And to the same Divine author of Every Good and Perfect Gift we are indebted for all those privileges and advantages, religious as well as civil, which are so richly enjoyed in this favored land."[8]

Now, two hundred years after those words were spoken, it is easy to feel discouraged, thinking our nation has gone off the rails after being laid by such godly proclamations. Although it is clear that our nation is drifting dangerously, it is easy to forget that many of those original blessings are still intact, and we are still beneficiaries of what our founders began. Despite our deep and serious problems, the blessings we still enjoy in America make us the envy of the world. In His providence, God has provided for America and still provides for it in many ways. Considering a few of those blessings may help us to see our nation's glass as half full instead of half empty.

The Blessing of Our Forefathers

Herbert Hoover, the thirty-first president of the United States, said, "Our Founding Fathers built for the United States a government new and different from all the governments of the Old World by three strokes of genius. . . . They enacted a written Constitution . . . they made a division of powers within the Federal and State governments by separating the Legislative and the Judiciary, and the Executive branches. And they reinforced all this by the declared purpose to establish a government of laws where every citizen was equal before the law."[9]

What was the source of these brilliant, revolutionary ideas? The Judeo-Christian Scriptures. Moses gave Israel a written constitution: a tripartite government of prophets, priests, and kings ruled a decentralized nation of twelve tribal states. All were equal before the throne of God. The Founding Fathers did not think America was Israel or the kingdom of God, but they certainly recognized the wisdom of how God governs and applied it freely to America's system of governance.

The Blessing of Our Freedom

The Pilgrims came to America to worship freely according to conscience. The Founding Fathers' generation fought for the right to be free citizens rather than restricted subjects of an earthly king. And ever since, America has welcomed those "yearning to breathe free" (as inscribed on the Statue of Liberty). More people have risked their lives to become Americans than to become citizens of any other country in the world—all because they yearned for freedom.

What Jesus said to the Jews in His day has broad sociological application to all humanity: "And you shall know the truth, and the truth shall make you free" (John 8:32). Freedom is the yearning of the human heart, and America's Declaration of Independence reflects the divine source of this yearning: "We hold these truths to be self-evident, that all men are created equal, that they are endowed by their Creator with certain unalienable Rights, that among these are Life, Liberty, and the pursuit of Happiness."

America is not the symbol of liberty to the whole world by accident. This nation was designed to reflect, corporately and individually, the biblical principle that man was created to be free. Nothing was to hinder the creature's relationship with his Creator—neither kings, nor governments, nor tyranny, nor the will of man. In a day when American soldiers are defending our right to live free from terrorism, it is incumbent upon us to thank God for a land in which freedom's bell has rung for 240 years.

We cannot enjoy the privileges of liberty without assuming commensurate responsibilities. I hope it will never be said of our generation that while we applauded those who purchased our freedom with their blood, we went to sleep on our watch and let that freedom slip through our fingers.

Somewhere along the way, we will have an opportunity to stand up and be counted. We will be called to express by word and action what the freedom of this nation truly means—the freedom to pray, the freedom to talk about God, the freedom to express our values and beliefs.

We must meet this challenge to purchase for our children the freedom we have known. For freedom is not static; it is dynamic. It is only as good as the caretakers who watch over it. Every generation has a responsibility to pass on to the next generation freedom as it was received. Those who take freedom for granted are in danger of taking for granted the Author of freedom.

While political freedom is to be cherished, we must remember that it is not the greatest freedom. The greatest freedom is freedom from sin. One can live in America and still be a slave to sin. Or one can live under the most oppressive political regimes on earth and still be completely free. Spirit-led Christians living in America have the best of both worlds—both political and spiritual freedom. While the former may be taken away, the latter can never be.

The Blessing of Our Fortunes

For nearly 250 years, Americans have been free to create, innovate, manufacture, and achieve in spectacular ways that have helped others both here and abroad. We have not used our blessings perfectly, but let's consider four significant blessings that have enabled our prosperity.

Financial Blessings

Individual wealth is not automatically a sign of God's blessing. In the Old Testament, however, Israel's wealth in its golden age was definitely a sign of God's blessing on obedient nations (Deuteronomy 28:1–14; 1 Kings 10:1–9).

Profit is built into God's creation. Every living thing on earth multiplies: animals, plants, microscopic life, and humans. Sow one seed in the earth, and reap hundreds from the resulting plant. Financial profit reflects nature's pattern. To sow one's talents and reap a profit is a godlike act (Matthew 25:14–30). Profit and abundance enable mankind to propagate the blessings of God to others.

For much of its history, America has led the world's nations in gross domestic product. We have the highest level of personal earnings and the most billionaires (more than five hundred). More than half of the world's twenty wealthiest people are Americans.[10]

Money is a means of measuring and transferring wealth. Its basic form has been precious metal, though it is most commonly represented today by paper certificates and digital entries. Money is neutral, neither good nor evil. It is what we *do* with our money, personally and nationally, that matters (1 Timothy 6:9–10, 17–19).

It is no coincidence that the wealthiest country in the world has also been the most generous country in the world. The United States gave more than $32 billion dollars in foreign aid in 2014—$12 billion more than any other nation. On a personal level, according to the World Giving Index, Americans ranked first, in both 2013 and 2014, and second in 2015, in the world in personal charitable giving and actions.[11] So both nationally and personally, America has a history of generosity.

What enables America to give so generously? The same thing that enabled King David and his people to give so generously to build the first temple in Jerusalem: "For all things come from You, and of Your own we have given You" (1 Chronicles 29:14). People who give freely receive freely. God told Malachi that if His people were generous in their giving, He would "open for you the windows of heaven and pour out for you such blessing that there will not be room enough to receive it" (Malachi 3:10). Everything we have is because of the generosity of God. Should we ever cease to be generous to others, could we expect God to continue being generous to us?

Intellectual Blessings

While American universities are by no means the oldest—the University of Bologna was founded in 1088 and the University of Oxford around 1096—they have become among the world's best. America's oldest universities were founded in New England in the seventeenth and eighteenth centuries, most of them with an emphasis on training ministers of the gospel. Just as the University of Oxford's motto betrays its original mission—"The Lord Is My Light"—so do the mottos of America's Ivy League universities:

- Harvard: "Truth"
- Yale: "Light and Truth"
- Princeton: "Under God's Power She Flourishes!"
- Brown: "In God We Hope"
- Columbia: "In Thy Light Shall We See Light"
- Dartmouth: "The Voice of One Crying Out in the Wilderness"

Sadly, all the original New England universities have abandoned their gospel-centered focus. But America's educational infrastructure is intact: We are home to eight of the top ten universities in the world, and fifty-two of the top one hundred.[12] Starting with Cal Tech, Stanford, and MIT, the United States has six of the top ten research universities in the world.[13]

Military Blessings

In the last two hundred years, only two major attacks by foreign enemies have occurred on American soil: Pearl Harbor and September 11. It is as if a hedge of protection has been placed around this nation.

The Preamble to the US Constitution states that one of the purposes of government is to "provide for the common defence [sic]." Article four, section four of the Constitution states specifically that the "United States shall guarantee to every state in this union a republican form of government, and shall protect each of them against invasion." It is a constitutional requirement that the federal government defend the nation. And it is a responsibility that has been fulfilled well.

Religious Blessings

According to one survey, 71 percent of American adults declare themselves to be Christians.[14] In terms of religious affiliation, America has been a Christian-consensus nation since its founding. But in the 1960s, the term "post-Christian" began to be applied to America. Christianity was still widely professed, but it was no longer the guiding worldview of American culture. The Christian consensus that shaped the first two centuries of America's national life is now essentially absent. The place of faith in the nation's future is an open question.

The Pew Research Center has charted the change in America's religious life from 2007 to 2014. The following declines are slight and slow, but they are declines nonetheless:

Evangelical Protestants	Declined by 0.9 percent
Catholics	Declined by 3.1 percent
Mainline Protestants	Declined by 3.4 percent

The rise of people who do not affiliate with any religious tradition is indicative of the secularization of American society and the marginalization of faith:

| Non-Christian Faiths | Increased by 1.2 percent |
| Unaffiliated | Increased by 6.7 percent[15] |

This is not to say the Christian faith cannot or will not begin to grow again in America. But the downward trend must reverse dramatically if the blessings of religion are to continue.

Does this mean our nation will not survive? Does the Bible offer any guidance concerning America's future?

AMERICA AND THE PLAN OF GOD

Joel Rosenberg has written many books addressing end-time events and has been consulted by leaders of nations, including Israel and the United States, concerning present realities and future possibilities. He has noted a shift in the questions he is most often asked when he speaks and does interviews. In the past, the most frequent question was "Joel, how can you be Jewish and believe that Jesus is the Messiah?" But since 2000, the most frequent question has been "What happens to America in the last days?" In the years before 2000, neither Rosenberg nor his wife recalls hearing anyone ask about the future of America relative to biblical prophecy. Obviously, something has changed.[16]

America is still a great nation by many measurements. But there is a gnawing feeling that, for whatever reasons, it is not as great as it once was. And that is a cause for concern. It explains why people now ask, "What does the future hold for our nation? Does the Bible say anything about America's future?"

Many modern nations find themselves (or their ancestors) mentioned in the Bible:

- Israel
- Jordan (biblical Ammon, Moab, and Edom)
- Egypt
- Sudan (Cush)
- Russia (Rosh)
- Iran (Persia)
- Iraq (Babylon)
- Europe (revived Roman Empire)
- Central Asia (Magog)
- Syria
- Greece
- Saudi Arabia (Sheba and Dedan)
- Libya (Put)
- Lebanon (Tyre)
- Turkey

But what about America? According to Rosenberg,

> The truth is, the United States of America simply is nowhere to be found in the Bible. This may be painful for many to hear. This may be difficult for many to accept. Nevertheless, the fact remains: The U.S. is never directly mentioned or specifically referenced in Bible history or in Bible prophecy. It just isn't.[17]

In 2008, I drew the same conclusion in my book *What in the World Is Going On?*: "Indeed, no specific mention of the United States or any other country in North or South America can be found in the Bible."[18]

Given all we know about America's past and present and what we know from Scripture about how events will unfold in the prophetic future, what is the likely outcome for America? Here is a summary of five possibilities.[19]

America May Be Included in the European Coalition

I believe the coming Antichrist will lead a coalition of ten nations that will comprise a modern revival of the ancient Roman Empire. Scholars expect this revived coalition to be centered in Europe. It will be the political vehicle of the Antichrist. It is possible that America will become part of this coalition for reasons of survival or submission to the Antichrist's power and authority. This outcome will happen only if America becomes so weak economically, morally, and militarily that it has no will or ability to resist. If this happens, then America will receive the same judgment God extends to the Antichrist and all who rebel against the second coming of Christ: utter destruction.

America May Be Incorporated into the One-World Money System

We have gone from having the world's reserve currency and being the greatest creditor nation in history to being the world's most indebted nation.[20] Financial mismanagement has driven us $19 trillion in debt and has burdened us with $127 trillion in unfunded liabilities.[21] We have become a slave-state—enslaved to those from whom we have borrowed. The bill has to come due at some point; no nation can live forever on borrowed money.

If America's inability to repay its trillions of dollars of debt leaves it so weakened as to be absorbed into the new world order and its global economy, the nation will inevitably lose its sovereignty and separate identity.

America May Be Invaded by Outside Forces

There was a time when the idea of America being attacked was nonsensical. America reinforced its formidable defenses by developing nuclear capability and using it twice against Japan in 1945. But today eight additional nations possess nuclear capability: Russia, United Kingdom, France, China, India, Pakistan, North Korea, and Israel. This proliferation of nuclear weapons—along with electromagnetic pulse (EMP) bombs, which can disrupt communications over a large area, and cyberattacks on large computer systems controlling power, transportation, nuclear stations, and public utilities—have changed the nature of warfare. September 11, 2001, was a wake-up call for America. The possibility of a nation our size being brought to its knees and taking decades to recover is no longer unthinkable. Such an attack could seriously weaken America's standing in the world.

America May Be Infected with Moral Decay

Many illustrations in Scripture warn us that even a long-suffering God will not forever strive with men. If we ignore divine directives, we cannot expect God's blessing.

The book of Judges is a twenty-one-chapter reminder that God will not be mocked. This one book records the fourfold cycle so common in Israel's history—rebellion, retribution, repentance, and restoration—that occurred thirteen times in that brief period of Israel's life. The nation stubbornly refused to learn.

Our nation's condition is similar. It has been popularly expressed this way: America is rolling in luxury, reveling in excesses, rollicking in pleasure, reeling in drunkenness, revolting in morals, and rotting in sin. America has rejected the God of its youth and has raised up in His place the idols made with its own hands. We have programmed God out of our schools, our government, our homes, and even our churches.

Once the downward spiral begins, it becomes very difficult to pull out of it. My seminary classmate Erwin Lutzer, pastor emeritus of the Moody Church in Chicago, shows us how quickly apathy can return after a period of renewal:

> When the 9/11 terrorist attacks happened, "God Bless America" signs were everywhere, even on marquees on porn shops. Everyone thought that surely God could be trusted to come to our side in this war against terror. . . . But once our nation felt secure again, God was safely tucked away, church attendance declined, and the so-called wall of separation of church and state was built a notch higher. . . . The God of the Bible will not endlessly tolerate idolatry and benign neglect. He graciously endures rejection and insults, but at some point, He might choose to bring a nation to its knees with severe discipline.[22]

America May Be Incapacitated Because of the Rapture

Imagine what would happen to the moral and spiritual health of America if the true church of Jesus Christ suddenly vanished. We don't know how many true Christians would disappear, of course, but estimates suggest that the US population might be reduced by as much as 70 percent.[23] More devastating than the number would be the absence of the Holy Spirit, who empowers Christians to be salt and light in society (Matthew 5:13–16). Without the Spirit's influence, all hell would break loose in America—literally—sending this nation into a devolution from which it would not recover (2 Thessalonians

2:5–12). This land would suffer the horrific judgments described in Revelation that are to fall upon the earth during the Tribulation.

Even if none of the preceding scenarios occur, this one eventually will. The Rapture of the church is coming, and we know what will happen to the nations during the following seven-year Tribulation, which I discuss in detail later, in chapters 9 and 10.

AMERICA AND THE PEOPLE OF GOD

When Arturo Toscanini was the conductor of the New York Philharmonic Orchestra, a letter written on crumpled notebook paper appeared in his mailbox.

"Dear Mr. Toscanini," read the rough scrawl. "I'm a sheepherder way out here in Wyoming. Your weekly concert sure is good company on them long nights out in these lonesome hills. But my radio batteries are fading out, and I've got an old violin I'd sure like to play when they go dead. But it's out of tune something awful. So I'm asking you a favor. At your concert next Sunday, do you reckon you could play a good, loud A for me? From that, I can tune up them other strings and make a bit of my own music."

The great conductor was touched by the request, and at the next concert, he announced that the orchestra would play an A for his lonely friend out in the Wyoming mountains. On the far side of the continent, the shepherd heard the note and retuned his instrument.[24]

I think we all agree that, today, America is out of tune. The nation has lost its pitch by removing God from its life, thus producing the dissonant chords of cynicism and apathy. Into this cacophony of hopelessness, God calls His people to sound a clear A so the world can hear above the discord the heavenly note of hope.

Peter's first epistle is a book of hope that provides a strong antidote to this age of apathy. The letter was written to a group of first-century believers who faced a situation in some ways similar to ours. They were trying to survive in a culture out of tune with their Creator—a culture that did not accept them or understand them (1 Peter 2:11–17).

Notice that Peter addressed these believers as "pilgrims"—that is, people living away from home, temporary residents, exiles, strangers, or foreigners. It's a reminder that we too are pilgrims passing through a sometimes treacherous world on the way to our true home in heaven.

In the opening verses of his letter, the apostle gave us three powerful truths that will help us live hopeful lives in an apathetic culture.

Our Living Hope Rests in the Power of the Resurrection

The first reason we can have hope is because Almighty God "has begotten us again to a living hope through the resurrection of Jesus Christ from the dead" (1 Peter 1:3). If Christ has overcome the last enemy—death—then surely there is no situation we face that cannot be overcome through Him. We are enormously blessed to have this one, solid reason for hope that remains certain regardless of the deterioration of our world or the difficulties of our lives. That reason is named Jesus!

Peter had walked closely with Christ throughout the three years of His public ministry, during which time he failed more than once. It is because of Peter's humanity that we readily identify with him. Peter's failings and resilience give us hope that we, despite our failures, can also serve the Lord just as well as he eventually did.

Peter had great hope that Jesus was the long-awaited Messiah who would set things right in Israel and throw off the yoke of Roman bondage. But when Jesus was crucified, Peter's world fell apart—just as it did for the other disciples and followers of Jesus. Had we been able to look into Peter's heart during the time between Jesus' crucifixion and resurrection, we would probably have seen a bottomless pit of despair. The man he thought was the Messiah had been killed, and all his hopes for the restoration of Israel died with Him.

But on the Sunday after the crucifixion, rumors began to spread that Jesus' tomb was empty. Peter and John ran to the tomb to see for themselves. When Peter looked inside and saw the empty grave clothes lying where Jesus' body had been, the reality of the resurrection began to sink in. Later, when he encountered the living Christ, he marveled at how this man who had been brutally executed could now be alive and whole again. Jesus had indeed risen from the dead. He was the risen Lord!

It is that background Peter called on when he wrote to those early Christians who were suffering for their faith. His message was this: "You have a living hope based on what Jesus Christ did when He walked out of the grave. Jesus defeated our greatest enemy—death— and thereby promises that no matter what happens in this life, you will defeat that enemy as well. If you are looking for hope while the nation descends into apathy around you, you need to look no further than the resurrected and living Christ."

The present world has only limited hope to offer—the hope of a life no better than our best efforts can make it, all of which eventually crumbles into the grave. If that is the best hope we have, "we are of all men the most pitiable" (1 Corinthians 15:19). How much better it is to have a "living hope"—the resources of heaven itself—when we are facing a hopeless situation.

Our Living Hope Rests in the Promise of Our Reward

Peter also had a living hope because the risen Christ had promised him an inheritance that is "incorruptible and undefiled and that does not fade away, reserved in heaven" (1 Peter 1:4). In that verse, Peter described this heavenly inheritance using four dynamic and descriptive statements.

An Untarnished Inheritance

The Greek word translated "incorruptible" could also be translated "unravaged." In the time when Peter wrote this letter, the Romans often sent marauding parties into areas of Palestine settled by Jews. Like conquerors taking the spoils of war, they would steal everything of value and leave a trail of devastation. They would "ravage" their defenseless victims. The Jews of that region lived in constant terror, knowing the spoilers could invade at any time. Peter reminded the believers that a day was coming when they would receive a reward that could never be ravaged or stolen.[25]

John Newton, the reformed profligate who became a great preacher, once visited a woman whose entire earthly estate had just been destroyed in a fire. Newton, who wrote our celebrated hymn "Amazing Grace," was known for his unorthodox ways. He walked into the grieving woman's presence and said, "Madam, I give you joy."

The look she shot at Newton could have burned a hole through him. "What? I just lost everything that I own! And you give me joy?"

With gentle compassion, Newton replied, "I give you joy that you have a treasure beyond the reach of the flames, that you have a better and more enduring substance in heaven, that you have an inheritance incorruptible."[26]

An Undefiled Inheritance

When a nation drifts into apathy, it also drifts into unrestrained indulgence of appetites. We see it all around us. Our entertainment, the Internet, and the media are saturated with enticement into activities that defile both our bodies and our souls. But Peter told us that the inheritance God offers through Christ is not stained or defiled. It is holy, pure, and clean. It is undefiled. In the land to which the believer belongs, there will be no evil.

The apostle John wrote of heaven, "There shall by no means enter it anything that defiles, or causes an abomination or a lie, but only those who are written in the Lamb's Book of Life" (Revelation 21:27).

An Unfading Inheritance

Jesus described our fallen world as a place "where moth and rust destroy and where thieves break in and steal" (Matthew 6:19). Living in such a world where everything tends to degenerate and fade away, we long for permanence, durability, everlasting solidity. But in heaven, where our reward is, Peter told us that nothing will ever fade away. There is no moth nor rust that can touch it—no thieves to break in and steal it. The things of God in heaven are things that never die and never fade.

An Uncontested Inheritance

How many news stories have you read or movies have you seen where members of a deceased person's family try to break the will and steal the fortune for themselves? Our inheritance is reserved in heaven specifically for us by a will that cannot be broken. It is securely held in the hand of God and cannot be stolen, lost, or destroyed. We know this inheritance is reserved for us because we have already received an advance payment: the Holy Spirit "who is the guarantee of our inheritance until the redemption of the purchased possession, to the praise of His glory" (Ephesians 1:14).

The Holy Spirit who lives within us is the guarantee that our inheritance in heaven is safely reserved by God Himself, who will deliver it to us at the moment of our arrival in heaven.

Our Living Hope Rests in Our Protection Until Christ's Return

Peter told us that as we await the time when we will receive the promised inheritance, we are "kept by the power of God through faith for salvation ready to be revealed in the last time" (1 Peter 1:5). An intriguing verbal counterpoint is used in verse 4, which says our inheritance is reserved in heaven for us; in verse 5 we are reserved for our inheritance in heaven. Here Peter gave us double assurance that the same God who is keeping the inheritance in heaven is also keeping His people for the inheritance. God not only protects our reward up there; He also protects us down here, assuring us with His absolute, unqualified promise that the reward and the inheritor will remain safe and intact until the day when they come together.

It is the hope of heaven that motivated the earliest Christians to live optimistic and godly lives. It also allowed them to lead quiet and respectful lives, loving their neighbors and honoring the governing authorities. The Epistle to Diognetus, written in the second century AD, provides an inspiring illustration of their lifestyle. The letter was written by an unbelieving Roman government official who had been observing the Christians salted throughout his territory. In his letter to Diognetus, he attempted to explain what these Christians were all about:

> Christians are not marked out from the rest of mankind by their country or their speech or their customs. . . . They dwell in cities both Greek and barbarian, each as his lot is cast, following the customs of the region in clothing and in food and in the outward things of life generally; yet they manifest the wonderful and openly paradoxical character of their own state. They inhabit the lands of their birth, but as temporary residents thereof; they take their

share of all responsibilities as citizens, and endure all disabilities as aliens. Every foreign land is their native land, and every native land a foreign land. . . . They pass their days upon earth, but their citizenship is in heaven.[27]

Not only does this letter paint a superb picture of ideal Christian citizenship, the fact that it was written by a pagan shows the powerful effect of Christian example.

Daniel Webster said, "Whatever makes men good Christians also makes them good citizens."[28] As Christians, we have a responsibility both to our nation and to God, and we dare not ignore either one. What are the specific responsibilities Christians have in relation to their nation? The New Testament names at least four.

Pray for Our Leaders

It is all too easy to complain about those in authority over us, whether they are government officials, civic leaders, or supervisors. But Paul told us to pray for these leaders:

> I exhort first of all that supplications, prayers, intercessions, and giving of thanks be made for all men, for kings and all who are in authority, that we may lead a quiet and peaceable life in all godliness and reverence. For this is good and acceptable in the sight of God our Savior. (1 Timothy 2:1–3)

In another epistle, Paul wrote that we should honor those in authority (Romans 13:7). If you think it is hard to honor and pray for some of our government leaders today, remember that Paul penned those words during the reign of Nero, the first and cruelest persecutor of Christians.

As I wrote in the notes of *The Jeremiah Study Bible*, "These intercessions should include requests for their wise and peaceable rule and also prayers for their salvation. Such prayers acknowledge that all authority is ultimately God's authority and that God is the ultimate King."[29]

Pay Our Taxes

Some Christians today wonder whether they should withhold part of their taxes because the government uses our tax money to finance causes antithetical to Christian morality and natural law. The early Christian father Justin Martyr answered this concern in an open letter to government officials:

> More even than others we try to pay the taxes and assessments to those whom you appoint, as we have been taught by [Jesus]. For once in his time some came to him and asked whether it were right to pay taxes to Caesar. And he answered, "Tell me, whose image is on the coin." They said, "Caesar's." And he answered them again, "Then give what is Caesar's to Caesar and what is God's to God" [Mark 12:17]. So we worship God only, but in other matters we gladly serve you, recognizing you as emperors and rulers of men, and praying that along with your imperial power you may also be found to have a sound mind.[30]

We will never have a perfect government until Christ returns and establishes His government on earth. Until then, we have to live under a secular government with which we do not always agree. God does not hold us responsible for the way the government uses our tax money. But we cannot remain in fellowship with Him if we avoid paying our taxes.

Participate in the Process

In the 2012 national election, approximately 25 million Christians who were registered to vote stayed home on election day.[31] Some tell me they do not vote because they do not believe their one vote makes any difference. This attitude is both illogical and irresponsible. Logic tells us that no majority would ever exist if not for the many single votes cast. Author and historian Edward Everett Hale emphasizes the responsibility of individual action: "I am only one, but still I am one. I cannot do everything, but I can do something. And because I cannot do everything, I will not refuse to do the something that I can do!"[32]

One vote sometimes makes the difference. Eight state House and state Senate elections in the United States have been decided by one vote.[33]

I fear the real reason so many Americans and evangelicals do not vote is simple apathy. Yet those non-voters are often the most vocal and critical when elected officials fail to meet their expectations.

The Bible tells us Christians that we are to be salt and light in the world. The time has come for us to let our voices be heard and our votes counted. But make them count responsibly:

- Don't vote your geographical location.
- Don't vote your religious denomination.
- Don't vote your political affiliation.
- Don't vote racial identification.
- Don't even vote your union obligation.

Instead, vote your values. Vote your beliefs. Vote your convictions. If candidates want your vote, let them earn it the old-fashioned way. Let them make commitments to your values, and let them know you intend to hold them responsible. It is my responsibility and yours to participate in the process. If we do not act soon, it may be too late. Let these words of Martin Niemoller, a pastor who lived during the Nazi regime in Germany, cement in your heart and mind the importance of your involvement:

> They came first for the Communists, and I didn't speak up because I wasn't a Communist. Then they came for the Jews, and I didn't speak up because I wasn't a Jew. Then they came for the trade unionists, and I didn't speak up because I wasn't a trade unionist. Then they came for the Catholics, and I didn't speak up because I was a Protestant. Then they came for me, and by that time no one was left to speak up.[34]

Persevere in the Race

The Greeks had one race in their Olympics that was truly unique. The prize did not go to the runner who merely finished first, but to the runner who finished first with his torch still lit.[35] That's a pretty good metaphor for the Christian life, isn't it? It's all about finishing the race with your torch still lit—with your influence still intact and your testimony still strong.

To persevere in the Christian race, "you have need of endurance" (Hebrews 10:36). Randy Alcorn writes, "We're called to a life of endurance empowered by Christ, and accompanied by joyful thanksgiving. Endurance requires patience, because reward for today's right choices will come, but it may be months or years from now, or not until we leave this world."[36]

How are Christians to persevere in a nation that is spiraling down into apathy?

In the opening scene of the classic 1952 movie *High Noon*, Marshal Will Kane (portrayed by Gary Cooper) has cleaned up the town and made it a decent and prosperous place to live. Now he is retiring to marry, leave town, and take up a new life as a storekeeper.

But immediately after his wedding, stunning news arrives. Frank Miller, whom Kane had sent to prison, has been paroled and is returning on the noon train to exact revenge. Kane knows if he leaves now, Miller will take the town back to its old lawless and debauched ways. He decides to delay his honeymoon just long enough to finish off Miller and his gang.

But as he attempts to round up a posse, every man he approaches finds an excuse not to get involved. Even when he tries the church, none of the citizens he has protected will join him in ridding the town of the evil that threatens it.

Is the apathy of Kane's town what we are witnessing in present-day America? Has our prosperity led us into such indulgence that we are no longer willing to leave our pleasures long enough to protect and heal the nation others sacrificed to give us? Even if America has reached that point, we Christians must rise above the apathy around us and, as Kane did, face our duty alone. We must remember that our hope is not dependent on the survival of our nation, but on our promised inheritance in heaven.

If we are diligent to reflect that hope to our neighbors, we may find that it is too early to write-off America. Even if Christianity becomes a minority, we must remember that only ten righteous men would have saved Sodom. I know that God stands ready to do for America what He promised Solomon He would do for Israel: "If My people who are called by My name will humble themselves, and pray and seek My face, and turn from their wicked ways, then I will hear from heaven, and will forgive their sin and heal their land" (2 Chronicles 7:14).

We Christians could well be the rudder that turns America's ship out of the doldrums of apathy and into the security of commitment.

CHAPTER 5

THE REMEDY OF REVIVAL

On the first day of high school, a short and skinny kid named Jeremy—five foot three—bounded into the building ready to play basketball and study hard, and in that order. He secretly dreamed of one day making it all the way to the NBA. But given his stature, few took him seriously. Undeterred, Jeremy developed a two-part strategy to increase his height: (1) he drank lots of milk, and (2) he hung from the monkey bars on the playground for long stretches of time. Incredibly, he shot up eleven inches during his high school years, made straight As, and excelled on the basketball court.[1]

During Jeremy's senior year, his coach tried and failed to land a basketball scholarship for him. So the young man leveraged his 4.2 grade point average and enrolled at Harvard, where he walked onto the team and, in four years, led the struggling Crimson to a winning season. This success stoked Jeremy's longtime dream of playing professional basketball, though one team after another passed him up. After all, there had never before been a Taiwanese-American NBA player. After several agonizing letdowns, Jeremy signed with the New York Knicks and moved into his brother's tiny Manhattan apartment, where he slept on the sofa.

On Valentine's Day of 2012, while Cupid's arrow was striking others, lightning struck for Jeremy Lin. He began playing the best basketball of his life. He almost single-handedly turned the Knicks' season around, and soon the rowdy crowds in Madison Square Garden found a new vocabulary: Linsanity. Lintensity. Lintelligence. Linvincible. Linspiration. Lincredible.

Since that magical season, however, Lin has battled injuries, surgeries, and ups and downs in his career. As I write, he is playing for the Charlotte Hornets, and he openly admits he battles discouragement at times. But things may be turning around for Lin. As the following headlines show, sportswriters have recently begun to detect evidences of a career revival: "It's Not Linsanity, but Jeremy Lin Is Experiencing a Revival in Charlotte."[2] "Linsanity Revived in Charlotte."[3] "The Quiet Revival of Linsanity."[4]

We often see the word *revival* in our headlines. Sportswriters use the word to describe slumping teams or athletes like Lin who rebound in competitiveness. Economists talk about economic revival or a revival in stocks, precious metals, or property values. The entertainment industry uses the word *revival* to describe vintage Broadway shows that find new life when restaged for today's audiences. This recent headline got my immediate attention: "Baltimore Needs a Comprehensive Revival Plan." But as I scanned the article, my hopes fell. It was not about spiritual revival at all. It advocated the recovery of deteriorating housing units.[5]

I cannot predict the future of Lin's basketball career, but I know for a fact he is deeply concerned about revival; it is on his mind day and night. His greatest concern, however, is not a revival of Linsanity, but a different kind of revival—a real revival, a revival of spiritual power in the United States and around the world. Lin is deeply committed to Christ, and his heart aches for a true revival of morality and faith.

Not long ago he sent a message to his fans, asking them to join him in praying for a worldwide awakening. "Please pray for global Christian revival," he pleaded. "Specific areas that I feel God has put on my heart are Asian-Americans in the U.S. who are lukewarm in their faith, the billions in China who don't know Christ and Taiwan/ Hong Kong. I obviously care about many other places, but these are very near and dear to my heart!"[6]

People may talk about one kind of revival or another, but I'm with Lin: The kind of revival we need is spiritual, and I believe it's the last hope for our nation and the world.

I am painfully aware that much of what I have written in the preceding pages of this book could leave us discouraged, and that is why I want to encourage you with the hope of revival. Yes, we should be burdened for our world. The prophet Jeremiah lived in days similar to ours, and when we read his writings, we are overwhelmed with the despair he felt for his culture. Jesus wept over unrepentant Jerusalem. Paul lamented, "I have great sorrow and continual grief in my heart . . . for my brethren, my countrymen according to the flesh" (Romans 9:2–3). Abraham's nephew, Lot, who lived in Sodom, was "distressed by the depraved conduct of the lawless" (2 Peter 2:7 NIV).

I cannot apologize for being frank and honest about our demoralizing times. We should carry a burden in our hearts for a fallen world and a sorrow for the accelerating pace of sin and suffering around us. Yet I want to challenge you to remain joyful. Even in darkening times, we have no need for pessimism. As Christians, we have the best of reasons to be realistic optimists and to be of good cheer. The Bible is packed with all the promises and power we need. Jesus Himself said:

"Son, be of good cheer; your sins are forgiven you." (Matthew 9:2)

"Be of good cheer, daughter; your faith has made you well." (9:22)

"Be of good cheer! It is I; do not be afraid." (14:27)

"Be of good cheer. Rise, He is calling you." (Mark 10:49)

"Be of good cheer, I have overcome the world." (John 16:33)

How can we be pessimistic when the future is in the hands of Him who knows the end from the beginning? Our nation is still filled with godly people who know how to pray. Around the world, the church is growing at an unprecedented rate. The upcoming generation is full of deeply committed Christian young people. And we can still hope for, pray about, and work toward a true spiritual revival in our land and an awakening in our world. The Bible even suggests a simple prayer for times like these:

> Will You not revive us again,
> That Your people may rejoice in You? (Psalm 85:6)

That is the prayer of my heart, and as I prayed over and crafted the chapters of this book, I knew I had to write about the remedy of revival. Things have been this bad before, and God has sent revivals that shifted the tides, reversed the trends, changed the culture, and propelled the gospel onward to a new generation. May He do it again! May He revive us again that His people can rejoice in Him!

REVIVAL IN THE BIBLE

According to the Bible, revival is God's work, a special season of rejuvenation He pours onto His church that spills over into evangelistic zeal. We cannot schedule or concoct revival. We cannot call fire down from heaven to light the altar, as Elijah did, but we can get the kindling ready and offer ourselves as Spirit-drenched firewood.

The Old Testament book of 2 Chronicles is the Bible's handbook on revival. The writer—it may have been Ezra—showed that God never gave up on the nation of Judah. He described one revival after another that reversed the nation's downward slide. Even after the eventual judgment and destruction of the nation, God stayed in the business of reviving His people. Second Chronicles 36 tells us that He sent a remnant back to Jerusalem to rebuild the temple and keep the progress of redemption alive. While the writer was realistic about Judah's apostasy, he always left room for revival; and the revivals made the difference.

It is impossible in the space I have here in this chapter to cover all the national Judean revivals described in 2 Chronicles, but we can take a prime example from chapters 34 and 35—the story of King Josiah. This young king ascended the throne during the darkest days Judah had ever known. One of the wickedest kings in the Bible, Manasseh, had sat on the throne for fifty-five years, and the nation had fallen under the influence of his arc of evil. During his reign, Judah sunk into a quagmire of idolatry, occultism, human sacrifice, lawlessness, violence, military weakness, and moral confusion.

Late in life, Manasseh turned to the Lord—there is hope for anyone!—but his spiritual conversion came too late to influence his nation. Upon his death, his hideously evil son Amon continued the reign of terror until he was assassinated in the second year of his reign by his own servants.

Enter Josiah, age eight. With his grandfather dead and his father murdered, Josiah ascended the throne. Remarkably, the boy had a heart for the Lord. Perhaps he had been influenced by his grandfather's late-in-life repentance. I can see old Manasseh, hands trembling with regret, taking his six-year-old grandson onto his lap and saying, "One day you will be king of Judah. Don't make the same mistakes I did. You must try to reverse the damage I caused. Give your heart to the Lord and lead this nation righteously."

Whatever the reason, Josiah did give his heart to the Lord and lead his nation righteously. "He did what was right in the sight of the LORD, and walked in the ways of his father David; he did not turn aside to the right hand or to the left" (34:2).

A Humble Leader

Since he was only eight when the crown descended on him, Josiah had little to do with running his nation until he began taking charge at age sixteen. Second Chronicles 34:3 says: "For in the eighth year of his reign, while he was still young, he began to seek the God of his father David; and in the twelfth year he began to purge Judah and Jerusalem of the high places, the wooden images, the carved images, and the molded images."

It is amazing what God can do with a teenager totally committed to Him! It is better to have a young leader who loves the Lord than an experienced one whose years have not been invested in righteousness.

In the eighteenth year of his reign, when Josiah was twenty-six, he became concerned about the condition of the massive temple of God on the hill above the palace, and he initiated an extensive renovation project to restore its glory. The needed money came in, and Josiah "gave it to the workmen who worked in the house of the LORD, to repair and restore the house. They gave it to the craftsmen and builders to buy hewn stone and timber for beams, and to floor the houses . . . and the men did the work faithfully" (vv. 10–12).

A Holy Book

That was when the workers made a great discovery: The temple renovation process uncovered a long-lost treasure. Hilkiah the priest found the Book of the Law of the Lord given by Moses (v. 14).

They brought the book to Josiah and read it to him. Each word struck the king like a dagger. The scriptures revealed that the sins of his father and grandfather were far worse than he had realized, and the nation was in great moral peril. Anguished over his guilt and that of his people, Josiah tore his clothes and earnestly sought to understand God's will more clearly than ever. He needed a prophet to instruct him, and God sent him Huldah, a prophetess whose husband managed the king's wardrobe.

Huldah told Josiah that Judah's sins were long, deep, and damning, but she added a personal word of encouragement from the Lord: "Because your heart was tender, and you humbled yourself before God when you heard His words against this place and against its inhabitants, and you humbled yourself before Me, and you tore your clothes and wept before Me, I also have heard you" (v. 27).

A Hungry People

Encouraged by Huldah's words, Josiah announced a revival meeting, and "all the men of Judah and the inhabitants of Jerusalem" gathered at the temple, where Josiah "read in their hearing all the words of the Book of the Covenant which had been found in the house of the LORD. Then the king stood in his place and made a covenant before the LORD, to follow the LORD, and to keep His commandments and His testimonies and His statutes with all his heart and all his soul" (vv. 30–31). The people, moved by the sight of their king, were burdened for revival and joined his commitment.

Can you imagine what would happen in our land if we could find such a young person, rediscover such an old book, and stir up such a burdened people? In Josiah's day, the result was electrifying, and the ensuing revival changed the complexion of Judah. Moral trends were turned upside down, spiritual zeal was turned right-side up, and impending judgment was turned aside for a generation: "All his days they did not depart from following the LORD God of their fathers" (v. 33).

The next chapter describes Josiah's renewal of one of the great festivals of Israel—the Passover. He instructed and encouraged the priests in their service, and the capital city erupted in praise and worship. "There had been no Passover kept in Israel like that since the days of Samuel the prophet; and none of the kings of Israel had kept such a Passover as Josiah kept" (35:18).

Josiah was only twenty-six, but God used him to revitalize his nation.

While King Josiah led the revival from the throne, the prophet Jeremiah assisted him in the pulpit, preaching in the streets, the squares, and the temple courtyards. Soon, other prophets such as Zephaniah and Nahum joined them. The national reformation of Judah was as radical and complete as anything Martin Luther, John Calvin, or John Knox undertook. Furthermore, the revival of Josiah's day inflamed a group of young people and propelled them into a lifetime of godly service—boys like Daniel and his three friends, Hananiah, Mishael, and Azariah (Shadrach, Meshach and Abed-Nego). I am convinced their exposure to Josiah and Jeremiah shaped the lives of these young people, preparing them to stand later for God in the midst of a perverted Chaldean culture. Revivals always induct new generations of zealous workers into the King's service.

This is the kind of revival overdue in our nation and world today. The great Scottish preacher Duncan Campbell wrote, "There is a growing conviction everywhere, and especially among thoughtful people, that unless revival comes, other forces will take the field, that will sink us deeper into the mire of humanism and materialism."[7]

REVIVAL IN AMERICA

The good news is that revival is possible—and we have the history to prove it. As dire as our present time appears, America has been at this low point before. We are prone to think our days are worse than those preceding us, but as I will show you in the following paragraphs, America's history is pockmarked with periods of spiritual jeopardy. Like ancient Judah, our nation has repeatedly sunk to the depths only to be saved from itself by timely seasons of revival. That's the grace of God! Perhaps a brief examination of past awakenings will help prepare us for a coming revival.

The Great Awakening: 1720s Through 1740s

The Great Awakening that occurred during the Colonial era is one of the most famous movements in the history of American Christianity. Many of the first settlers on the eastern seaboard came here inflamed with the gospel and hungry for religious liberty. An almost-forgotten monument stands today in a little circular park on Allerton Street in Plymouth, Massachusetts. It is called the National Monument to the Forefathers, formerly known as the Pilgrim Monument—the largest solid granite sculpture in the United States. Deeply infused with overt Christian symbolism, it has stood as a silent witness to the Christian origins of our country since 1889.

This towering statue features a woman personifying faith. She points upward toward heaven with her right hand and clutches a Bible in her left. On each of the four sides of her pedestal sit smaller statues representing the values of morality, law, education, and liberty. The monument is a fitting tribute to the biblical faith and Christian values of our forefathers.

As J. Stephen Lang and Mark A. Noll observe, "For the early New Englanders, religious and social history were inseparable. It was assumed since the landing of the Pilgrims in 1620 that the settlers were (or should be) Christians, and that God would bless the building up of a godly commonwealth in the new land."[8]

After the Pilgrims came the Puritans, who founded Harvard College to train ministers and Christian leaders shortly after their arrival. The colonies were, according to one historian, "the most Protestant, Reformed, and Puritan commonwealths in the world."[9]

Yet throughout the 1600s, the spiritual and moral condition of the Colonies declined at a rate that alarmed genuine believers. The following paraphrase, from a sermon preached in 1702 by a New England pastor named Increase Mather, could well be what that pastor would say from a pulpit today:

> We are the posterity of godly people, our forefathers who followed the Lord. But look at how the glory is departing. You that are aged can remember fifty years ago when the churches were in their glory. Is there not a sad decay of that glory? What a change there has been! Time was when the churches were beautiful. Many people were converted and willingly declared what God had done for their souls. And there were added to the churches daily such as should be saved. But conversions have become rare in this day. Look into the pulpits and see if there is such a glory as there once was. The glory is gone. The special design of providence in this country seems to be now over. We may weep to think about it.[10]

Another observer, the Rev. Samuel Torrey, preached a sermon on May 16, 1683, titled "A Plea for the Life of Dying Religion" in which he said,

> There hath been a vital Decay, a Decay upon the very Vitals of Religion, by a deep Declension in the Life, and Power of it; that there is already a great Death upon Religion, little more than a name to live; that the things which remain are ready to die; and that we are in great Danger of dying together with it.[11]

In the early 1720s, God unleashed a small revival in New Jersey that would eventually blaze through the rest of the Colonies and change history. A New Jersey Dutchman named Theodore Frelinghuysen began preaching evangelism in his church. He preached a pure gospel. He preached that people needed to be born again. Oddly, the older people did not accept his message, but young people responded with enthusiasm, and revival broke out.

The revival began to spread, and eventually it reached Northampton, Massachusetts, where the flame was fanned by a New England pastor named Jonathan Edwards. Like Josiah, Edwards had benefited from the influence of his grandfather, a revivalist named Solomon Stoddard. Stoddard was a large man who preached powerful evangelistic sermons without notes and believed God had brought the forefathers to the New World for an exceptional purpose.

Young Edwards was brilliant. At six he studied Latin. He entered Yale when he was not quite thirteen and graduated when he was barely fifteen. Ordained at age nineteen, Edwards taught at Yale by age twenty and later became president of Princeton. Harvard granted him both a bachelor's and a master's degree on the same day. But he is best known for his "Sinners in the Hands of an Angry God"—the most famous sermon in American history.

Edwards preached the sermon on Sunday, July 8, 1741, while ministering in tiny Enfield, Connecticut. A group of women had spent the previous night praying for revival. When Edwards rose to speak, he quietly announced that his text was Deuteronomy 32:35, "their foot shall slip in due time." This "hellfire and brimstone" approach was somewhat a departure for Edwards. Of his many written sermons, few are of this type.

He spoke softly and simply, warning the unconverted that they were dangling over hell like a spider over the fire. "O sinner! Consider the fearful danger you are in. . . . Unconverted men walk over the pit of hell on a rotten covering, and there are innumerable places in this covering so weak that they won't bear their weight, and these places are not seen."[12]

Edwards's voice was suddenly lost amid cries and commotion from the crowd. He paused, appealing for calm. Then he concluded: "Let everyone that is out of Christ, now awake and fly from the wrath to come. The wrath of Almighty God is now undoubtedly hanging over a great part of this congregation: let everyone fly out of Sodom."[13]

It is reported that strong men held to pews and posts, feeling they were sliding into hell. Others trembled uncontrollably and rolled on the floor. Throughout the night cries of men and women arose in the village as people begged God to save them. Five hundred were converted that evening, sparking a revival that swept thousands into the kingdom.[14]

At the same time, John Wesley and his Methodists were riding the crest of a similar revival in England. And the powerful George Whitefield was traveling back and forth between America and England, lending his powerful voice to the evangelization of sinners. And when I say powerful voice, that is exactly what I mean. Without amplification, his words would carry in the wind for a mile and reach thirty thousand sets of ears.[15]

As thousands of converts filled the Colonies, new theological training colleges opened, including Princeton, Rutgers, Dartmouth, and Brown universities. Missionaries ventured into the wilderness to evangelize Native Americans. The effects of the Great Awakening shaped the American political scene and set the stage for the American Revolution. Historian Benjamin Rice Lacy Jr. wrote, "The course of events which led to the Declaration of Independence, the enthusiasm and constancy which finally eventuated in the victory of the Colonies . . . would not have been possible during the years 1775–1788 had there been no Great Awakening."[16]

The Second Great Awakening: Early 1800s

After the Revolutionary War, Christianity in America spiraled into another decline. As people plunged into the business of building a new nation, they neglected their spiritual well-being. French rationalism swept through the colleges. Large numbers of people moved inland and began populating territories west of the Appalachian Mountains, west of the Blue Ridge, into what was called the American frontier, where few churches existed. People drifted away from the Lord and the Bible. Society became godless. During the Great Awakening, as many as 40 to 50 percent of the population attended church, but by the 1790s the number was down to 5 to 10 percent—far fewer than even today.[17]

John Marshall, the Chief Justice of the Supreme Court, wrote to "Bishop Madison" and said, "The church is too far gone ever to be redeemed."[18] Overseas in France, Voltaire predicted that "in two generations Christianity would altogether disappear."[19]

Voltaire's disciple in America, Thomas Paine, the great Revolutionary War penman, attacked Christianity with vicious hatred. "Of all the systems of religion that were ever invented," he wrote, "there is none more derogatory to the Almighty, more unedifying to man, more repugnant to reason, and more contradictory in itself, than this thing called Christianity. Too absurd for belief, too impossible to convince, and to inconsistent for practice, it renders the heart torpid or produces only atheists and fanatics."[20]

Things became so bad that among the students at Princeton, only two professed to be Christians. According to Dr. J. Edwin Orr,

> The typical Harvard student was atheist. Students at William College conducted a mock celebration of Holy Communion. When the Dean at Princeton opened the chapel Bible to read, a pack of playing cards fell out, some radical having cut a rectangle out of each page to fit the pack. Christians were so unpopular that they met in secret and kept their minutes in code. . . . The last two decades of the eighteenth century were the darkest period, spiritually and morally, in the history of American Christianity.[21]

But another revival came. The first stirrings of the Second Great Awakening occurred at Hampden-Sydney College in Virginia when a few students locked themselves in a room for fear of other students and began praying for revival. This created a near-riot, and the college president showed up to investigate. After inviting the Christian students to his office, he joined them in prayer, and within a short time more than half the student body had been converted.[22] This revival spread to other campuses and became a forerunner to what occurred shortly afterward on the American frontier.

In 1800, plainspoken evangelists like the Rev. James McGready began holding brush arbor meetings in southern Kentucky. Crowds materialized in unprecedented numbers, thousands upon thousands, clogging the roads and overwhelming the locations. Tremendous conviction of sin broke out with people weeping and wailing as they found God.

The most famous of these camp meetings occurred in Cane Ridge, Kentucky, in August 1801. Here is an eyewitness account by James B. Finley of Highland County, Ohio, who visited the revival to see what was happening:

> The noise was like the roar of Niagara. The vast sea of human beings seemed to be agitated as if by a storm. I counted seven ministers all preaching at one time, some on stumps, others on wagons. . . . Some of the people were singing, others praying, some crying for mercy in the most piteous accents . . . while others were shouting most vociferously. While witnessing these scenes, a peculiarly strange sensation such as I had never felt before, came over me. My heart beat tumultuously, my knees trembled, my lips quivered, and I felt as though I must fall to the ground. A strange supernatural power seemed to pervade the entire mass of my mind. . . . At times it seemed as if all the sins I had ever committed in my life were vividly brought up in array before my terrified imagination, and under their awful pressure I felt that I must die if I did not get relief.[23]

Finley was so overcome that he left to find a nearby tavern where he could settle his nerves with brandy. He slept fitfully that night in a nearby barn, and the next morning, mounted his horse to return home; but en route he was gloriously converted and later became a traveling Methodist preacher.

Among the results of the Second Great Awakening, several deserve special mention. Out of this revival came a generation of circuit-riding preachers like Finley, Peter Cartwright, and Charles Finney, who took the gospel to every part of the nation. But the Holy Spirit had a wider field in mind. In 1806 some students at Williams College hid in a haystack to avoid a thunderstorm, and there they joined in prayer and committed themselves to go into all the world, wherever God might lead. On February 19, 1812, Adoniram and Ann Judson sailed out of Salem, Massachusetts, as America's first foreign missionaries. They were soon followed by thousands more as American churches began sending missionaries around the globe. The birth of the modern missionary movement can be traced back to the "Haystack Prayer Meeting" and the Second Great Awakening.

The revival also stirred up righteous indignation against slavery, which led to its abolition in America, though it took the Civil War to achieve it.

A flood of humanitarian causes flowed like river currents from the Second Great Awakening, including prison reform, child labor laws, women's rights, and rescue missions. Thousands of organizations sprang up to advance education, temperance, world peace, Sabbath observance, and overseas evangelism. The Second Great Awakening gave birth to the American Bible Society, the American Sunday School Union, the American Board of Commissioners for Foreign Missions, the American Tract Society, the American Temperance Society, the American Baptist Home Missionary Society, and many other organizations, societies, and movements that took the gospel in word and deed around the world.

The Third Great Awakening: 1850s and '60s

After some years, the passion of revival died, and America sank once again into spiritual lethargy and godlessness. But in 1857 another national revival broke out. Historians have given it many names—the Third Great Awakening, the Fulton Street Revival, the Businessman's Revival, the Prayer Revival, and the Layman's Revival.

Among the catalysts for this revival was Jeremiah Lanphier, who announced a prayer meeting to be held on September 23, 1857, in a

Dutch Reformed Church building on Fulton Street in New York City.[24] Almost no one came to his first meeting, but within a few months more than fifty thousand people a day were gathering for prayer all over New York. The revival spread from one city to the next—Cleveland, Detroit, Chicago, Cincinnati—and between one and two million people are estimated to have found Christ as their Savior.

One story of particular interest occurred during this time. A New York harbor pilot who was a Christian boarded a European cargo ship to guide it into port. He told the captain and crew about the revival, and a strange but powerful sense of conviction gripped those on the ship. By the time it docked, most of the crew had given their lives to Christ.[25]

At the height of the revival, offices and stores across the nation closed for prayer at noon. Newspapers spread the story, and even telegraph companies set aside certain hours during which businessmen could wire one another with news of the revival. This third revival also became the launching pad of an array of new ministries, such as the Young Men's Christian Association (YMCA), Moody Bible Institute, and several denominational youth organizations.

Even when the Civil War tore the nation apart, God's Spirit was still at work. Major revivals broke out in both armies. Between 100,000 and 200,000 Union Army soldiers and approximately 150,000 Confederate troops converted to Christ. Sometimes churches held preaching and praying services twenty-four hours a day, and chapels could not accommodate the soldiers wanting to get inside. "A 'Great Revival' occurred among Robert E. Lee's forces in the fall of 1863 and winter of 1864, during which some 7,000 soldiers were converted."[26]

These revivals amid the Civil War birthed the ministry of military chaplains, with one of the first being a young firebrand named

Dwight L. Moody. He and others distributed millions of tracts, preached thousands of sermons, and baptized countless converts. At least one baptism service occurred in a pond exposed to enemy fire, causing several of the converts to be "wounded while the ordinance was being administered."[27]

Out of this revival came the gospel era of Moody, Ira Sankey, and Fanny Crosby and the birth of a new phase in our hymnody with millions singing warm, heart-lifting, popular gospel songs like "Revive Us Again" and "Blessed Assurance."

The Global Revival: Early 1900s

Despite revival fires among the troops and the ministry of the nineteenth-century evangelists, the lamp of the church again dimmed in the wake of the Civil War. America became overwhelmed by the economic, political, and spiritual devastation from the war; the assassination of Abraham Lincoln; and the burden of Reconstruction.

Then almost out of the blue, one of the greatest revivals in Christian history erupted in the first decade of the twentieth century. It is hard to pinpoint its origin, but a major epicenter was undoubtedly Wales. The person most associated with the Welsh Revival is a young coal miner named Evan Roberts. The first spark of revival flashed when Roberts, a Bible college student, took a break from school and returned to his home village of Loughor to preach his first sermon. The sermon featured four main points:

1. Confess any known sin to God and put away any wrong done to others.
2. Put away any doubtful habit.
3. Obey the Holy Spirit promptly.
4. Confess faith in Christ openly.

Only seventeen people showed up for Roberts's sermon, but by the end of the week, sixty people had been converted and a revival broke out. Within three months, one hundred thousand converts were added to the churches in Wales. All across the nation, theaters closed, jails emptied, churches filled, and soccer matches were canceled to avoid conflicting with revival services. Welsh miners were so thoroughly converted that their ponies and mules had to be retrained to work without the prodding of curse words.

On March 29, 1905, Roberts opened a series of meetings at Shaw Street Chapel in Liverpool—out of Wales and into England, out of the country and into the city. Thousands thronged around the church, and people poured in from all parts of England, Scotland, Ireland, the Continent, and America. Multitudes were converted or found new joy in Christ. Often Roberts did not even preach. The very sight of him sent rivers of emotion flowing through the crowds. When he did speak, his message was quiet and simple: "Obedience to Jesus, complete consecration to his service, receiving the Holy Spirit, and allowing ourselves to be ruled by him."[28]

One man who experienced this revival, the Rev. R. B. Jones, said the sense of God's presence in Wales was all-pervasive:

> It mattered not where one went, the consciousness of the reality
> and nearness of God followed . . . in the revival gatherings . . . in
> the homes, on the streets, in the mines and factories, in the schools,
> yea, and even in the theatres and drinking saloons. The strange
> result was that wherever people gathered became a place of awe,
> and places of amusement . . . were practically emptied.[29]

The revival spread through England, Scotland, and Scandinavia and throughout Europe. Accounts of the history of Christianity in

South Africa, India, Korea, and China report revival fires igniting everywhere in the last half of the first decade of the 1900s. In Indonesia, the number of Christians tripled.[30] Thousands came to Christ in Japan, and in Brazil the Baptists "experienced the equivalent of twenty-five years of growth in three years, from 1905 to 1907."[31]

In America, the Methodists of Philadelphia reported ten thousad conversions in a four-month period; in Atlantic City so many people were saved that some reports could only find fifty or so people among a population of sixty thousand who did not profess faith in Christ. It is believed that in New England, more people were added to the churches in April 1905 than at any other time on record.[32]

Half the students at Rutgers University were swept into Bible studies, and more than 70 percent of the students at Princeton. At Trinity College in Durham, North Carolina, a third of the students proclaimed Christ as Lord, and only twenty-five students remained nonresponsive. Baylor University experienced what was called "an extraordinary upheaval."[33]

At Asbury College, four male students met in a private room to pray, and at about ten o'clock that night, "the Holy Spirit seemed to enter the room." Other students came running, and few slept that night. The next morning, the revival spread over the campus like a tidal wave, and for three days all classes were suspended as students got their lives right with God.[34]

An awakening hit Seattle Pacific College on December 19, 1905, that was hard for participants to describe. Students gathered, and "wave after wave of blessings, billow after billow of divine glory rolled over the entire congregation. . . . So great was the power of God that the unsaved were unable to resist. . . . The meeting continued in power and interest until long after midnight."[35]

Portland, Oregon, had such a visitation of the Spirit that the occasion is still called "Portland's Pentecost."[36]

In Atlanta, stores, factories, and offices—even the Supreme Court—closed so people could attend prayer meetings. In Louisville, the press reported thousands of conversions, and fifty-eight leading business firms closed at noon for prayer meetings.[37] In Colorado, the State Legislature suspended its proceedings so members could attend prayer meetings.[38]

In California, the Azusa Street Revival, which began in 1906, changed the face of Christianity in America and the world by initiating the Pentecostal movement.[39]

In state after state throughout America, revival spread like wildfire, even to the most remote areas. My friend Robert Morgan tells of his grandfather, an itinerate preacher in the remote mountains of East Tennessee and North Carolina, who reported hundreds of converts in the years between 1905 and 1910. When you drive through those mountains today, there are little churches in every hollow and up every road, and many of them were started in the 1905 revival.

While the world has not experienced such a global, history-altering revival since that time (we are due for another!), occasional revival-like movements did mark the subsequent years of the twentieth century. Following World War II, for example, there was an outbreak of Christian ministries that shaped the remainder of the century. Among these were Campus Crusade for Christ, Youth for Christ, evangelists such as Billy Graham, numerous radio and television ministries, and Bible colleges and seminaries.

The Jesus Movement: 1970s

Yet our nation once again fell on hard times, morally and spiritually. Those my age can never forget the dark days of the 1960s, when it seemed that an entire generation of young people "Turned On, Tuned In, and Dropped Out," as Timothy Leary put it.[40] President John F. Kennedy was shot in 1963. The Cold War pitted the United States against the USSR. Racial conflict raged in the South, and in 1968 Dr. Martin Luther King Jr. was assassinated in Memphis, followed by the tragic slaying of Bobby Kennedy. Riots erupted in the streets. The Vietnam War ripped apart the fabric of our national life.

Richard Nixon was elected president. Students took over university campuses, bombs went off, people were killed, institutions of all kinds were attacked. Hallucinogenic drugs were popularized. Long hair, short skirts, transcendental meditation, Eastern Mysticism, and Maharishi Mehesh Yogi—all these forces were swallowing up an entire generation. Watergate sent our politics into chaos, and students battled the National Guard on college campuses, sometimes with tragic results.

Ground zero for the emerging youth culture of this distressed generation was San Francisco's Haight-Ashbury district (called "Hashbury" by the hippies). There, disillusioned and long-haired youth adopted countercultural values, turned to drugs, dropped out of society, and protested the "establishment."[41]

At the height of the Hashbury bedlam in 1968, a Christian couple opened an evangelistic coffeehouse called The Living Room. Other Christian coffeehouses soon opened up and down the West Coast. Ministries started, souls were saved, and the winds of revival swept thousands of hippies into the Pacific Ocean to be baptized. This was the beginning of the Jesus Movement.[42]

Many Christians initially viewed "Jesus People" skeptically. But on January 1, 1971, Billy Graham rode through Pasadena as grand marshal of the Tournament of Roses Parade, and a sea of newly converted hippies surrounded him, pointing index fingers to heaven and shouting "One Way." Deeply moved, Graham committed himself to encouraging these young people who were seeking Christ out of despair. He called them "The Jesus Generation" and penned a book by that title.[43]

The media also noticed. *Look* magazine reported in its February 9, 1971, edition: "A crusade . . . has caught hold in California, and it shows every sign of sweeping east and becoming a national preoccupation. It's an old-time, Bible-toting, witness-giving kind of revival, and the new evangelists are the young." The magazine continued:

> The Jesus movement seems to be springing up simultaneously in a miscellany of places, and often in the last places you would think to look. But maybe, because this is California, this should be the first place to look. In Orange County, an entire motorcycle gang converted. . . . Dozens of go-go clubs throughout the state have been turned into religious coffeehouses, where kids go to sing and pray. . . . Religious clubs are forming on the campuses of California—Stanford, Berkeley, and UCLA. It's a revival, there's no getting around it. Jesus is rising in California. He's the latest movement, the latest thing to groove on.[44]

Time magazine featured a purple Jesus on its cover, encircled by a rainbow bearing the words "The Jesus Revolution." The magazine described Christ as a "notorious leader of an underground liberation movement," who bore the appearance of a "typical hippie type—long hair, beard, robe, sandals."[45]

Yet He was changing lives. Thousands of the "Jesus Freaks," as they were sometimes called, flooded churches like Calvary Chapel in Costa Mesa, where Chuck Smith was pastor. Congregations welcomed the unconventional converts and encouraged them to play their guitars, enjoy their folk-rock sounds, and write new songs to the Lord, thus nurturing the emergence of praise and worship music. Ripples of revival spread into youth groups and churches around the world. Explo '72, a six-day gathering in Dallas, drew eighty thousand young people. Campus revivals shook colleges like Wheaton and Asbury.

As in any revival or movement, there were pockets of immaturity. Not everyone was doctrinally or morally sound. In the confusion of the times, some pastors hardly knew what to think. But yesterday's "Jesus People" are today's church leaders. Their passion for Jesus has never dimmed. Fueled by the revival of those days, an army of Christian workers has labored on mission fields for a generation. Many have advanced the cause of Christ on university campuses and in churches around the world. Their songs have changed the way we worship, adding fresh notes to our hymnody and giving us a new era of Christian music.[46]

We need another spark today, another touch of the fire of heaven. America cannot be saved by politics. It is not going to be saved by Republicans, Democrats, or Independents. While we need wise and godly national leaders, the real answer to our problems is not political but spiritual. We are not going to be saved by our economists or educators. The answer is not found in being liberal or conservative, but in being committed to Jesus Christ.

As I said regarding Josiah's revival, there is powerful chemistry in the union of a humble leader, a holy book, and a hungry people. The key verse of the Bible's manual on revival is 2 Chronicles 7:14: "If My people who are called by My name will humble themselves, and pray and seek My face, and turn from their wicked ways, then I will hear from heaven, and will forgive their sin and heal their land."

In his book, *The Secret of Christian Joy*, Vance Havner wrote:

The greatest need of America is an old-fashioned, heaven-born, God-sent revival. Throughout the history of the church, when clouds have hung lowest, when sin has seemed blackest and faith has been weakest, there have always been a faithful few who have not sold out to the devil nor bowed the knee to Baal, who have feared the Lord and thought upon his Name and have not forsaken the assembling of themselves together. These have besought the Lord to revive his work in the midst of the years, and in the midst of the fears and tears, and in wrath to remember mercy. God has always answered such supplication, filling each heart with his love, rekindling each soul with fire from above.[47]

A TWO-FOLD PLAN FOR REVIVAL

We cannot orchestrate revival, but we can lay the groundwork in two ways.

Pray for Revival Personally

First, let's rededicate ourselves to praying "Revive us!" If you want, you can put it this way: "Revive US." As we have seen, revival often starts with a handful of praying people who develop an insatiable desire to plead with heaven for revival. Remember that wonderful prayer the Lord gave us in Psalm 85:6: "Will You not revive us again, that Your people may rejoice in You?"

The Old Testament scribe Ezra wrote, "And now for a little while grace has been shown from the Lord our God, to leave us a remnant to escape, and to give us a peg in His holy place, that our God may enlighten our eyes and give us a measure of revival" (Ezra 9:8).

Oh, how we need to pray for that measure of revival! Psalm 80:18 says, "Revive us, and we will call upon Your name."

Practice Revival Personally

Second, rededicate yourself to living a life of personal holiness and perpetual revival. You and I do not have to wait for a global or national revival. We can let it begin with us by living in a state of ongoing, personal revival. This is what the apostle Paul meant when he said these words:

> Be filled with the Spirit, speaking to one another in psalms and hymns and spiritual songs, singing and making melody in your heart to the Lord, giving thanks always for all things to God the Father in the name of our Lord Jesus Christ, submitting to one another in the fear of God. (Ephesians 5:18–21)

It is important to pray "Revive us!" but equally vital to pray "Revive me!" Let's pray as did a hymnist of yesteryear: "Let the Holy Spirit come and take control, and send a great revival in my soul."[48] That is the recurring prayer found in the longest chapter in the Bible, Psalm 119. Look at how the author pleaded with God for personal revival:

> Revive me according to Your word. (v. 25)
>
> Revive me in Your way. (v. 37)
>
> Revive me in Your righteousness. (v. 40)
>
> Revive me according to Your lovingkindness. (v. 88)
>
> Revive me, O Lord, according to Your word. (v. 107)
>
> Revive me according to Your justice. (v. 149)
>
> Revive me according to Your word. (v. 154)
>
> Revive me according to Your judgments. (v. 156)
>
> Revive me, O Lord, according to Your lovingkindness. (v. 159)

If we are to change the world, we must first let the Lord change us. And then we pass on to others the flame He ignited in our hearts.

He longs to grant you perpetual joy, everlasting hope, and empowered living. In the middle of a darkened culture, we can confess and turn from sin and let the revival fires of the Holy Spirit burn within us like a divine furnace.

Have you lost the fervor of your love for Him? Has sin dampened your spiritual zeal and hindered your testimony? Has the world seeped into your soul and into your habits? What changes need to occur in your life to open your heart to be filled with the Holy Spirit, to walk in the Spirit, to labor in the power of the Spirit? Whatever it takes, put away sin, put Christ first, and become kindling wood for Him. Jesus came to set the world on fire, and it only takes a spark to do it. Let it begin with you. Let it begin today.

Will You not revive us again, that Your people may rejoice in You?

PART II

IS THIS THE END FOR THE WORLD?

CHAPTER 6

THE ISOLATION OF ISRAEL

On October 13, 2015, Richard Lakin walked out of a doctor's office after a routine appointment and decided to take the bus home rather than walk. Tensions were high in Jerusalem streets due to recent waves of Palestinian terrorism. The bus, he thought, would offer more safety.

Two Arab men sat in seats near the front of the bus, watching the passengers as they entered. After all were boarded, the door closed, and the two suddenly rose up brandishing knives and screaming, "Allahu Akbar." Before anyone could react, they rampaged through the aisle stabbing passengers, killing two and injuring sixteen others. Lakin was one of their victims.

When news of the attack broke on television, Karen Lakin and their son began frantically dialing Richard Lakin's phone. Finally, a nurse answered and urged them to come to the hospital as soon as possible.

The surgical team struggled valiantly to save Lakin's life, but his multiple injuries were too extensive. He died in the hospital two weeks later. Lakin was not an enemy to the Palestinians. He was, in fact, a highly respected teacher of English to both Israeli and Arab children.[1] He was killed randomly simply because he was an Isracli.[2]

Most people in Israel know someone who was a victim of Palestinian terrorism. One Israeli recently blogged, "Everywhere in Israel we can feel the terror tension, by rockets, stones, riots, or Molotov cocktails. . . . Today the Palestinians managed to shoot rockets nearly as far as Haifa, which is about 165 km from Northern Gaza."[3] In some sections of Israel, herding one's family to a bomb shelter is an almost routine experience.

Israelis live daily with this kind of terror hanging over their heads. "Although many Palestinians genuinely desire an end to hostilities, 'Palestinian nationalism' continues to be based on one issue alone—the death of Israel. From the beginning of the Second Intifada in 2000, the Palestinians have supported the slaughter of over 100 Israeli children; murdered teenagers studying in their schools, civilians in their buses and cafes, and have attempted to murder children in nursery schools and child care centers."[4] The Palestinian leaders pay stipends to terrorists and their families who kill Israelis, financed in part by the Israel-hating regime of Iran, now flush with funds after their arms treaty with the Obama administration gave them a 100-billion-dollar windfall.

Author Ramon Bennett believes the Arab-Israeli conflict can be summarized in one word, *Islam*: "The advent of the recreated State of Israel in 1948 created the ultimate challenge to the Islamic world. . . . A recreated Israel proves the Bible to be true and the teaching of the Koran to be false. Not only does a recreated Israel thrust a sword through the heart of Islamic belief, but it also adds insult to the injury by being recreated in the very center of the Islamic heartland!"[5]

Modern Israel is surrounded on all sides by enemies who do not recognize its right to exist and openly vow to annihilate it. These nations occupy a land mass of more than five million square miles. Tiny Israel occupies a land mass of almost nine thousand square miles.

In his book *Fast Facts on the Middle East Conflict,* Dr. Randall Price provides a map that graphically illustrates the vulnerable situation the citizens of Israel wake up to every morning. With his permission, I have included that map here:

Modern Israel has been forced to maintain a continual state of warfare throughout its sixty-eight years of existence. The problem seems to be that very few in the West will admit that Israel is in a fight for its very survival. The subtitle of an article by WORLD News Group editor in chief Marvin Olasky succinctly summarizes the nation's dilemma: "Slammed If You Do, Dead If You Don't." When Israelis take the tough but necessary measures to defend themselves, they are slammed by world censure. If they fail to take those measures, they are left vulnerable to hostile neighbors. In that article, Olasky files this explanation of the impossible situation in which Israelis find themselves today:

The Holocaust's 6 million murders led to the creation of the Israeli state in 1948 and the willingness of Jews to fight for it against enormous odds. . . . The hardened men and women who founded the state of Israel and fought to defend it in the 1950s, 1960s, and 1970s, became known for saying, "Never again." Never again would they make it easy for mass killers. Never again would they go down without a fight. For several decades, non-Jewish Americans and Europeans understood that resolve. . . . But then a generation grew up that did not know Adolf [Hitler]. Those without a visceral awareness of the background saw Israelis not as victims trying to survive but as overlords acting unjustly to poor Palestinians. Manipulators took the opportunity to re-package the old anti-Semitism as sympathy for an oppressed third-world population.[6]

Sam Harris, a strident atheist, is a hero to many on the left, which is why his defense of Israel should impact those who see the Israelis as villainous and the Palestinians as victims. He wrote:

The truth is that there is an obvious, undeniable, and hugely consequential moral difference between Israel and her enemies. The Israelis are surrounded by people who have explicitly genocidal intentions towards them. The discourse in the Muslim world about Jews is utterly shocking. Not only is there Holocaust denial— there's Holocaust denial that then asserts that we will do it for real if given the chance. . . . There are children's shows in the Palestinian territories and elsewhere that teach five-year-olds about the glories of martyrdom and about the necessity of killing Jews.[7]

Oppression and opposition to Jews is nothing new in world history. As they were growing into a nation, they were slaves in Egypt for four hundred years. After conquering their promised homeland, the people of the young nation were continually attacked by hostile tribes. When the glory days of the United Kingdom ended, the Jews were beleaguered by wars with neighboring countries. In 722 BC, the Assyrians conquered northern Israel and deported its people. In 586 BC, Babylon conquered southern Israel and exiled its citizens. The Jews returned to their homeland seventy years later, but the Romans finally crushed them in AD 70 and dispersed them to the four winds, leaving them without a country for 1,878 years.

Even in the countries of their exile, the Jews were oppressed, denied rights, isolated in ghettos, and persecuted relentlessly. The worst of these persecutions came in the 1930s and early 1940s when the despotic madman Adolf Hitler exterminated about six million Jews.[8]

Considering all that the Jews have endured, there is no human explanation for their continued existence. No other people in the world have been driven from their homeland, have maintained their identity through eighteen-plus centuries of exile, and then have reemerged as an intact nation.

The Bible makes it clear why the Jews have endured despite these centuries of hardship. They are God's special people, chosen for a specific purpose. The prophet Ezekiel answered the natural question: If the Jews are God's special people, why have they endured so much hardship?

> Therefore say to the house of Israel, "Thus says the Lord God: 'I do not do this for your sake, O house of Israel, but for My holy name's sake, which you have profaned among the nations wherever you went. And I will sanctify My great name, which has been profaned among the nations, which you have profaned in their midst; and the nations shall know that I am the Lord,' says the Lord God, 'when I am hallowed in you before their eyes.'" (Ezekiel 36:22–23)

Agreeing with Ezekiel, the prophet Isaiah suggested that many of Israel's hardships have been God's discipline for the nation's failures. Having made the Jews His special people, He required much of them; thus they received double punishment for their transgressions: "Speak comfort to Jerusalem, and cry out to her, that her warfare is ended, that her iniquity is pardoned; for she has received from the Lord's hand double for all her sins" (Isaiah 40:2).

Yet because God has an eternal purpose for Israel, He has protected the nation throughout those centuries of oppression, and as this verse tells us, one day its sins will be pardoned and its warfare will end. Peace will come to Israel in the future; meanwhile it continues to suffer.

In the classic musical *Fiddler on the Roof*, the poor Jewish milkman Tevye is burdened with poverty while trying to maintain long-standing traditions and cope with oppression from the anti-Semitic Russians. At one point, he cries out to God, "I know, I know. We are Your chosen people. But, once in a while, can't You choose someone else?"

While poor Tevye was aware he was one of God's chosen people, it is not likely he understood why God chose the Jews. When I first started to study prophecy, I remember reading a little quip about Israel. It went like this:

> How odd of God,
> To choose the Jews.

Out of all the nations of the world, why did God choose Israel? In the book of Deuteronomy, Moses explained why:

> For you are a holy people to the Lord your God; the Lord your God has chosen you to be a people for Himself, a special treasure

above all the peoples on the face of the earth. The LORD did not set His love on you nor choose you because you were more in number than any other people, for you were the least of all peoples; but because the LORD loves you, and because He would keep the oath which He swore to your fathers. (Deuteronomy 7:6–8)

The Israelites became God's chosen people for two reasons: (1) because of a promise God made to Abraham and (2) because of God's faithful love in keeping His promises. Notice that both of these reasons have nothing to do with Israel's merit and everything to do with God's love.

When Abraham was living with his family in the Mesopotamian city of Haran, God made this covenant with him:

> "Get out of your country,
> From your family
> And from your father's house,
> To a land that I will show you.
> I will make you a great nation;
> I will bless you
> And make your name great;
> And you shall be a blessing.
> I will bless those who bless you,
> And I will curse him who curses you;
> And in you all the families of the earth shall be blessed."
> (Genesis 12:1–3)

Here, in the first book of the Bible, we encounter one of the most important passages in all Scripture. It reveals God's covenant with Abraham, which explains the ultimate purpose of the nation of Israel and places it in the center of the geopolitical world of our day. These three verses reveal both the mission and future of God's chosen nation.

The Abrahamic covenant is filled with several far-reaching promises that resound through ages past and reach into ages to come. Studying these promises will give us great help in understanding the present unrest in the Middle East, the future of the Israeli nation, and how the destiny of today's nations will be affected by their stance toward God's chosen people.

When we unpack this historic document, we discover seven important features. The Abrahamic covenant is . . .

start here

AN UNCONDITIONAL COVENANT

Seven times in Genesis 12:1–3, God declared in emphatic terms what He would do for Abraham. There was no ambiguity: it was all "I will . . . I will . . . I will." God's covenant with Abraham was unconditional, and He ratified it in a special ceremony described in Genesis 15. In *The Jeremiah Study Bible*, I explain the meaning of this ceremony:

> To establish and confirm a covenant in Abram's day, usually the two parties would walk between the pieces of the sacrificial animals, saying, in effect, "May what has happened to these creatures happen to me if I break the covenant." The Hebrew expression "to cut a covenant" pertains to the act of cutting the sacrificial animals in two (Genesis 15:18).
>
> Because this was God's sovereign covenant with Abram, not an agreement between equals, symbols of God (a smoking oven and a burning torch) passed between those pieces; Abram did not. The Lord made the covenant with no conditions—independent of Abram—and He would fulfill it in His time.[9]

Paul Wilkinson notes that God alone signed and sealed the covenant, "since only He passed through the animal pieces (Genesis 15:12–21). The inference drawn from Ancient Near Eastern custom is that in so doing, God invoked a curse upon Himself, should He ever break His promise."[10]

No provision was made for this covenant to be revoked, and it was not subject to amendment or annulment.

A PERSONAL COVENANT

Notice that in the covenant with Abraham, God promised extravagant blessings not only to Abraham's descendants but also to Abraham himself: "I will bless you and make your name great" (12:2).

In Genesis 12:1–3, God addressed Abraham using the personal pronouns *you* and *your* eleven times. The promises are ultimately far-reaching and eternal, but they were made first of all to Abraham personally; and each has been fulfilled.

God directed Abraham to travel to the land He promised to his descendants, and Abraham was abundantly blessed as he lived on that land. He found it to be, as Moses later described, a rich land "flowing with milk and honey" (Exodus 3:8, 17; 13:5; 33:3). His flocks and herds increased exponentially, and he became an extremely wealthy man who commanded 318 trained servants (Genesis 14:14). Yes, this land would be the eternal possession of his descendants, but it was also Abraham's personal home throughout the rest of his life (25:7–8).

God's promise to make Abraham's name great has also been lavishly fulfilled. Today, four thousand years after he lived, Abraham continues to inspire devotion from the followers of Judaism, Christianity, and Islam.

Even in his own time, Abraham's name became famous. He was known throughout the land as a rich and powerful leader who was highly respected and feared (Genesis 14).

A NATIONAL COVENANT

In the second verse of God's covenant with Abraham, He said, "I will make you a great nation." The ultimate greatness of the nation of Israel awaits the Millennium, but by all the common standards of evaluation, Israel is a great nation today. Professor Amnon Rubinstein gives us an impressive summary of Israel's national achievements:

> Minute in size, not much bigger than a sliver of Mediterranean coastline, it has withstood continuing Arab onslaughts, wars, boycotts and terrorism; it has turned itself from a poor, rural country to an industrial and post-industrial powerhouse. . . . It has reduced social, educational and health gaps . . . between Arabs and Jews. Some of its achievements are unprecedented: Israeli Arabs have a higher life expectancy than European whites.
>
> Inside Israel proper, democracy functions even in times of great national emergency. . . . It has maintained freedom of the press in time of war; it stands out as a singular democratic, First World island in an Arab and Muslim sea of poverty and backwardness.[11]

A TERRITORIAL COVENANT

The Abrahamic covenant included God's promise to give Abraham "a land" (12:1). Abraham left his home in Haran and followed God's leading to the area at the east end of the Mediterranean Sea. At that time the land was called Canaan. When Abraham settled into this new land, we read that the Lord made a covenant with him, saying: "To your descendants I have given this land, from the river of Egypt to the great river, the River Euphrates" (15:18).

Not only did God promise this land to Abraham, He also promised it to Abraham's son Isaac (26:2–5); to Isaac's son Jacob (28:13; 35:12); and to Jacob's twelve sons and their descendants (Exodus 33:1–3).

The land promised to Abraham and his descendants was described in definite terms with clear geographical boundaries. It takes in all the land from the Mediterranean Sea as the western boundary to the Euphrates River as the eastern boundary. The prophet Ezekiel fixed the northern boundary at Hamath, 100 miles north of Damascus (Ezekiel 48:1), and the southern boundary at Kadesh, about 100 miles south of Jerusalem (v. 28). If Israelis were currently occupying all the land that God gave to them, they would control all the holdings of present-day Israel, Lebanon, and the West Bank of Jordan, plus substantial portions of Syria, Iraq, and Saudi Arabia.

The strange thing is, Israel has never, in its long history, occupied anywhere near this much land—not even at the height of its glory days under David and Solomon. This fact has caused many biblical scholars to spiritualize the meaning of the term *land* and equate it with heaven. Others claim these promises were conditional and were forfeited by Israel's disobedience. In refutation of these interpretations, Dr. John F. Walvoord wrote:

The term *land* . . . used in the Bible, means exactly what it says. It is not talking about heaven. It is talking about a piece of real estate in the Middle East. After all, if all God was promising Abraham was heaven, he could have stayed in Ur of the Chaldees. Why go on the long journey? Why be a pilgrim and a wanderer? No, God meant *land*.[12]

Any normal reading of Scripture recognizes Canaan as an actual place, a piece of real estate, an expanse of soil that will belong to Abraham's descendants forever.

The land of Israel has been described as "'the most important piece of real estate on earth,' . . . 'the geographical platform on which the story of the Bible is staged,' . . . 'the centre of Divine dealings with nations,' 'the spiritual navel of the world,' . . . 'ground zero for the end times,' . . . 'the only city on earth not up for negotiations with anyone at any time for any reason.'"[13]

The fact that Israel has been dispossessed of the land in three periods of its history is not an argument against its ultimate possession. Occupation is not the same as ownership. After each dispossession God has brought Israel back to its originally promised land. No matter how often the nation turns faithless and self-destructs, God has consistently kept His promise to Abraham. And that gives us absolute assurance that He will keep it in the future.

The writings of the Old Testament prophets, both major and minor, are filled with promises that Israel will return to this land God promised to Abraham. Here is a sampling of these prophecies. (In each case, the emphasis on the word *land* is added.)

> "Behold, I will gather them out of all countries where I have driven them in My anger, in My fury, and in great wrath; I will bring them back to this place, and I will cause them to dwell safely. . . . Yes, I will rejoice over them to do them good, and I will assuredly plant them in this *land*, with all My heart and with all My soul." (Jeremiah 32:37, 41)

"Thus says the Lord God: 'I will gather you from the peoples, assemble you from the countries where you have been scattered, and I will give you the *land* of Israel.'" (Ezekiel 11:17)

"Then you shall know that I am the Lord, when I bring you into the *land* of Israel, into the country for which I raised My hand in an oath to give to your fathers." (20:42)

"And I will bring them out from the peoples and gather them from the countries, and will bring them to their own *land*; I will feed them on the mountains of Israel, in the valleys and in all the inhabited places of the country." (34:13)

"Thus says the Lord God: 'Surely I will take the children of Israel from among the nations, wherever they have gone, and will gather them from every side and bring them into their own *land*. . . . Then they shall dwell in the *land* that I have given to Jacob My servant, where your fathers dwelt; and they shall dwell there, they, their children, and their children's children, forever.'" (37:21, 25)

"Then they shall know that I am the Lord their God, who sent them into captivity among the nations, but also brought them back to their *land*, and left none of them captive any longer." (39:28)

> "'I will bring back the captives of My people Israel;
> They shall build the waste cities and inhabit them;
> They shall plant vineyards and drink wine from them;
> They shall also make gardens and eat fruit from them.
> I will plant them in their *land*,
> And no longer shall they be pulled up

> From the *land* I have given them,'
>
> Says the LORD your God." (Amos 9:14–15)

What does it mean to take these prophecies at face value? Look again at the last phrase in the prophecy of Amos above: "And no longer shall they be pulled up from the land I have given them." This could not apply to any of the Jews' repossessions of their land in ancient history. It could not apply to Joshua's repossession of the land after the Canaanites had settled it following Jacob's migration to Egypt, because the Jews were "pulled up from the land" in the Assyrian and Babylonian conquests. And we must remember that all the many prophecies of Israel's restoration were made long after Joshua and his generation had come and gone. Nor could the restoration apply to the Jews' return to their homeland after the Babylonian captivity because after that particular return they were again "pulled up from the land" and dispersed by the Romans in AD 70.

From the time of the Roman dispossession, the dispersed Jews had no homeland until the modern state of Israel was established in 1948. Even then, the United Nations partitioned off a large section of what had been ancient Israel—Judea and Samaria, now called the West Bank—and gave it to the Islamic Palestinians in the area. In the famous Six-Day War of 1967, Israel won back the West Bank territory.

Although the outcome of that war did wonders for Israel's morale and international prestige, it also created the controversy that has led to Israel's increasing isolation. This land rightfully belongs to the Israelis by any standard of justice. They won it while defending themselves against hostile attacks, and they are determined to keep it to enhance their defense against the terrorism that has poured out of that area. But most important, this disputed piece of land rightfully belongs to Israel through God's historic covenant with Abraham.

Every single Old Testament prophet, with the exception of Malachi, repeated the land promise, a fact which, as Dr. Walvoord noted, makes it all the more astonishing that Israel's right to the land is not more widely recognized:

> Only by indiscriminate spiritualization of all the terms and promises relating to the land can these prophecies be nullified. The fact that they are stated and restated so many times in so many different periods of Israel's history, even in times of apostasy and departure from God as in the days of Jeremiah and Ezekiel, and by so many of the minor prophets makes clear that God intended them to be taken at their face value.[14]

Today, the land clause in the Abrahamic covenant is utterly ignored by our secularized world. Allies and enemies alike are strongly urging Israel to give up the West Bank portion of their God-ordained land in the interest of "peace" in the Middle East. The debate over turning it into a Palestinian state is in the news almost every day. This turmoil over Israel's right to its land will not cease till the end, for as we noted earlier, the land provision of the Abrahamic covenant is at the core of the hatred of Middle Eastern nations for Israel today.

But ignoring God's care and protection of Israel puts one in an extremely dangerous position. The land of Israel is so important to God that, according to Deuteronomy 11:12, it is "a land for which the LORD your God cares; the eyes of the LORD your God are always on it, from the beginning of the year to the very end of the year."

If you wonder why my exposition of the land clause of the Abrahamic covenant is way out of proportion to my treatment of the rest of the covenant, we have now reached the point where I can explain. I have written about the importance of Israel's land in previous books, but until I researched all the passages where that land clause is mentioned, I did not realize how very carefully the Spirit of God has protected the truth we are about to unveil.

The significance of Israel's modern emergence as a nation in its ancient homeland is that this had to occur in order to set the stage for the final fulfillment of biblical prophecies about the future. Without the existence of the nation of Israel, we would not be able to say with certainty that we are in the last days. The 1948 return of the Jews to its homeland is the most prominent sign that we are living in the final moments before the coming of Jesus.

Israel's restoration to its land has been described as "God's time clock," "God's barometer," "God's prophetic clock," "the powder keg fuse for the final world conflict," "the touchstone of world politics," and "the evidence that God is the God of history."[15]

A RECIPROCAL COVENANT

God also promised protection to the nation that would descend from Abraham: "I will bless those who bless you, and I will curse him who curses you" (Genesis 12:3).

Leaders and nations that ally with Israel to preserve, protect, and defend it will likewise be preserved, protected, and defended. On the other hand, those who stand in the way of Israel's wellbeing will find themselves standing against God—which means they will not long stand at all.

The prophet Zechariah reiterated the warning in this covenant several times in his prophecy: He declared that God would plunder the nations that plunder Israel, "for he who touches [Israel] touches the apple of His eye" (Zechariah 2:8). A little later Zechariah sounded a roll call of peoples who would fall under God's judgment for lifting a hand against His chosen nation: Hadrach, Damascus, Hamath, Tyre, Sidon, Ashkelon, Gaza, Ekron, and Ashdod (9:1–7). Then in the next verse, he recorded God's warning against those who would harm Israel in the future: "I will set up camp in my home country and defend it against invaders. Nobody is going to hurt my people ever again. I'm keeping my eye on them" (v. 8 THE MESSAGE). Finally, in the twelfth chapter of his prophecy, Zechariah said, "Behold, I will make Jerusalem a cup of drunkenness to all the surrounding peoples, when they lay siege against Judah and Jerusalem. And it shall happen in that day that I will make Jerusalem a very heavy stone for all peoples; all who would heave it away will surely be cut in pieces, though all nations of the earth are gathered against it" (vv. 2–3).

History tells the tragic story of what has happened to nations and leaders who dared to oppress Israel. Egypt, the first nation to enslave Israel, was brought to its knees by ten devastating plagues (Exodus 7–11). The Amorites, who resisted Israel's march toward their promised land, were soundly defeated (Numbers 21:21–30).

One of the most notable examples of God's vengeance against an enemy of Israel was the annihilation of the Midianites who joined with Moab in trying to stop Israel. After their failure to bribe the prophet Balaam into pronouncing a curse on Israel, they resorted to Balaam's plan B. They used Midianite women to seduce Israel's men into immorality and idolatry. Moses prepared Israel for war "to take vengeance for the LORD on Midian" (31:3). The battle was quick and decisive. After the dust settled, all five Midianite kings had been killed, along with every Midianite male and married female. All the Midianite cities were burned to the ground, and the Israelites took as plunder massive amounts of gold, silver, bronze, tin, lead, and wood, along with 808,000 head of cattle, sheep, and donkeys (Numbers 31; Revelation 2:14).

Babylon, the empire that destroyed Jerusalem and the temple and deported the Jews from their homeland, was soundly defeated seventy years later by the Persians. One of history's worst persecutors of the Jews, the Greek-Seleucid ruler Antiochus IV, died a horrible death shortly after hearing that his army had been defeated in the Jewish Maccabean rebellion. Breathing rage against the Jews, he rushed to Israel to put down the rebellion. On the road he was suddenly afflicted with painful intestinal disorders so severe that he fell from his chariot. Internal worms began to eat his body, flesh fell from it, and he emitted such a foul stench that his men could not remain in his presence. Days later he died in horrible agony.[16]

In modern times, Russia confined Jews to ghettos and harassed them with pogroms under the czars, who were subsequently overthrown in the communist rebellion of 1917. The Jews fared even worse under communism. They were forbidden to practice their religious rites, and many were arrested, deported, or executed. Communism disintegrated in 1989. Hitler's Germany, which destroyed some six million Jews, was crushed in World War II.

Earlier I mentioned Israel's Six-Day War of 1967. It stands today as the most spectacular modern example of God's punishment on those who curse Israel. Although Israel became an independent nation in 1948, the Palestinians and Islamic states surrounding it never recognized its statehood and vowed its extermination. In 1967, the United Arab Republic (UAR), allied with Jordan, Syria, and Palestinian guerrillas, combined to attack Israel from the north, south, and east. Israel was hopelessly outmanned. The Arab armies numbered more than 500,000 men; Israel had only 75,000. The Arabs fielded 5,000 tanks and 900 combat aircraft, whereas the Israeli total was only 1,000 tanks and 175 planes. Yet when the smoke cleared six days later, the UAR had lost almost its entire air force, about 20,000 lives, and Israel had taken over significant Arab-controlled territory, including the Sinai Peninsula, Golan Heights, Gaza Strip, and West Bank.[17]

Here is how the *Encyclopedia Britannica* summarized the war: "The Arab countries' losses in the conflict were disastrous. Egypt's casualties numbered more than 11,000, with 6,000 for Jordan and 1,000 for Syria, compared with only 700 for Israel. The Arab armies also suffered crippling losses of weaponry and equipment. The lopsidedness of the defeat demoralized both the Arab public and the political elite."[18]

In a powerful speech to the United Nations General Assembly on October 1, 2015, Israeli Prime Minister Benjamin Netanyahu summarized Israel's long fight for existence, described the miraculous preservation of the Jewish people, and detailed the punishment that fell on those who opposed them:

In every generation, there were those who rose up to destroy our people. In antiquity, we faced destruction from the ancient empires of Babylon and Rome. In the Middle Ages, we faced inquisition and expulsion. And in modern times, we faced pogroms and the Holocaust. Yet the Jewish people persevered.

And now another regime has arisen, swearing to destroy Israel. That regime would be wise to consider this: I stand here today representing Israel, a country 67 years young, but the nation-state of a people nearly 4,000 years old. Yet the empires of Babylon and Rome are not represented in this hall of nations. Neither is the Thousand Year Reich. Those seemingly invincible empires are long gone. But Israel lives. The people of Israel live.[19]

Do not forget the other half of the reciprocal covenant. God also promises that those who bless Israel will be blessed. The United States was the first country to recognize the modern state of Israel and, up to now, has been its strongest ally and supporter. No one can deny that in the years following that 1948 event, our country has been blessed beyond measure with burgeoning prosperity, power, and prestige. We must pray that the current strain in US-Israeli relations will be resolved before we too join the Hall of Shame of nations that have tried to stand in the way of God's blessings on Israel. History records that Israel stands at the graves of all its enemies.

A UNIVERSAL COVENANT

Here we reach the overarching reason for all the promises we have studied in God's covenant with Abraham: "In you all the families of the earth shall be blessed" (Genesis 12:3).

This is the root of God's promise to Abraham and His purpose in creating a new people for Himself. It was not to exclude the rest of humanity from His favor; in fact, it was the very opposite—Abraham's descendants were to become the repository of God's glory, wisdom, love, and redemptive grace. This saving grace was to overflow from the Jews to the rest of the world's people. Through Abraham God gave His written Word to the world:

The Bible's human authors were almost exclusively Jewish people. From Moses, the author of Genesis, to the apostle John, the author of Revelation, the books of the Bible are the result of Jewish writers who were guided by the Holy Spirit to produce the words that guide our Christian faith today. With the possible exception of Luke, who authored the Gospel of Luke and Acts, every book of the Bible was authored by a Jewish writer.[20]

And through Abraham, God gave His Son to the world, blessing all humanity with the means of escaping the grip of sin and death, "that the blessing of Abraham might come upon the Gentiles in Christ Jesus, that we might receive the promise of the Spirit through faith" (Galatians 3:14).

All the other promises in God's covenant with Abraham are in support of this one universal promise that affects every person who has ever lived upon the earth.

Let's also remember that the city of Jerusalem came to us through Abraham. As I was writing this chapter, I took time out to lead a group of 650 people to Israel. One of my favorite experiences when I come to this blessed land is the opportunity to preach to our touring congregation from the southern steps of the Holy City, the city where God's Son died for the sins of the world. When I stand on those steps to deliver my message, I can look off to my right and see the place from which our Lord ascended to heaven after He completed His earthly work of redemption. I am reminded that it is to this very same place He will someday return to set up His kingdom on this earth. The blessings of Abraham, as God promised, are continually being poured out upon our world.

AN ETERNAL COVENANT

God's promise to Abraham came in three stages. It was initiated in Genesis 12:1–3, formalized in Genesis 15:1–21, and then amplified in Genesis 17:1–18.[21] In Genesis 17, Abraham was approaching his one hundredth birthday, his faith was frail—it had been nearly twenty-five years since his first encounter with the Lord—and doubts were beginning to cloud his mind. Then God appeared, reminding Abraham that His promise was still in force. It was a forever promise, an eternal promise "between Me and you and your descendants after you in their generations, for an *everlasting* covenant, to be God to you and your descendants after you. Also I give to you and your descendants after you the land in which you are a stranger, all the land of Canaan, as an *everlasting* possession; and I will be their God" (vv. 7–8).

The promise to Abraham is an everlasting promise because it is an unconditional covenant based on the grace and sovereignty of Almighty God. There may be delays, postponements, and chastisements, but an eternal covenant cannot be abrogated by a God who cannot deny Himself.

> Thus says the LORD,
> Who gives the sun for a light by day,
> The ordinances of the moon and the stars for a light by night,
> Who disturbs the sea,
> And its waves roar
> (The LORD of hosts is His name):
>
> "If those ordinances depart
> From before Me, says the LORD,
> Then the seed of Israel shall also cease
> From being a nation before Me forever."

Thus says the LORD:

> "If heaven above can be measured,
> And the foundations of the earth searched out beneath,

I will also cast off all the seed of Israel.
For all that they have done, says the LORD." (Jeremiah 31:35–37)

He remembers His covenant forever,
The word which He commanded, for a thousand generations,
The covenant which He made with Abraham,
And His oath to Isaac. (Psalm 105:8–9)

When I was growing up, I loved to hear visiting college choirs sing an old spiritual that had these words in its chorus:

Dem bones, dem bones, dem dry bones.
Dem bones, dem bones, dem dry bones.
Dem bones, dem bones gonna rise again.
Dem bones, dem bones gonna rise again.
Now hear the word of the Lord.

It was one of my favorite spirituals. I loved the toe-tapping, hand-clapping rhythm of it. But at my young age, it never occurred to me that the song might have any particular meaning. How wrong I was! It is built on a startling and eerie vision of the prophet Ezekiel, who suddenly found himself standing in a grim valley completely covered with human bones, all dry, dismembered, and scattered:

The hand of the LORD came upon me and brought me out in the Spirit of the LORD, and set me down in the midst of the valley; and it was full of bones. Then He caused me to pass by them all around, and behold, there were very many in the open valley; and indeed they were very dry. And He said to me, "Son of man, can these bones live?"

So I answered, "O Lord God, You know."

Again He said to me, "Prophesy to these bones and say to them, 'O dry bones, hear the word of the Lord! Thus says the Lord God to these bones: "Surely I will cause breath to enter into you, and you shall live. I will put sinews on you and bring flesh upon you, cover you with skin and put breath in you; and you shall live. Then you shall know that I am the Lord."'"

So I prophesied as I was commanded; and as I prophesied, there was a noise, and suddenly a rattling; and the bones came together, bone to bone. Indeed, as I looked, the sinews and the flesh came upon them, and the skin covered them over; but there was no breath in them. (Ezekiel 37:1–8)

We can only wonder how Ezekiel reacted when God enabled these bones to hear his message and come together. But we need not wonder about the meaning of the phenomenon. Like so many other prophetic passages in the Bible, this one is self-interpreting. Ezekiel 37:11–14 tell us expressly what the vision means:

> These bones are the whole house of Israel. They indeed say, "Our bones are dry, our hope is lost, and we ourselves are cut off!" Therefore prophesy and say to them, "Thus says the Lord God: 'Behold, O My people, I will open your graves and cause you to come up from your graves, and bring you into the land of Israel. Then you shall know that I am the Lord, when I have opened your graves, O My people, and brought you up from your graves. I will put My Spirit in you, and you shall live, and I will place you in your own land.'"

God made it clear to Ezekiel that the dry bones in this vision represented the scattered nation of Israel, buried in the graves of Gentile nations around the world. But, as Ezekiel said, "there was no breath in them" (v. 8). They were merely recycled corpses.

Let's stop for a moment and look at what Ezekiel's vision tells us. Just as these scattered, dry bones reassembled into their original human forms, the Jews who had been scattered all over the world would be reassembled in their original land. Yet the re-gathered nation would have no breath. It would be without spiritual life.

This is exactly what we have seen happen. Israel is finally back in its original land, but in a twist of irony, the one nation founded and chosen by God Himself is today among the most alienated from His Son, Jesus Christ.

According to a 2015 WIN/Gallup poll, 65 percent of the Israeli population "said that they are either not religious or convinced atheists, compared to just 30% who say that they are religious."[22] Of this religious 30 percent, only 2.1 percent practice Christianity in any form, and about 80 percent of these are Arab Christians.[23] So the actual number of ethnic Israelis who are Christians is one-half of 1 percent of Israel's entire population.

The Jews have returned to their land, just as Ezekiel and so many other biblical prophets predicted. In Ezekiel's terms, the bones have gathered and formed a body. But spiritually speaking, it is a dead body.

During my years as a pastor, I have been asked many times whether I believe that Israel's return to its land fulfills all the biblical prophecies concerning its future. What they are really asking is this: Now that Israel is restored to its land, is this the end?

Ezekiel 37 enables me to answer that question, and the answer is no. Israel is in its land: The dismembered, dry bones have been reconnected, fulfilling the part of Ezekiel's prophecy that we have considered so far. But Ezekiel recorded one more prophecy that is yet to be fulfilled.

What we have read in Ezekiel describes Israel in its current state today. The bones have reassembled, but "there [is] no breath in them" (v. 8). The Old Testament word for *breath* is the Hebrew *ruach*[24], which can also mean "wind" or "spirit." Its New Testament Greek equivalent is *pneuma*, which often denotes the presence of God's Holy Spirit.[25] We know that since the death and resurrection of Jesus Christ, the Holy Spirit has been imparted to mankind through belief in Him, and the presence of the Holy Spirit in one's life is the seal of redemption, the mark of God's people (Ephesians 1:13–14; 4:30; 2 Corinthians 1:21–22). The nation of Israel does not know Christ; therefore, it does not have "breath." Its people do not have God's Holy Spirit. Israel is present in its land, but it is as spiritually dead as Ezekiel's reconstituted corpses.

But as God showed Ezekiel in these next verses, this will not be Israel's permanent condition:

"Prophesy to the breath, prophesy, son of man, and say to the breath, 'Thus says the Lord GOD: "Come from the four winds, O breath, and breathe on these slain, that they may live."'" So I prophesied as He commanded me, and breath came into them, and they lived, and stood upon their feet, an exceedingly great army. (Ezekiel 37:9–10)

Here Ezekiel told us that God will, in time, put breath into the reassembled corpse of Israel. Obviously, this has not yet happened. But we can be assured that it will happen, just as God promised in many other prophecies besides those of Ezekiel:

"I will pour on the house of David and on the inhabitants of Jerusalem the Spirit of grace and supplication; then they will look on Me whom they pierced." (Zechariah 12:10)

"And so all Israel will be saved, as it is written:

'The Deliverer will come out of Zion,

And He will turn away ungodliness from Jacob;

For this is My covenant with them,

When I take away their sins.'" (Romans 11:26–27)

We have learned that there are still two pivotal prophecies concerning Israel that have not yet been fulfilled: Israel does not yet occupy all the land originally promised to it, and its people have not yet turned to Christ. The numerous prophecies of Israel's return to its homeland were explicitly fulfilled in 1948 when Israel began to be restored to its land. This gives us absolute assurance that full restoration is on the horizon and that the prophecies concerning Israel's return to God will also be explicitly fulfilled.

As we wait for the fulfillment of these prophecies, Israel continues to grow as a nation. Against all odds, the people of Israel lead the Middle East in productivity, wealth, order, freedom, and military power. Yet as these assets increase, the nation becomes more and more isolated, threatened with extinction and continually terrorized by the murderous hostility of its surrounding neighbors.

When I first began to learn about this nation, Israel was to the world an example of courage and resilience in times of great suffering and persecution. The Jews had endured the Holocaust, and stories about people such as Corrie ten Boom and her courageous family reminded us of the best in people. Steven Spielberg's 1993 movie *Schindler's List* brilliantly told the story of an accomplished industrialist who risked his life and went into bankruptcy to save more than one thousand Jews from death in Nazi concentration camps by employing them in his factory.

These stories and many others raised our level of love and respect for the Jewish people and for the many Europeans and Americans who came to their aid during one of the darkest hours of human history. But sadly, today, the tide of public opinion has turned against the Jewish nation. Former Associated Press reporter Matti Friedman wrote a serious description of how Israel is treated by the European and American press:

> You don't need to be a history professor, or a psychiatrist, to understand what's going on. Having rehabilitated themselves against considerable odds in a minute corner of the earth, the descendants of powerless people who were pushed out of Europe and the Islamic Middle East have become what their grandparents were—the pool into which the world spits. The Jews of Israel are the screen onto which it has become socially acceptable to project the things you hate about yourself and your own country. The tool through which this psychological projection is executed is the international press.[26]

Today Israel longs for peace—even desperately, it seems, at times. But its peace will not come until its Messiah comes and sets up His kingdom on earth. The last chapters in the book of Ezekiel (40–48) speak of that kingdom. Then and only then will the second part of Ezekiel's prophecy be fulfilled. When we pray for the peace of Israel, we are asking God for more than we often realize.

I was seven years old when the nation of Israel was established in 1948. I now believe that the restoration of the Jewish people to their land is the most important prophetic sign to have occurred in my lifetime. More than anything else we are writing about in this book, the prophetic future of the nation of Israel answers the question, "Is this the end?"

The return of the Jewish people to their homeland is considered by many to be the greatest prophetic miracle of all time. But an even greater prophetic fulfillment awaits an unknown future day: the return of the Jewish Messiah to the Jewish people!

CHAPTER 7

THE INSURGENCY OF ISIS

It was not a large gathering. Only a few dozen worshippers assembled in the courtyard of the Virgin Mary Church in the village of al-Our, 150 miles south of Cairo, Egypt. A preacher stood and spoke in somber tones to the equally somber group: "The life we live is but numbered days that will quickly pass, the Bible says."[1]

He was not beginning a sermon on time management or stewardship. He was addressing the reason the congregation had grown smaller. Just a few days earlier, in February 2015, the organization known as the Islamic State of Iraq and Syria (ISIS) had decapitated thirteen of their members on a beach in Libya.

These Coptic Christian men were among twenty that ISIS murdered on that day. All twenty hailed from Egyptian farming communities and had traveled to Libya in search of work. But they had been kidnapped in late December and early January and held in the Libyan coastal town of Sirte.

A month later, the condemned men were led single file onto a beach, where they were lined up on their knees with one black-clad ISIS soldier, each with knife in hand, standing behind each man. The Christians were dressed in orange coveralls in malicious mockery of the orange suits worn by radical Muslims incarcerated at the American Guantanamo Bay prison in Cuba. The prisoners were given the opportunity to recant their faith, but each refused. In the video of the executions released by ISIS, the Christian men can be seen, on their knees, mouthing prayers and praise to their Lord.

When these Christian men were kidnapped, it was as if they had dropped off the face of the earth. The church at al-Our lost all contact with them and had no idea what might have happened. But they did not lose hope. The local Coptic priest, Father Makar Issa, reported:

> In the month and a half when the people were kidnapped, the whole congregation was coming to the church to pray for their return, but in their prayers later on, they asked that if they died, they die for their faith. . . . The congregation is actually growing, psychologically and spiritually.[2]

This spiritual growth was evident in the remarkable maturity shown by relatives of the deceased. Bashir Kamel, whose two brothers and cousin were among the murdered, said, "I felt peace knowing that they died as martyrs in the name of Christ."[3]

Bishop Feloubes Fawzy, who lost a nephew and four cousins in the slaughter, said, "I am happy for my relatives. They had faith in God. They had faith in Jesus Christ. And that is what matters. They died for their faith. They died for Christianity."[4]

The mother of twenty-five-year-old laborer Malak Ibrahim, one of those martyred, told reporters, "I'm proud of my son. He did not change his faith [even at] the last moment of death. I thank God. Malak is with his father now. Jesus . . . is taking care of him."[5]

Despite her grief, the mother of Samuel Abraham expressed the ultimate meaning and triumph that shone like beams of glory from the death of her son and his companions: "Now more people believe in Christianity because of them. ISIS showed what Christianity is. We thank God that our relatives are in heaven. He chose them."[6]

In their heroic deaths, these men did indeed show the world and ISIS the power of faith over fear. They demonstrated with their last breath the ultimate reality of God and a love more powerful than death.

These twenty Christian believers represent just a few who have fallen under the knives of ISIS. Many more, both men and women, have been shot, tortured, raped, forced into ISIS marriages, sold into sexual slavery, and driven from their villages to become refugees. ISIS has firmly established itself in Iraq and Syria, but its tentacles now reach into other nations of Asia, the Middle East, and Africa, where its franchises commit the same atrocities. Since September 11, 2001, we in the West have learned that Islamic militants no longer limit their terrorism to the Middle East. America and Europe—notably New York, London, Paris, and Brussels—have also suffered attacks from ISIS and its forerunner, al-Qaeda. The group's battlefield is now the world.

But let's be clear: The use of terms like *Islamic militants* and *Islamic terrorism* should not be seen as an indictment of all the world's Muslims. Those terms simply acknowledge what is obvious: Most of the terrorism inflicted on the world today is motivated by militant Islamic ideology.

In a 2014 opinion column for the *Washington Post*, the Indian-born American journalist Fareed Zakaria wrote:

> Let's be honest. Islam has a problem today. The places that have trouble accommodating themselves to the modern world are disproportionately Muslim.

In 2013, of the top 10 groups that perpetrated terrorist attacks, seven were Muslim. Of the top 10 countries where terrorist attacks took place, seven were Muslim-majority. The Pew Research Center rates countries on the level of restrictions that governments impose on the free exercise of religion. Of the 24 most restrictive countries, 19 are Muslim-majority. Of the 21 countries that have laws against apostasy, all have Muslim majorities.

There is a cancer of extremism within Islam today. A small minority of Muslims celebrates violence and intolerance and harbors deeply reactionary attitudes toward women and minorities. While some confront these extremists, not enough do so, and the protests are not loud enough. How many mass rallies have been held against the Islamic State (also known as ISIS) in the Arab world today?[7]

In his widely quoted 2014 Rosh Hashanah sermon, the noted Atlanta Rabbi Shalom Lewis said,

There are one billion Muslims in the world and authorities agree that 5% are committed Islamists who embrace terror and wish to see, by any means possible, the Muslim flag fly over every capital, on every continent. I was relieved when I heard only 5%. Thank God it's only 5%. Now I could sleep soundly. But wait . . . 5% of a billion is 50 million Koran-waving, Allah Akbar–howling Muslim murderers out there planning to slit our throats, blow us up or forcibly convert us.[8]

Those of us who know biblical prophecy cannot but see a foreshadowing of the future in the barbarous actions of radical Islamists and ISIS. John the apostle saw in his revelation, "the woman, drunk with the blood of the saints and with the blood of the martyrs of Jesus" (Revelation 17:6). Today we are getting a taste of what John foresaw—the religious fanaticism that will one day cover the earth via the rule of the Antichrist and his False Prophet. Like the twenty martyrs on the Libyan beach, many more Christians will lay down their lives for Jesus in the days ahead.

Members of ISIS have publicly vowed to bring their agenda to America. In a five-part video documentary on the rise of ISIS produced by Vice News, an ISIS press officer reads this formal statement: "I say to America that the Islamic Caliphate has been established. . . . Don't be cowards and attack us with drones. Instead send your soldiers, the ones we humiliated in Iraq. We will humiliate them everywhere, God willing, and we will raise the flag of Allah in the White House."[9] If ISIS does not bring its unholy war to the United States, it won't be for feebleness of desire or lack of trying.

Who and what is ISIS, and how should we, as Christians, respond to its threat?

THE DEVELOPMENT OF ISIS

In the few short years of its existence, the organization we now know as ISIS has gone by different names. Tracing the chronological evolution of those names will give us a glimpse into the developing character of the organization.

- **AQI (AL-QAEDA IN IRAQ).** In 2003, a US-led coalition of nations invaded Iraq in response to 9/11. In retaliation, Osama bin Laden began funding an al-Qaeda branch in Iraq. This branch was referred to as AQI. AQI served as the cradle of ISIS.

- **ISIS (ISLAMIC STATE OF IRAQ AND SYRIA).** Since early 2014, ISIS has gained control of large swaths of northern Iraq and Syria. It has taken over oil production; banks in Mosul, Iraq; and stockpiles of American military hardware left behind by the fleeing Iraqi army. It took the name ISIS because it operated primarily in Iraq and Syria. It is the name under which the organization gained worldwide recognition.

- **ISIL (ISLAMIC STATE OF IRAQ AND THE LEVANT).** As ISIS expanded its operation throughout 2014 and 2015, its name changed to reflect its wider range of influence. The Levant is an ancient designation for the territory now occupied by Syria, Jordan, Lebanon, Israel, Iraq, Turkey, Egypt, Palestine, and Cyprus—an umbrella term for "Middle East." ISIL has become familiar to Americans because it is the name now used by President Obama and the White House.

- **DAESH (OR DA'ISH).** The names defined above are English acronyms; DAESH is an Arabic acronym meaning the same thing as ISIL. ISIS detests the name DAESH because it sounds much like the Arabic words *daes* ("one who crushes or tramples underfoot") and *dahes* ("one who sows discord"). Muslim opponents of ISIS refer to the organization as DAESH to express their scorn or derision. Many government officials around the world—including US Secretary of State John Kerry—use DAESH as a way to remove the connotation of the organization being an Islamic State, as implied by the terms ISIS or ISIL. And they may derive a bit of backhanded pleasure from knowing the term gets under the skin of ISIS leaders. And does it ever! ISIS officials reportedly threatened to cut out the tongue of anyone publicly referring to ISIS as DAESH.[10]

- **IS (ISLAMIC STATE).** Islamic State is the current name for the organization. It is the name preferred by its own leaders for two reasons. First, it includes "Islam" and "state," which summarizes its goal of uniting the Muslim religion into a single, powerful political entity. Second, the new name eliminates geographical references, which would suggest the organization is nothing less than a worldwide movement.

It may seem that ISIS just popped up in the past two or three decades as a catalyst for the anger and ambitions of militant Muslims. But in reality, its history is ancient and complex. It has its geo-political roots in the Soviet invasion of Afghanistan in the 1980s, its theological roots in the founding of Islam, and its ethnic roots in the family of Abraham. Let's sort out this history in order to get an accurate picture of how ISIS has developed.

The Ancient History of ISIS

Most Bible students know the story of Abraham and his two sons, Ishmael and Isaac (Genesis 16, 21). God had promised to make Abraham the father of a great nation (12:1–3), and that meant, of course, that he would need to have a son. Abraham had no children at the time, but he depended on God's promise that one would come (15:4). But by the time Abraham was eighty-five years old and his wife, Sarah, was seventy-five, the promised heir had not yet arrived. Sarah, therefore, fell back upon Mesopotamian law codes and suggested that Abraham follow the ancient custom allowed in their homeland. When a wife could not conceive, her female servant could step in as a surrogate and bear a child for the couple. So Sarah's servant, Hagar, bore Abraham a son, whom they named Ishmael.

But Ishmael was not the son God had promised. That son would come through Abraham and Sarah. Yet God took Ishmael into account and gave him a place in history. An angel of the Lord spoke to Hagar, saying, "He shall be a wild man; his hand shall be against every man, and every man's hand against him" (16:12). God also promised that Ishmael would be the father of multitudes (17:20).

Fourteen years after Ishmael's birth, when Abraham was one hundred years old and Sarah was ninety, they had a son whom they named Isaac—the son of the covenant promise. Isaac became the patriarch through whom would flow the great nation promised to Abraham. Abraham loved Ishmael (v. 18), but there could be only one son of promise, and that was Isaac.

Things did not go well between the two mothers of Abraham's sons. Tensions and jealousy poisoned the home atmosphere. On the day when Isaac was weaned, his mother, Sarah, "saw Ishmael—the son of Abraham and her Egyptian servant Hagar—making fun of her son, Isaac" (21:9 NLT). In a rage, she had Ishmael and his mother banished from the home. The animosity that broke up Abraham's household was a portent of things to come.

Ishmael fathered twelve sons who became the progenitors of the modern Arab peoples. Almost all Arabs— including Muhammad, the founder of Islam—look to Ishmael as their father just as Jews look to Jacob (Israel), the son of Isaac, as their father.

Fast forward a few thousand years from the births of Abraham's sons, and we see the modern manifestation of that ancient animosity in the Arab-Israeli conflict. It simmered throughout the centuries but finally flared into a raging conflagration in 1948, when Israel regained nationhood.

To understand how ISIS links into that historical chain, we must look at the two primary factors that fuel the ongoing Arab-Jew hostility—race and religion. It is a racial/ethnic conflict first and a religious conflict second. The racial rift grew out of the Ishmael-Isaac enmity, which began around 1900 BC. The religious conflict arose in the AD 600s with the establishment of Islam.

The ISIS-against-everybody syndrome that plagues the world today has virtually nothing to do with the Ishmael-Isaac divide. Radical Islam's quarrel is not just with Judaism; it is with *all* other religions, including even moderate Muslims who do not subscribe to the extreme ideology of ISIS. So when ISIS targets Jews, they do so for reasons both racial (strains of the Ishmael-Isaac rift) and religious (because Jews are not Muslims).

With ISIS, religion, not ethnicity, is always the primary source of conflict. In fact, most Muslims are not Arabs. There are large popula- tions of non-Arabic Muslims in Turkey, Iran, and Indonesia. And not all Arabs are Muslims—there are Arab Christians as well as Arabs of other religions. Not even all members of ISIS are Arabs (though the majority are), but they are definitely all Muslim. You cannot be a member of ISIS without subscribing to radical Islamic theology and ideology.

In summary, ISIS targets anyone whose religion differs from Islam or who occupies land that Muslims previously conquered in the name of Allah—which includes the land of Israel, now occupied by the Jews.

The Modern History of ISIS

The previously given history describes the ancient soil in which ISIS is rooted. The organization itself, though only a few decades old, is shaped by those many centuries of religious conflict and racial tension. It was not created in any methodical sense of the word, but more or less self-generated in response to a crisis and then evolved like a mutating cancer through increasingly radical stages. (I am indebted to the work of Charles Dyer and Mark Tobey for the following five-part outline.)[11]

Stage 1: The Mujahideen

Arab Muslims brought Islam to Afghanistan in the mid-600s, and it has been a Muslim nation ever since. Political turmoil in the 1970s led to a coup that deposed the reigning king, Mohammed Zahir Shah, and put the nation under the communist-leaning Mohammed Daoud Khan. When the people of Afghanistan rose up against Khan, he appealed to Moscow for help. And in 1979, Russian forces invaded Afghanistan to put down the conservative Islamic tribal factions.

The conservative Muslims who waged guerilla warfare (jihad) against the godless infidels from Russia were known as *mujahideen*, which means "holy warriors." Islamic mujahideen from all over the Middle East streamed into Afghanistan to aid in the fight, including the son of a Saudi billionaire: Osama bin Laden. By 1989, the Russians withdrew, leaving Afghanistan in chaos.

Stage 2: The Taliban

The withdrawal of the Russians left a leadership vacuum in Afghanistan. Mullah Mohammed Omar was a mujahideen commander and war hero in the civil war that ousted the Russians. A religious zealot, Omar started a movement with fifty followers that became known as the Taliban ("the students"). The Taliban movement grew rapidly, increasing Omar's influence to the point that in the late 1990s, he gained control of the government. His goal was to make Afghanistan a perfect Islamic state operating under sharia law. Bin Laden pledged his loyalty to Omar and the Taliban.

Stage 3: Al-Qaeda

Two years after the Russians left Afghanistan, a US-led coalition invaded Kuwait to drive out Saddam Hussein's Iraqi army (the First Gulf War). Muslims such as bin Laden viewed the US action as yet another invasion of Islamic lands. Bin Laden founded al-Qaeda ("the base") to focus on driving Westerners out of the Middle East by attacking Western targets. The most high-profile of these attacks occurred on September 11, 2001, bringing down the twin towers of the World Trade Center in New York City. Al-Qaeda became the world's most high-profile terrorist organization and its leader, bin Laden, the world's most wanted man.

Stage 4: Al-Qaeda in Iraq

When the United States invaded Afghanistan in search of bin Laden and his lieutenants, al-Qaeda decentralized. Its leaders went into hiding, and franchise operations were set up in many different nations—most notably Iraq, following the ouster of Saddam Hussein in 2003 by American and coalition forces.

Al-Qaeda in Iraq, under Abu Musab al-Zarqawi, was the most ruthless of all the franchises. It attacked American forces and other Muslims equally. Its members popularized suicide bombings, utilized improvised explosive devices (IEDs), and introduced beheadings to instill fear in its enemies.

Americans killed al-Zarqawi in 2006 and bin Laden in 2011. With both men out of the picture, President Obama announced on November 1, 2012, that al-Qaeda had been destroyed and the war in Iraq was over—and almost over in Afghanistan. But his victory claim was premature.

Stage 5: ISIS

Within the Islamic religion is a schism between two sects, the Shiites and the Sunnites, which plays into what happened next. Both groups claim their origin to the prophet Muhammad, both rely on the Qur'an, and the rituals of both are similar.

When America pulled out of Iraq, Shiite Muslims returned to power, which reanimated Sunnite insurgents (al-Qaeda) against them. A new al-Qaeda leader, Abu Bakr al-Baghdadi, took advantage of a leadership vacuum in the organization and quickly rose to the top. This man was more ruthless than any of his predecessors. Al-Qaeda in Iraq became known as ISI—the Islamic State in Iraq. When the Arab Spring revolts reached Syria, a civil war broke out, and al-Baghdadi saw it as an opportunity to gain more power. He moved his Sunnite forces into Syria to fight against President Bashar al-Assad's Shiite government forces, and he brought his ruthless tactics with him: beheadings, rapes, selling women into sex slavery and unwanted marriages, throwing homosexuals off buildings, and mutilating lawbreakers. People fled before the onslaught of barbarism, and al-Baghdadi's forces took over the vacated territory, bringing vast swaths of land under their control.

Al-Baghdadi broke away from al-Qaeda in 2013 to announce the formation of ISIS—a new Islamic state (caliphate) with himself as the leader (caliph). Being a Sunnite Muslim put al-Baghdadi on a collision course with the 10 to 15 percent of Muslims who are Shiites and with more moderate Sunnites who do not condone his extremism. But as of this writing, no one in the Islamic world is challenging his leadership role. And so his radical agenda, implemented by tens of thousands of militant followers, pushes forward.

THE DESCRIPTION OF ISIS

A brief profile of the Islamic State will help us to clarify their beliefs and learn what sets them apart from the majority of the world's Muslims.

ISIS Teachings

Within the framework of Islam, the mission of ISIS is to take Muslims "back to the Qur'an" to restore the purity of the religious teachings that Muhammad supposedly received from Allah and recorded for the faithful.

Second only to the Qur'an as a primary source of instruction for Muslims is Hadith, the record of Muhammad's teachings and activities during his tenure as caliph of Islam. Hadith is a collection based on oral traditions gathered over the two centuries following Muhammad's death, and it serves to illuminate the doctrines laid down in the Qur'an. There are several versions of Hadith, none of which is officially sanctioned. The result is that each of the many groups of Muslims adopts its own preferred version.[12]

All Muslims embrace the Qur'an and Hadith, but in varying ways. Many modern Muslims de-emphasize the teachings prescribing jihad against infidels, hatred of Jews and Christians, subjugation of women, and overly strict lifestyle regulations. But not ISIS. It embraces every detail of what Muhammad wrote, said, and did concerning the conquest of lands and people for Allah's sake.

ISIS Traditions

On September 10, 2014, President Obama said, "ISIL is not 'Islamic'. No religion condones the killing of innocents, and the vast majority of ISIL's victims have been Muslims. . . . ISIL is a terrorist organization, pure and simple."[13]

The president received significant pushback on his claim that "ISIL is not Islamic," especially since ISIS calls itself the "Islamic State." Regardless of whether President Obama or anyone else agrees, ISIS thinks it is Islamic.

In his article "What ISIS Really Wants," contributing editor at *The Atlantic* Graeme Wood addressed the issue of whether ISIS is Islamic:

> The reality is that the Islamic State is Islamic. *Very* Islamic. Yes, it has attracted psychopaths and adventure seekers, drawn largely from the disaffected populations of the Middle East and Europe. But the religion preached by its most ardent followers derives from coherent and even learned interpretations of Islam. Virtually every major decision and law promulgated by the Islamic State adheres to what it calls, in its press and pronouncements, and on its billboards, license plates, stationery, and coins, "the Prophetic methodology," which means following the prophecy and example of Muhammad, in punctilious detail.[14]

Although the vast majority of modern Muslims do not support ISIS, Wood is telling us that it is actually the most strictly religious of any Islamic entity. ISIS has gone back in time to the seventh-century foundations of the religion, which it is determined to follow in its exact form. In following Muhammad's example to the letter, ISIS is, in essence, the purest form of the original expression of Islam. ISIS makes it clear that its mission is religious—Islamic—as it understands Muhammad's original intent to carry out jihad against infidels.

If there is a tradition of Islam as a "religion of peace," it is not found in the teaching of the Qur'an or the actions of Muhammad. In his book *Understanding Jihad*, David Cook noted that in the last nine years of Muhammad's life, he participated in eighty-six battles—more than nine per year, on average.[15] And the claim that *Islam* means peace is likewise unfounded. The word means "surrender," which was demanded of the enemies of Islam and enforced by military might.[16] The peace that can be attributed to Islam is that which occurs after its enemies lay down their arms in the face of violent jihad.

Former Muslim Nabeel Qureshi, who is now a Christian scholar, has summarized Islam's history of warfare:

> Within two centuries of the advent of Islam, Muslim conquests expanded Islamic territory from the shores of the Atlantic well into the valleys of India. At the end of that era, the most influential hadith collectors gathered whole books documenting Muhammad's conduct and commands during times of warfare. Shortly after them, the great Islamic jurists systematically codified *sharia*, Islamic law, devoting whole branches of jurisprudence to the proper practice of warfare.
>
> For these reasons, no one can claim that "Islam is a religion of peace" in the sense that the religion has been historically devoid of violence, neither in its origins nor in the history of the global Muslim community. Apart from the first thirteen years of Islamic history, when there were not enough Muslims to fight, Islam has always had an elaborate practice or doctrine of war.[17]

ISIS has merely renewed this historical Islamic tradition of warfare, which it is now directing toward Jews, Christians, moderate Muslims, and the irreligious. When facing ISIS, the options are either to convert, pay an impossibly burdensome annual tax, leave your country, or die.

ISIS Training

ISIS does not have a navy or an air force, but it does have an army of tens of thousands of soldiers. In an open war against any developed nation's military, they would not last long. But against armed civilians in sandals, and unarmed villagers fleeing with their children and household goods in hand, they are formidable.

The military training of the ISIS army is superb, but the indoctrination that precedes it is what makes ISIS such a threat to the civilized world today.

THE TRAINING OF ADULTS. No Islamic community is without its mosques and community centers. But where ISIS is running things—as in its headquarters city, Raqqa, Syria—those institutions become hotbeds of indoctrination, radicalization, and recruitment. ISIS teaches its brand of radical Sunnite theology to adults and children alike. Outside these centers, ISIS "enforcers" walk the streets brandishing automatic weapons to impose strict adherence to sharia law. Everything from diet to dress to business dealings to music is subject to inspection and correction. Life under ISIS is a closed, controlled system where every aspect is part of the training.

THE TRAINING OF MALE CHILDREN. ISIS education of children centers on its close adherence to the original teachings of the Qur'an. Preteen boys are recruited into "Caliphate Clubs" to begin training for the ISIS army of the future. ISIS actually pays the parents of boys who enlist between $250 and $350 per child per month. They entice the boys with videos of ISIS exploits and video games in which ISIS always wins.

The boys are sent first to "Sharia Camps" to be indoctrinated in sharia and ISIS ideology, after which they swear loyalty to al-Baghdadi as caliph. Once they are ready, the boys move into military barracks to begin physical and military training. In addition to infusing skill in the art of warfare, training includes cutting off the heads of dolls and, more appalling, carrying around the actual decapitated heads of ISIS victims, all in an attempt to desensitize the trainees against what they will be called upon to do as ISIS soldiers.

Boys who excel in physical and military skills are sent into combat or assigned suicide missions. The others are sent back into the community as spies and informants against their own people. They become operatives in a version of a police state similar to Hussein's Iraq or al-Assad's Syria, reporting anyone who speaks or acts against ISIS or violates sharia law. Parents live in fear of their own sons, whose loyalty to ISIS supersedes family ties.

Child soldiering is a violation of international law, but this does not deter ISIS. The Syrian Observatory for Human Rights reported that between January and August 2015, ISIS recruited 1,100 Syrian children below age sixteen. ISIS plays by its own rules.[18]

ISIS Tactics

The basic tactics employed to achieve the goals of ISIS are those originated by Muhammad and his successors in the first two centuries of Islam: conquer, plunder, suppress (by conversion, taxation, death, or emigration), and rule. ISIS is clear about its goal, which is a worldwide Islamic caliphate based on sharia law. Not content merely to attack camel caravans of traders, ISIS has plundered oil reserves in northern Iraq and Syria, seized Iraqi military equipment (supplied by the United States), and stolen money from Iraqi and Syrian banks.

Today ISIS employs modern tactics unavailable to the original Muslims. It has fired up a highly effective publicity engine via the Internet. ISIS produces videos that spread its message through all contemporary social media platforms. Its online magazine, *Dabiq*, is as slick as anything published in New York. These tools are used primarily for recruitment purposes—and they are working.

These tools have a secondary effect, which aids ISIS even when they do not result in overt recruitment, as the United States has learned in tragic ways. On December 2, 2015, an ISIS-inspired married couple entered a building in San Bernardino, California, and shot to death fourteen people.[19] Six months later, in the early morning of

June 12, 2016, Omar Mateen walked into a gay nightclub in Orlando, Florida, and opened fire with an assault rifle and pistol. Before he finished his rampage, forty-nine lay dead and another fifty-three were wounded—the worst terrorist attack on America since the destruction of New York's World Trade Center towers in 2001. While Mateen was not a member of ISIS, he pledged allegiance to the terrorist organization and supported its goals.[20]

A word of warning to the West: Because the primary tool of ISIS is violence and these ISIS-inspired attacks have been random and sporadic, it is easy for those outside of the Middle East not to take the threat of a worldwide Islamic caliphate seriously. The combined military forces of Europe and America could easily defeat ISIS in battle. Many Western governments seem to be biding their time until their collective wills coalesce around the goal of crushing ISIS. At that point they will stage a war against ISIS on its home turf in Iraq and Syria. Then, they believe, the threat of a worldwide Islamic caliphate will be over.

Nothing could be further from the truth. ISIS is not the only branch of Islam pursuing world domination. The others are working primarily through nonviolent methods, though they will resort to jihad if needed.

For example, the century-old Muslim Brotherhood is a "Sunni, pan-Islamic organization based in Cairo, Egypt whose ultimate aim is the re-establishment of the global Islamic caliphate."[21] According to Elliot Friedland, Clarion Project research fellow, "they have branches in approximately 80 countries worldwide and have been the leading source of inspiration behind other Islamist organizations including Al Qaeda and the Islamic State."[22]

In recent years Muslim Brotherhood documents have come to light detailing a six-phase plan of gradualism designed to overturn Western cultures—slowly infiltrating, persuading, proselytizing, and transforming societies into Islamic, sharia-based cultures without a shot being fired.[23]

In 2007, the Brotherhood's spiritual leader, Sheikh Yusuf al-Qaradawi, publicly explained Islamic gradualism when he said, "The conquest of Rome, the conquest of Italy and Europe means that Islam will return to Europe once again. Must this conquest necessarily be through war? No, it is not necessary. There is such a thing as a peaceful conquest. The peaceful conquest has foundations in this religion. So I imagine that Islam will conquer Europe without using violence. It will do so through predication and ideology."[24] In a 2012 interview he revealed something of his concept of gradualism when he said there should be "no chopping off hands for the first five years."[25]

General Georges Sada graduated from Iraq's Air Academy in 1959 and was trained as a fighter pilot and military leader in England, America, and Russia. He was the top fighter pilot in Iraq's air force and became Saddam Hussein's air vice-marshal. He would have risen even higher in Hussein's cabinet except for the fact that he was not an Arab Muslim, but a Persian Christian. He was the only cabinet minister who was not a member of the Ba'ath Party. Sada rose as high as he did only because he was the only military leader Hussein trusted to tell him the truth instead of rubber-stamping, out of fear, whatever the dictator wanted to do.

Three years after the capture of Hussein in 2003, General Sada wrote his memoirs detailing his life as a Christian working in Hussein's militant Sunnite Islamic government. His book included a sobering warning to the West concerning the usually non-violent gradualism we see occurring in several nations today:

In some cases this means moving thousands of Muslim families into a foreign land—by building mosques and changing the culture from the inside out, and by refusing to assimilate or adopt the beliefs or values of that nation—to conquer the land for Islam.

A military invasion will not succeed [in many places], but in countries such as England today, we can witness a modern nation in the process of being conquered by the militant form of Fatah, in a slow, systematic, and unrelenting overpowering of British culture.

The way of life in Great Britain has been transformed by followers of Islam. This is also true in countries such as France, Germany, and the Netherlands, as well as the Scandinavian countries.

What we're seeing in many places is a "demographic revolution." Some experts have projected that by the year 2040, fully 80 percent of the population of France will be Muslim. At that point, the Muslim majority will control commerce, industry, education, and religion in that country. They will also, of course, control the government, as well, and occupy all of the key positions in the French Parliament. And a Muslim will be president.[26]

These are challenging thoughts. It is easier to respond to an ISIS army determined to conquer through overt violence than to the frog-in-the-kettle incrementalism of gradual conquest.

ISIS Treachery

We need not dwell long on the treachery of ISIS; it is well documented in the media. As I write these words, Syrian forces have just retaken the city of Palmyra, which ISIS had held for ten months. Shortly afterward, the Syrians uncovered a mass grave containing forty-two civilians and soldiers, including three children. ISIS had shot some of the victims and beheaded the rest.[27] Many more discoveries such as this one are inevitable as territory currently held by ISIS is recovered.

Point-blank murder, public beheading, torture, amputations, rape, forcing women into marriage and sex slavery, throwing lawbreakers off buildings to their death, using children as soldiers and suicide bombers—there is no limit to ISIS barbarity. And they justify it all in the name of religion—their strict adherence to the Qur'an and Hadith.

ISIS is known for treachery, butchery, and barbarity—all tactics designed to instill fear that leads either to conversion to Islam, payment of exorbitant taxes, exile, or death.

We know that ISIS perpetuates such violence in order to achieve its goal, which is the imposition of Islam on the entire world. But we have to ask, why is this so important to its members? It is all based on their eschatology—their view of the future and the end of the age. Let's look at what this means.

THE DESIRES OF ISIS

Jesus taught His disciples to pray for two eschatological outcomes: "Your kingdom come. Your will be done on earth as it is in heaven" (Matthew 6:10). Those two outcomes will converge in the second coming of Jesus Christ and the establishment of His millennial kingdom of righteousness on earth. Surprisingly, the eschatology of Islam follows a similar pattern: the return of their Mahdi ("messiah") and his rule over a worldwide caliphate (kingdom) based on sharia law. Christian theology seems to provide a paradigm for Islamic eschatology.

Given these similarities, we sometimes hear uninformed people say, "See, both Christians and Muslims want the same thing. King and kingdom—what's the difference?" Believe me, the difference is enormous. Aside from the obvious facts that Muslims do *not* worship Jesus Christ as Lord, do *not* look to Him as mankind's only Savior, and do *not* expect Him to be their returning messiah, Islam's ultimate goal differs radically from that of Christianity. Its goal is the establishment of a theocratic caliphate (a kingdom ruled by Allah) mediated by the twelfth ruler (imam or Mahdi) since Muhammad. ISIS believes the continued escalation of war and violence will lead to a final apocalypse, the appearing of the Mahdi, and the establishment of the worldwide caliphate.

Revival of the Caliphate

In preparation for this final apocalypse, ISIS wants to retake all the lands that belonged to the last great Islamic caliphate, the Ottoman Empire. That empire was divided up after World War I by Britain and France, creating the present Middle Eastern countries (except for Israel, which was partitioned in 1948). ISIS intends to recapture that land and make it the seat of the future worldwide caliphate.

The current self-appointed caliph of ISIS is al-Baghdadi, who believes four more caliphs will follow him before the twelfth caliph, the Mahdi, returns and rules the worldwide caliphate. Both now and in the future, the Islamic caliphate will be governed by sharia law. This is not a written law like the Ten Commandments. It includes the collective teachings of the Qur'an, Hadith, and accepted authorities through the centuries, applied on a contextual and case-by-case basis by sharia courts.

Today's Iran is the clearest example of an Islamic theocracy. It has an elected government, but the real power is held by religious clerics of the Guardian Council and the supreme leader, who can overrule the elected officials at will. A passage from Iran's constitution summarizes how an Islamic theocracy works:

All civil, penal, financial, economic, administrative, cultural, military, political, and other laws and regulations must be based on Islamic criteria. This principle applies absolutely and generally to all articles of the Constitution as well as to all other laws and regulations, and the [wise persons] of the Guardian Council are judges in this matter.[28]

The headquarters of ISIS is in Raqqa, Syria. The way that city is run gives us an indication of what a worldwide caliphate, as envisioned by ISIS, would look like. There are schools and Islamic centers where Islamic doctrine is drilled into children and adults. Welfare and health systems are subject to strict social regulation enforced by Islamic judges and courts. Robed "religious police" roam the streets, automatic weapons slung over their shoulders, pointing out citizens whose dress, religious life, commercial practices, recreational activities, or social conduct falls short of sharia standards.

In a worldwide ISIS-style caliphate, Christians, Jews, and nonbelievers would be allowed to live, but they would be subject to heavy taxation and forced to submit to sharia law. All houses of worship belonging to non-Islamic religions would be destroyed, as they are today in Raqqa. If ISIS has its way, this is a preview of the coming worldwide caliphate.

Return of the Messiah

Both Sunnite and Shiite Muslims look for the return of the Islamic messiah, or Muhammad al-Mahdi. Both sects agree that he is the twelfth successor to Muhammad, but they differ on who he is and how he will return.

Sunnites believe the Mahdi will arrive at some point in the future, for the line of twelve caliphs has not yet been completed. Shiite Muslims believe the twelfth caliph has already arrived. He was born in AD 869 and has been in hiding (occultation) since 874, awaiting the proper time to be revealed.[29]

The Islamic eschatological calendar is not precise, but all Muslims agree that the following major events will occur:

- A final apocalyptic conflagration between the armies of Islam and the armies of the infidels at Dabiq, Syria, where the infidels will be defeated.
- The rise of a false messiah figure in the end times who must be defeated.
- The return of Jesus (or Isa, an Islamic prophet who never died but was taken to heaven), to defeat the false messiah, accompanied by the return or appearance of the twelfth Imam, the Mahdi.
- The final judgment of all who are found wanting, according to Islamic standards.
- The establishment of the worldwide caliphate.

Because the final apocalyptic battle between Islam and the world causes the Mahdi to appear, all militant Muslims view violence and struggle as a way to hasten that day. ISIS soldiers are motivated to fight by dangling before them a win-win option: If they die in battle, they gain paradise. If they live to see the apocalypse, they get to welcome the Mahdi.

THE DEFEAT OF ISIS

Islamic expansion poses a dilemma for Christians around the world. Whether we face the overt violence of ISIS as Christians must in the Middle East or the non-violent gradualism that is eating away at the West—how are we to respond?

We cannot help but wonder whether our Islamic neighbors or

coworkers support ISIS. Or do they support the non-violent expansion of Islam, the imposition of sharia law, and the repression of all non-Islamic religions? Or are they Muslims who want to coexist peacefully in a live-and-let-live pluralistic society?

The point of those questions is not to accuse but to bring us face to face with reality. Islam is the second-largest, but fastest-growing, religion in the world. Christians everywhere must realize that their response to this worldwide religious phenomenon can have life-or-death implications. The madness of radical Islam is now part of our lives because the always-on news cycle has shrunk the world to the size of our smartphone screens. We cannot escape the fact that radical Islam poses an existential threat to all of us, but especially to our Christian brothers and sisters in many parts of the world who endure severe persecution at the hands of ISIS and its sister organizations.

So what do we do?

Remember

The principle of Hebrews 13:3 applies here: "Remember the prisoners as if chained with them—those who are mistreated—since you yourselves are in the body also." Christians around the world are one body in Christ. We must pray for the persecuted church that is suffering under ISIS. We must stand with them in unity (Ephesians 4:4–6) and empathy: "Rejoice with those who rejoice, and weep with those who weep" (Romans 12:15).

Reach Out

Because love is the greatest of all virtues (1 Corinthians 13:13), we have an automatic responsibility to love not only our persecuted brothers and sisters, but also those who persecute them (Matthew 5:44). We must demonstrate the love of Christ in order to reveal the person of Christ. Loving our Islamic friends and neighbors will show them that we belong to Jesus (John 13:35). Muslims honor Jesus as a great prophet; we have the opportunity to manifest Him as a great Savior, Lord, and Friend.

Realize

Scripture tells us in several places that the Christian's primary battle is not against national armies, but against invisible spiritual powers under the influence of the devil (2 Corinthians 10:3–4; Ephesians 6:12; 1 John 5:19). Sometimes, however, spiritual battles spill over the ramparts of heaven and ravage the earth. God has ordained human governments on earth to protect the good from the onslaught of evil (Romans 13:1–4). Sometimes those governments must call citizens to war in defense of an orderly society. This has created a dilemma in the minds of many well-intentioned, peace-loving Christians who believe military service to be antithetical to Christian principles. But mainstream Christian tradition has long relied on the precepts of Saint Augustine and Thomas Aquinas, both of whom supported the idea of "just wars" for Christians.[30]

War may be terrible, but it is sometimes better than allowing evil to run rampant. Years ago during the Vietnam War, a GI helicopter pilot was killed, and on his tombstone in New Hampshire, his parents had these nineteenth century words of John Stuart Mill inscribed:

> War is an ugly thing, but not the ugliest of things. The decayed and degraded state of moral and patriotic feeling, which thinks nothing is worth a war, is worse. A man who has nothing which he cares more about than his own personal safety is a miserable creature, and has no chance of being free unless he is made free and kept so by the exertions of better men than himself.[31]

After fighting first on our knees, we may also be called to fight on our feet. Reality in a fallen world can be challenging and conflicting, but those who remain Christ-centered will find their way toward right conclusions.

Radicalize

Let's not let Islamic terrorists own the word *radical*. As Dr. David Platt reminded the church in his book *Radical: Taking Back Your Faith from the American Dream*, authentically following Jesus into the kingdom of God is a radical act:

> You and I can choose to continue with business as usual in the Christian life and in the church as a whole, enjoying success based on the standards defined by the culture around us. Or we can take an honest look at the Jesus of the Bible and dare to ask what the consequences might be if we really believed him and really obeyed him. . . . We may discover that satisfaction in our lives and success in the church are not found in what our culture deems most important but in radical abandonment to Jesus.[32]

If you are amazed at the willingness of ISIS fighters to die for what they believe in, ask yourself this: Who first called for that kind of commitment? The answer is found in Luke 14:27: "Whoever does not bear his cross and come after Me cannot be My disciple." Jesus, not Muhammad, is history's most radical figure. He calls us to give everything because He gave everything. He despises lukewarmness (Revelation 3:16). As His followers, we must display to the world and our Muslim friends what may seem radical to them: love, sacrifice, courage, and commitment to spreading the good news of the gospel in the world (Matthew 28:19–20).

Rely

We need not fear that ISIS will destroy the church; it is invincible. As Jesus told Peter, "the gates of Hades shall not prevail against it" (16:18). ISIS can drive Christians away, even behead them and destroy their churches; but they will never prevail over the church of Jesus Christ. We must rely on that truth.

In the opening story of this chapter, I told you that ISIS had beheaded twenty Christians on that Libyan beach. But the actual number beheaded was twenty-one. I withheld the name of the last one so I could end this chapter with his inspiring story. When ISIS published the video of the mass beheading, there was one face among the Egyptians who no one could identify. It was later learned that he was an African from Chad, Mathew Ayairga, who had migrated to Libya to find work. He was not a Christian at all. For reasons that are not clear, he had been swept up with the twenty Egyptian Coptic Christians and marched to the beach to die.

Ayairga knelt in his orange suit at the end of the line as the ISIS executioners asked each of the Christians to reject Christ and then beheaded them when they refused. Finally, the butchers reached Ayairga. Although he was not a Christian, they demanded that he reject the Christian's God. "Do you reject Christ?" they asked.

Having observed the faith and courage of the Egyptian Christians throughout the ordeal, Ayairga was deeply moved by the unbending power of their belief. At that moment he knew he wanted what they had more than life itself. He calmly confessed to his captors, "Their God is my God."

Moments later, like the repentant thief on the cross who confessed his faith in Christ (Luke 23:39–43), I believe Ayairga entered paradise along with his fellow martyrs. In attempting to shrink the size of the church triumphant, ISIS actually caused it to grow by one. Heaven will one day reveal how many others, like Ayairga, will have entered paradise after witnessing the faith and martyrdom of those twenty Egyptian Christians.

We do not know what the future holds in the Middle East or in the West. But we do know who holds the future. While we wait for the day when swords will be beat into plowshares and spears into pruning hooks (Isaiah 2:4), let us faithfully represent Christ to all who do not yet know Him—even to those who are the enemies of His church.

CHAPTER 8

THE RESURRECTION OF RUSSIA

Russian president Vladimir Putin, dressed in ordinary casual clothes, stepped from the dock onto the swaying deck of a miniature submarine. He squeezed inside the capsule, the glass-viewing bubble closed on him, and the craft descended into the depths of the Black Sea. The purpose of Putin's excursion, as people were told, was to view the wreckage of an ancient ship on the sea floor. But as underwater cameras followed the descent some ninety feet down, it became clear that archeology was the last thing on Putin's mind. The craft leveled out and moved toward the Crimean coastal city of Sevastopol. It surfaced near a waiting yacht, which sped the Russian president to the seaport and deposited him on Crimean soil.

The date was mid-August 2015, less than eighteen months after Russia seized the Crimean Peninsula from its parent nation Ukraine—a takeover approved by Crimean voters weeks later. At the time of the takeover, Ukraine had been making overtures to the West with the possibility of joining the European Union. To prevent such a move—which would impede Putin's ambitions for a reunited Soviet bloc—he had not only annexed Crimea but also infiltrated eastern Ukraine with Russian soldiers in unmarked uniforms. His purpose was to stir that nation, already reeling from political turmoil, into utter chaos. Confrontations between Russians and Ukrainian nationalists had already cost some six thousand lives. It was inevitable that the Ukrainian government would be incensed by Putin's drop-in Crimean visit, condemning it as an arrogant show of power intended to increase the already exploding tensions between the two countries.

In fact, that seemed to be the primary purpose of Putin's visit. It was his way of saying, "Crimea is Russian territory. I don't need an invitation. I don't need to go through formalities. I don't need to inform anyone of my arrival. I can come here any time I want in any way I want."

Moments after Putin landed at Sevastopol, a BBC reporter questioned the legitimacy of the takeover, citing the fact that the Ukrainian administration saw it as an illegitimate power grab. Putin replied, "The future of Crimea was determined by the people who live on this land. They voted to be united with Russia. That's it."[1] The president's face and voice were every bit as stern and unyielding as his words. It was clear that he had no intention of considering the possibility that Crimea might be returned to Ukraine.

Given Putin's history, this aggressive takeover and hard-nosed attitude is not surprising. He began his career as a Russian KGB officer in 1975 when Russia, the ruling nation of the USSR (Union of Soviet Socialist Republics), was a major world power second only to the United States. Russia was feared around the globe for its massive nuclear armaments and threats of communist takeover. Putin retired from the KGB in 1991, and immediately entered politics, rising to power under Boris Yeltsin's administration. When Yeltsin resigned in December 1999 for political and health reasons, Putin became acting president. He was officially elected in March 2000 and subsequently held the offices of president (2000–2008) and prime minister (1999, 2008–2012), before being elected president again in 2012.

At the midpoint of Putin's rise to power, President Ronald Reagan's policies brought down the Soviet-Russian threat without firing a shot. The fall of communism and the disintegration of the USSR must have been a bitter blow to the ambitious, young politician. Many believe that from that moment on, Putin was driven by his determination to restore Russia to its former glory. "Putin has always had one overriding foreign policy goal: the creation of a 'Eurasian Union' to act as a counter-weight to the European Union."[2] The takeover of Crimea was merely the first step in that direction. But other steps were soon to follow.

In mid-August 2015, Putin made a deal with Iran to deliver a sophisticated air defense missile system to that belligerent and hostile nation. These new armaments will make it much more difficult should either the United States or Israel decide to mount air strikes against Iran's nuclear manufacturing facilities. According to an article in *USA Today*, "Russia and Iran are increasingly cooperating in multiple arenas, notably their joint efforts to preserve the regime of Syria's President Bashar Assad in his civil war by providing military support and diplomatic pressure on his behalf."[3]

Putin's support of the Assad regime came shortly after his Iran deal. In the fall of 2015, he sent ground forces and planes to Syria under the pretext of aiding the war against ISIS, the so-called Islamic State. But it soon became clear that Russia's interest in Syria was not ISIS when they began attacking Syrian rebel forces who were attempting to oust the despotic Assad from power.

While Russia's Syrian intervention has secured Assad's loyalty, it has also dealt misery to the people of Syria, where over 470,000 have been killed at this writing and half the population has been forced to flee their homes, creating a major refugee crisis. It has also increased unbalance and chaos in Middle East diplomacy.

THE RUSSIAN AWAKENING

Two-thirds of the US population is old enough to remember the Cold War between Russia and the United States that lasted from 1947 to 1991. Soviet saber-rattling kept nations in fear of Russian encroachment. The possibility of nuclear war loomed over the world like a dark cloud. But that fear was moderated by US military might, strong western alliances, and leaders with the will to move boldly. But now, in the absence of American will and the collapse of order in the Middle East, what will keep the world's old nemesis, Russia, from rising again?

It appears that Putin realizes this is his moment of opportunity and is taking advantage of it. As one journalist writes, "Since resuming the presidency in 2012, Mr. Putin has worked to restore some of the great-power status Russia lost with the disintegration of the Soviet Union, not least by cultivating relations with countries hostile to the United States, like Venezuela and, to some extent, China."[4] Another journalist claims, "Russia's strongman has restored his country's status as a major international player."[5]

Putin obviously wants to be recognized as a world leader of a world power. Where will his ambitions lead? Will the old Russian Bear come out of its quarter-century hibernation and again sound a roar that shakes the world? As much as we would like to think Putin's manipulations and power grabs merely reflect the antics of an overreaching dreamer, we have good reason to believe the Russian threat is real. In fact, we have evidence that, at some point, Russia will ignite a pivotal world war like none ever seen or imagined. According to the prophet Ezekiel, this is a sure thing. Russia's aggressive moves today cast a long shadow into a future explicitly described in Ezekiel's prophecy.

THE RUSSIAN AGGRESSION

Approximately twenty-five hundred years ago, Ezekiel predicted Russia's return to power in the latter days. In chapters 38 and 39 of his prophecy, he described the invasion of the land of Israel by Russia and a coalition of mostly Islamic nations. In these two chapters, God gave to Ezekiel the most detailed prophecy concerning war in the entire Bible.

The prophecy begins with a list of ten proper names, one of a man (Gog) and the rest of nations that are in alliance and preparing for an enormous war (38:1–6):

1. Gog (v. 2)
2. Magog (v. 2)
3. Rosh (v. 2)
4. Meshech (v. 2)
5. Tubal (v. 2)
6. Persia (v. 5)
7. Ethiopia (v. 5)
8. Libya (v. 5)
9. Gomer (v. 6)
10. Togarmah (v. 6)

THE RUSSIAN ASSUMPTION

You will not find the name *Russia* in these two prophetic chapters or anywhere else in the Bible. But the nation we know as Russia figures very prominently in these scriptures. In Ezekiel's list of ten proper names, the third name, Rosh, is the most important, for it identifies the nation ruled by the leader of the coalition that will attack Israel.

We have at least two strong reasons for believing that Rosh and Russia are one and the same.

The Language Argument

The term *Rosh* is found three times in Ezekiel's prophecy: 38:2, 38:3, and 39:1. It is not hard to see the phonetic similarity between the words *Rosh* and *Russia*. Dr. John F. Walvoord tells us that "in the study of how ancient words came into modern language, it is quite common for the consonants to remain the same and the vowels to be changed. In the word 'Rosh,' if the vowel 'o' is changed to 'u' it becomes the root of the modern word, Russia."[6]

Wilhelm Gesenius, the famous nineteenth-century lexicographer, increases the certainty of that assumption when he assures us that *Rosh* in Ezekiel 38 and 39 is "undoubtedly the Russians, who are mentioned by the Byzantine writers of the tenth century, under the name *Ros*."[7]

The Location Argument

It is significant that the Bible refers to the location of Israel as "the middle" of the earth: "Thus says the Lord GOD: 'This is Jerusalem; I have set her in the midst of the nations and the countries all around her'" (5:5). The Hebrew word translated *midst* in this verse is more literally translated "navel."[8] Jewish rabbis saw Jerusalem as the center of the world's compass:

> As the navel is set in the centre of the human body, so is the land of
> Israel the navel of the world . . . situated in the centre of the world,
> and Jerusalem in the centre of the land of Israel, and the sanctuary in
> the centre of Jerusalem, and the holy place in the centre of the sanc-
> tuary, and the ark in the centre of the holy place, and the foundation
> stone before the holy place, because from it the world was founded.[9]

The prophets assumed Israel to be the hub of the world. This means that whenever we find compass points or geographical directions in prophecy, they are given in relation to the position of Israel. North means north of Israel; south means south of Israel, and so on.

The prophet Daniel used the phrase "king of the North" to describe the ruler featured in Ezekiel's prophecy who would lead an attack against Israel in the latter days (Daniel 11:5–35). Ezekiel's prophecy meshes perfectly with Daniel's in saying the invading armies will come to Israel "from the *far* north" (Ezekiel 38:6, 15). In the translation of the Hebrew found in the American Standard Version, the phrase is rendered "the uttermost part of the north," that is, "the extreme north."

Dr. Walvoord clarified the importance of this geographical specification:

> If one takes any map of the world and draws a line north of the land of Israel he will inevitably come to the nation of Russia. As soon as the line is drawn to the far north beyond Asia Minor and the Black Sea it is in Russia and continues to be in Russia for many hundreds of miles all the way to the Arctic Circle. . . . On the basis of geography alone, it seems quite clear that the only nation which could possibly be referred to as coming from the far north would be the nation Russia.[10]

Only one country occupies a geographical position in "the uttermost part of the north" in relation to Israel. That nation is Russia, whose landmass stretches all the way from the Baltic to the Bering Seas.

THE RUSSIAN ALLIANCE

Now that we have identified Ezekiel's Rosh as today's Russia, we will turn to the other nine names listed in the opening of his prophecy—names that identify the leader and the nations forming the alliance that will attack Israel.

The Commander of the Alliance

The first two verses of Ezekiel 38 read, "Now the word of the LORD came to me, saying, 'Son of man, set your face against Gog, of the land of Magog, the prince of Rosh, Meshech, and Tubal.'" The word *Gog* is found twelve times in Ezekiel 38 and 39, and it means "high," "supreme," "a height," or "a high mountain."[11] Unlike the other names in this prophecy, Gog refers not to a nation but to a person. Several times in these chapters, God speaks to Gog as one speaks to an individual.

Some scholars believe that Gog is not a personal name but a title, much like "President" or "Caesar" or "Pharaoh." Gog is from the land of Magog and has somehow become the prince of three other lands: Rosh, Meshech, and Tubal (v. 3). He has amassed the power to become the leader of the armies that will invade Israel. God commands Gog to be a guard for these nations: "Prepare yourself and be ready, you and all your companies that are gathered about you; and be a guard for them" (v. 7).

Matthew Henry explained the use of the term *guard* in this verse: "As commander-in-chief, let him engage to take care of them and their safety; let him pass his word for their security, and take them under his particular protection."[12] In other words, God enjoins Gog to be an effective commander of this massive alliance.

The Countries in the Alliance

Magog

Ezekiel told us that Gog, the commander of the alliance, will come from the land of Magog. According to Genesis 10:2, Magog was the second son of Japheth and the grandson of Noah. His name is also mentioned in 1 Chronicles 1:5; Ezekiel 38:2; Ezekiel 39:6; and Revelation 20:8.

Most scholars identify the ancient land that Magog founded as the former domain of the Scythians, who lived in the mountains around the Black and Caspian seas. In *The Jeremiah Study Bible*, I identify this area as the homeland of the "-stan" countries, all of them states of the former Soviet Empire: Kazakhstan, Kyrgyzstan, Uzbekistan, Turkmenistan, Tajikistan, and perhaps Afghanistan.[13] According to Mark Hitchcock, "All of these nations have one thing in common: *Islam*. And within their borders they have a population of 60 million."[14]

Meshech and Tubal

Meshech and Tubal were the fifth and sixth sons of Japheth and, therefore, grandsons of Noah (Genesis 10:2). The descendants of these two men established cities or territories bearing their names. C. I. Scofield identifies Meshech as "Moscow" and Tubal as "Tobolsk."[15] But many other scholars and experts identify them as territories in modern Turkey.

Persia

The words *Persia, Persian,* or *Persians* occur thirty-six times in the Old Testament. According to Ezekiel 38:5, Persia will also participate in Russia's invasion of Israel. Persia changed its name to Iran in March 1935 and then, in 1979, changed it again to the Islamic Republic of Iran. Iran and Russia will be the leading forces in this final attempt to wipe Israel off the map. Today, with its 77 million people, Iran is wielding its malevolent influence not only in the Middle East but in the West as well.

Under the leadership of President Obama, the United States has entered into an agreement with Iran that baffles allies and enemies alike. It involves allowing that country to develop nuclear weapons and access some $100 billion.[16] More than one pundit has argued that the United States is now the leading financier of terrorism in the world!

Why the Obama administration has chosen to trust Iran is a great mystery. It is one of the most belligerent nations in the world today. Despite the fact that the US nuclear agreement has aided Iran in its pursuit of power, that country has not slackened its hatred toward Americans or Israelis. The Iranian leaders call America "The Great Satan," and they still openly vow to wipe Israel off the face of the earth. Their hatred is intense and unyielding.

Every year Muslims celebrate Quds Day on the last Friday of Ramadan, which in 2015 occurred on July 10. Quds Day has historically been a time to call for violence against the Jewish state. Shortly before the 2015 Quds Day, "Iranian President Hassan Rouhani urged the entire country to 'shout its hatred for the Zionists' and back Palestinian efforts to seize territory from Israel."[17]

What disturbs the Western nations as well as most of the Middle East is the fact that the Iran deal gives Iran the means to act on that hatred. According to the *Washington Post*,

> None of Iran's nuclear facilities . . . will be closed. Not one of the country's 19,000 centrifuges will be dismantled. . . . In effect, Iran's nuclear infrastructure will remain intact. . . . When the accord lapses, the Islamic republic will instantly become a threshold nuclear state. . . . The proposed accord will provide Iran a huge economic boost that will allow it to wage more aggressively the wars it is already fighting or sponsoring across the region.[18]

What may be worse, the loose and unenforceable inspection terms outlined in the treaty play into the hands of Russia's growing ties with Iran. "The agreement would be vulnerable to the greed of other international actors, particularly Vladimir Putin. If the Russians, among others, cheated when it came to monitoring Saddam Hussein's activities, you can be sure they'll do the same with Iran."[19]

It is clear that the new and increasing accords between Russia and Iran reveal a trajectory that points toward the ultimate fulfillment of Ezekiel's prophecy.

Ethiopia

This is the first of two North African nations named as part of this coalition. Ethiopia was founded by Cush, the grandson of Noah through his second son Ham (Genesis 10:6). When Ezekiel made this prophecy, Ethiopia was the name of the land south of Egypt. Today that region is the modern country of Sudan. Along with Iran, Sudan is one of Israel's fiercest enemies.

Libya

Libya is the land west of Egypt—the only country on Ezekiel's list that retains its ancient name today. Like Ethiopia, it too was founded by a son of Ham, Put (Genesis 10:6). Today's Libya, along with Iran and Syria, is another of Russia's friends among the Islamic states.

Modern Libya was ruled for forty-one years by the notorious dictator Muammar Gaddafi. He was killed in the aftermath of the Arab Spring uprisings of 2011, in which rebels in several Arab countries attempted to overthrow dictatorial governments. Even now Gaddafi's legacy continues to haunt Libya, which is still wracked by civil war and street violence (including the attack on the US compound in Benghazi on September 11, 2012) as militant Islamists vie for control. The current Libyan government is renewing ties with Russia in hopes of purchasing military armaments.[20]

Gomer

Gomer was the first son of Japheth and the grandson of Noah (vv. 2–3). Because of the similarity between the words, many have taught that Gomer was the founder of the nation that is now Germany. Believing that Gomer represents modern Germany, John Phillips wrote of the death and chaos that nation has inflicted in the past—especially against the Jews:

> Single-handedly a united and greater Germany ("Gomer, and all his bands") had come within a hair of winning World War II. The Nazis' attempt to achieve global power had cost thirty-five million lives. On the battlefields, 1 out of every 22 Russians had been killed, 1 out of every 25 Germans, and 1 out of every 150 Britishers. In addition, 2 out of every 3 European Jews had been systematically exterminated. It had taken all the combined might of the British Empire, the Soviet Union, and the United States to fight Germany to a standstill. What if a united and anti-Semitic Germany were to seek its future fortunes while allied to an anti-Semitic Russia?[21]

Togarmah

Togarmah was the third son of Gomer, son of Japheth (v. 3) and, thus, the great-grandson of Noah. Ezekiel specifically located this nation for us: "the house of Togarmah from the far north and all its troops" (Ezekiel 38:6). Some commentators identify Togarmah with Turkey, noting a possible etymological connection between the name Togarmah and the names Turkey and Turkestan.[22]

These are the nations that will ultimately form a coalition and march against the nation of Israel, setting the stage for this gigantic world war that has the Holy Land as its focal point. The map that follows shows that these nations literally surround Israel. Though the northern armies of Russia and Turkey will lead the coalition, they will be joined by Iran from the east, Sudan and Libya from the south, and (possibly) Germany from the west in the form of a revived European coalition of nations. To darken the picture for Israel, remember that Ezekiel listed only Russia's *chief* allies in the invasion. But he added that the nation will have "many peoples" on its side (v. 9). When Russia is ready to move against Israel, it will have as its allies at least the Arab states of the Near East and likely the nations in the former Soviet bloc.

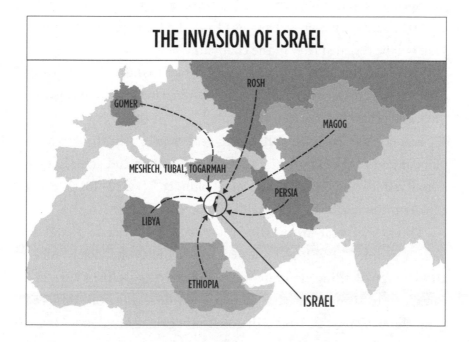

THE INVASION OF ISRAEL

THE RUSSIAN ATTACK

After listing the assemblage of Russian allies, Ezekiel went on to describe the actual invasion of Israel (vv. 7–17). As you read this section of Scripture, remember that this is a prophecy *against* Russia and the invading nations. "Thus says the Lord GOD: 'Behold, I am *against* you'" (v. 3). The term *you* refers to Russia, and the terms *they* and *them* refer to Israel in this section.

No doubt at this point you are asking: Why is God urging nations He opposes to attack His chosen people? We will learn the answer to that question shortly.

Why Will Russia and Its Allies Attack Israel?

What is the purpose of this invasion? Ezekiel gave us three answers that spring from the evil hearts of Israel's attackers. (There is actually a fourth, deeper answer that springs from the heart of God Himself. That will be revealed later in the chapter.)

First, the Russians will go to *seize* Israel's land: "'I will go up against a land of unwalled villages . . .' to stretch out your hand against the waste places that are again inhabited" (vv. 11–12).

Second, the purpose will be to *steal* Israel's wealth: "To take plunder and to take booty . . . 'to carry away silver and gold, to take away livestock and goods, to take great plunder'" (vv. 12–13). We will explore the extent of Israel's wealth later in this chapter.

Third, the great army from the North will seek to *slaughter* Israel's people: "'I will go to a peaceful people, who dwell safely, all of them dwelling without walls, and having neither bars nor gates' . . . to stretch out your hand . . . against a people gathered from the nations. . . . 'You will come up against My people Israel like a cloud, to cover the land'" (vv. 11–12, 16). We have already noted the Islamic hatred of Israel, a hatred that has existed since Abraham exiled Ishmael from the presence of Isaac (Genesis 21:8–19). That hatred can only be satisfied by the annihilation of the Jewish nation.

Where Will the Russian Invasion Occur?

Ezekiel identified the country to be invaded as "the land of those brought back from the sword and gathered from many people on the mountains of Israel" (Ezekiel 38:8).

At least five times in chapter 38, Ezekiel affirmed that Israel will be the target of the Russian coalition. This fact alone makes Ezekiel's prophecy an amazing thing because Israel is one of the smallest nations on earth. It is one-nineteenth the size of California and roughly the size of New Jersey. Russia is 785 times larger than Israel. Israel measures approximately 290 miles at its longest, 85 miles at its widest, and 9 miles at its narrowest.[23] Yet here the nation is at the center of one of the world's final global wars, the target of a massive coalition led by a world superpower.

When Will the Russian Invasion Occur?

Ezekiel prophesied that three events must take place before Russia invades Israel. Two of these events are already history; the third is yet to be fulfilled.

Israel Must Be Present in Its Land

Ezekiel told us six times in chapters 38 and 39 that the dispersed people of Israel will be re-gathered to their original homeland (twice in 38:8; also in 38:12 and 39:25, 27, 28). He also recorded this promise of God in a previous chapter: "For I will take you from among the nations, gather you out of all countries, and bring you into your own land" (36:24).

In the time of Ezekiel, the only remaining tribes of Israel—Judah and Benjamin—had been deported from their homeland by the Babylonians. When Cyrus the Persian conquered Babylon, he and successive Persian rulers allowed the Jews to return to their land. But about six hundred years later, in AD 70, the Roman general Titus conquered Jerusalem, utterly destroying the city and slaughtering hundreds of thousands of Jews. Roman soldiers later went throughout the entire land, razing every building, sawing down or uprooting trees, and doing everything possible to render the land uninhabitable. Israel lay waste for several generations afterward, and the Jews were scattered over the face of the earth—the great Jewish diaspora.

As a result of Middle Eastern realignments after World War I, Palestine (the area of the original Israel) became a British protectorate. At the close of World War II, the horrific German persecution of the Jewish people generated pressure to allow them to return to their ancient homeland. Jews began to pour into Palestine in large numbers. In May 1948, the newly established Israel was recognized by the United States as a nation-state. Within a few years, for the first time in almost twenty centuries, more than five hundred thousand Jews had come back to their original homeland. It was the largest return of Jews to their land since the days of the exodus.

Out of the 14 million Jews in the world today, 6.3 million live in Israel.[24] This is about the same number of Jews that were killed in the Holocaust. The total population of Israel is about 8.5 million, with 1.7 million Arabs making up most of the difference.[25]

Obviously, Ezekiel's prophecy could not have been fulfilled prior to 1948, for the Jewish people had not yet re-gathered to their ancient land.

Ezekiel added one more item concerning Israel's occupation of its land before the Russian invasion. He told us that Gog, the coalition leader, will "come into the land of those brought back from the sword and gathered from many people on the mountains of Israel, which had long been desolate" (38:8). Not only will the Jews return to their homeland, but they will also occupy "the mountains of Israel." Mark Hitchcock explains the meaning of this prophecy and how it has already been fulfilled: "The famous Six-Day War in Israel in 1967 helped set the stage to fulfill this prophecy. Before the Six-Day War the mountains of Israel were in the hands of the Jordanian Arabs, with the exception of a small strip of West Jerusalem. Only since that war have the mountains *of* Israel been *in* Israel."[26]

Ezekiel 36–37, the two chapters preceding the description of the Russian invasion, predict the re-gathering of the nation of Israel. That gathering marks the *national* rebirth of Israel, and as we have shown above, that has already occurred. Ezekiel 40–48, the chapters that fol low Ezekiel's description of the invasion, is about the Millennium, which will be the time of Israel's *spiritual* rebirth. The invasion of Gog and Magog will take place between the *national* and *spiritual* rebirths of Israel.

Israel Must Be Prosperous in Its Land

Ezekiel further prophesied that when the Jewish people have returned to their homeland, God will bless them beyond anything they had previously known: "I will multiply upon you man and beast; and they shall increase and bear young; I will make you inhabited as in former times, and do better for you than at your beginnings. Then you shall know that I am the LORD" (36:11).

We have already noted that one of the reasons for Russia's invasion of Israel will be to seize the nation's great wealth (38:12). Ezekiel predicted that after the nation of Israel is reestablished, it will become extremely wealthy and the envy of the hostile nations surrounding it.

Israelis tell a joke about a Jew who begins to read only Arab newspapers. A puzzled friend asks him why. "When I read the Israeli papers," he replies, "all I find is bad news about us—how we are vulnerable to terrorism and attack, problems with Palestinian settlements, political turmoil, and growing isolation. But the Arab papers tell nothing but good news about us: They constantly claim we're all rich, successful, and rule the world."[27]

These Arab newspapers may see Israel's wealth as material corruption, but they are spot-on accurate about its reality. Here are several examples:

- "The Tel Aviv Stock Exchange lists 616 companies, meaning Israel has one public company for every 12,500 citizens. By comparison, the U.S. has one public company for every 47,000 citizens."[28]
- Israel "has the most non-U.S. Nasdaq-listed companies in the world—more than China, India, Korea, Japan, Canada or the entire European continent."[29]
- Israel's economy has been ranked the world's third most innovative, behind Finland and Switzerland and just ahead of Japan and the United States.[30]
- For a nation of just eight million people, Israel generates about five hundred start-ups every year—more than every other country except the United States. By comparison, the entire continent of Europe, with a population of some seven-hundred-million people, produces only six hundred to seven hundred start-up companies each year.[31]
- Israel is home to seventeen billionaires and more than eighty-eight thousand millionaires.[32]
- Of the five hundred wealthiest people in the world, nine are Israeli. And of the top fifty billionaires, ten are Jews.[33]

The prosperity of today's Israel is beyond question. God has blessed that nation in ways it has never known, not even in the days of King Solomon. This means the second of the three conditions that will exist before the Russian invasion is in place.

Israel Must Be Peaceful in Its Land

The third condition of Israel that will be in place before the Russian invasion is peace. Ezekiel told us that the northern coalition will descend on a people whose peace is so secure they do not bother to maintain weapons or take defensive measures. The arrogant Gog boasts, "I will go up against a land of unwalled villages; I will go to a peaceful people, who dwell safely, all of them dwelling without walls, having neither bars nor gates" (v. 11; see also vv. 8, 14).

In ancient times, whenever a city prospered and became prominent, a wall was built around it. As my wife and I have traveled in Europe and the Middle East, we have often seen still-standing portions of these ancient city walls. But the prophet Ezekiel, guided by God, described a time in Israel's future when there will be no walls, a time when Israel will dwell in peace and safety without concern for defensive measures.

This is clearly one condition that has not yet occurred. There has never been a time in Israel's existence, ancient or modern, when it has not been concerned about defense. Israel has always been surrounded by enemies. Even today Israel is constantly threatened from all sides by extremely hostile neighbors many times its size. It has already fought three major wars in its brief modern history, and Israel's close neighbor Iran is rabidly eager to annihilate it.

There is no country on earth as massively armed for its size and as constantly vigilant as Israel. Every young Israeli man is required to undergo three years of military training, and every young woman trains for two years. Visit Israel today and you will see its readiness for war on display everywhere. Armed soldiers are stationed in every strategic location, and security is the highest priority. One cannot enter a shop or restaurant without going through a metal detector. No, Israel is not at peace or anywhere close to it. That means the Russian invasion is not imminent.

A time is coming, however, when Israel will be at peace in its land. The prophet Daniel told us how this peace will come about: "Then he [the Antichrist] shall confirm a covenant with many for one week" (Daniel 9:27).

Daniel told us when the Antichrist appears, one of his first projects will be to settle the perpetual Arab-Israeli dispute. On behalf of the European coalition of nations, he will make a covenant with the Jews to guarantee their safety. This covenant, which will be contracted for a period of seven years (v. 27), will cause Israel to let down its guard and turn its attention toward prosperity. Israel will, for the first time, be a nation of "unwalled villages" and, therefore, a ripe target for Russian aggression.

The Bible tells us this invasion will take place in "the latter years" (Ezekiel 38:8) and in "the latter days" (v. 16). According to J. Dwight Pentecost, the terms *last days* and *latter days* have "specific reference to the latter years and days of God's dealing with the nation Israel, which, since it is before the millennial age (Ezekiel 40), must place it during God's dealing with Israel in the seventieth week of Daniel's prophecy," the seven-year Tribulation Period.[34]

Thus, we have the time of the Russian invasion of Israel pinpointed. To summarize, it will come after Israel returns to its homeland, after it has become highly prosperous, and after the implementation of the seven-year peace treaty with the Antichrist.

THE RUSSIAN ANNIHILATION

Anyone observing the advance of this horde of armies will have already pronounced the doom of Israel. Israel has always been outnumbered in its wars, but in this instance, it will be so grossly mismatched that there will be no human way for the nation to survive. Here is Ezekiel's description of the coalition's advance: "Then you will come from your place out of the far north, you and many peoples with you . . . a great company and a mighty army. You will come up against My people Israel like a cloud, to cover the land" (38:15–16).

Some have suggested that the reference to a cloud means massive air strikes. But it is more likely that the prophet used this metaphor to describe the gargantuan nature of the invasion. As a cloud covers the land with its shadow, so the armies of the Russian alliance will cover the land of Israel.

What happens next in this astounding narrative defies imagination. When all hope for Israel's survival is gone, God intervenes: "'And it will come to pass at the same time, when Gog comes against the land of Israel,' says the Lord GOD, 'that My fury will show in My face. For in My jealousy and in the fire of My wrath I have spoken'" (vv. 18–19).

Remember that when we were outlining the three reasons for Russia's attack on Israel, I alluded to a fourth reason that overrides all the others—a reason that the invading coalition will know nothing about. That reason is to set the stage for God's punishment of Russia and its allies for their history of rebellion against Him. Here is Ezekiel's explanation:

"'So I will make My holy name known in the midst of My people Israel, and I will not let them profane My holy name anymore. Then the nations shall know that I am the LORD, the Holy One in

Israel. Surely it is coming, and it shall be done,' says the Lord GOD. 'This is the day of which I have spoken.'" (39:7–8)

God will use the evil tendencies of these allied nations—their greed, hatred, and bloodlust—to goad them into attacking Israel so He can execute His judgment against them for their long history of human oppression. This judgment will come down in a series of disasters even more spectacular and catastrophic than the plagues God inflicted on ancient Egypt. Ezekiel described four key calamities that will descend on the invading armies when God intervenes to protect His people.

Monumental Convulsions

The first calamity Ezekiel prophesied was an earthquake:

"'Surely in that day there shall be a great earthquake in the land of Israel, so that the fish of the sea, the birds of the heavens, the beasts of the field, all creeping things that creep on the earth, and all men who are on the face of the earth shall shake at My presence. The mountains shall be thrown down, the steep places shall fall, and every wall shall fall to the ground.'" (38:19–20)

This earthquake will be like none ever seen on earth. It will register completely off the Richter scale. Towering buildings and even mountains will come crashing down. Though Israel will be the epicenter, every living creature on the earth will feel the effects of this colossal quake.

Military Confusion

The movement, wreckage, and billowing clouds of dust and smoke from the quake will generate mass confusion among the invading armies (v. 21). Here is Dr. Walvoord's description of the chaos:

In the pandemonium, communication between the invading armies will break down and they will begin attacking each other. Every man's sword will be against his brother. Fear and panic will sweep through the forces so each army will shoot indiscriminately at the others.[35]

John Phillips gives us an added dimension to the attackers' self-destruction:

> The Russian leaders will underestimate the hatred nursed by many ethnic groups against the Russians themselves. Also Russia's allies, though motivated by a common hatred of Israel, will probably have had more than enough of Russian arrogance and dominance. In any case, a long-smoldering revolt will break out and the invaders will turn on each other.[36]

This event will be a repeat of a similar one from Israel's history, but on an exponentially larger scale. In the days of King Jehoshaphat, the enemies of Israel destroyed themselves by turning on one another (2 Chronicles 20:22–25). God will protect His people in the future as He has done in the past.

Major Contagion

God's third weapon against the Russian coalition will be an epidemic breakout of disease: "I will bring him to judgment with pestilence and bloodshed" (Ezekiel 38:22). Unburied dead bodies will lie everywhere, causing a malignant plague to infect the land. Thousands more of the invaders will die.

Multiple Calamities

A deluge of fire and brimstone will fall on Russia and its allies just as God rained fire and brimstone down on Sodom and Gomorrah (v. 22).

If the coalition's troubles on the battlefield were not enough, these God-inflicted calamities will extend to the Magog homelands as well. "And I will send fire on Magog and on those who live in security in the coastlands. Then they shall know that I am the LORD" (Ezekiel 39:6). Those who remain home in Magog will not escape punishment. Remember, *Magog* is the term that covers the Middle Eastern nations that were once part of the Soviet Union: Kazakhstan, Kyrgyzstan, Uzbekistan, Turkmenistan, Tajikistan, and perhaps Afghanistan.

THE RUSSIAN AFTERMATH

God's supernatural intervention to protect Israel and bring judgment on the Russians will leave all of Israel's fields, mountains, plains, gullies, and lakes strewn and piled with masses of the invaders' bodies. It will be a grisly testament to the ignoble end of those who defy God to the end. The final disposal of these corpses can be summed up in these words: the birds and the beasts, the burials, and the burning. All three operations are described in Ezekiel 39. Just as Ezekiel 38 details the *destruction* of the northern armies, chapter 39 describes their *disposal*.

The Birds and the Beasts

Ezekiel recorded God's invitation to all the birds of the world and the beasts of the field to come to Israel and devour the multiple thousands of bodies that will be scattered across the land. God calls it a "sacrificial meal" for the scavengers that will do His bidding and clean up the land for His people:

> "Assemble yourselves and come;
> Gather together from all sides to My sacrificial meal

Which I am sacrificing for you,

A great sacrificial meal on the mountains of Israel,

That you may eat flesh and drink blood.

You shall eat the flesh of the mighty,

Drink the blood of the princes of the earth . . .

You shall be filled at My table

With horses and riders,

With mighty men

And with all the men of war," says the Lord GOD. (39:17–20)

The Burnings

Not only will the failed Russian invasion leave masses of bodies, but it will also leave all the coalition's military equipment littering the landscape everywhere. How will these now-useless weapons be discarded?

> "'Then those who dwell in the cities of Israel will go out and set on fire and burn the weapons, both the shields and bucklers, the bows and arrows, the javelins and spears; and they will make fires with them for seven years. They will not take wood from the field nor cut down any from the forests, because they will make fires with the weapons; and they will plunder those who plundered them, and pillage those who pillaged them,' says the Lord GOD." (vv. 9–10)

It will take seven years to burn the enormous number of weapons the Russian allies will leave in Israel. In a previous book, I addressed a question people often ask about these weapons. Ezekiel described them as ancient devices—shields and bucklers, bows and arrows, javelins, and spears. We know this future battle will surely be fought with sophisticated modern weaponry—rifles, artillery, tanks, planes, bombs, missiles, and possibly even nuclear devices. Doesn't Ezekiel present us with an anachronistic discrepancy here?

In answer, I wrote that "we must allow common sense to prevail in our reading of Ezekiel. He did what all prophets have done: He spoke of the future using terms and descriptions that he and the people of his day would understand. If he had written of tanks and missiles and bombs, those living in his time would have been utterly mystified, and his message would have had no meaning to them."[37]

The Burials

The vultures and scavengers God will invite to devour the bodies of the fallen invaders will leave a residue of bones and other inedible parts. It will be necessary for the Israelis to bury what the scavengers leave. In the following passage, God specifies the place of the burial:

> "'It will come to pass in that day that I will give Gog a burial place there in Israel, the valley of those who pass by east of the sea; and it will obstruct travelers, because there they will bury Gog and all his multitude. Therefore they will call it the Valley of Hamon Gog. For seven months the house of Israel will be burying them, in order to cleanse the land.'" (vv. 11–12)

The fact that it will take seven months to bury the dead gives us an indication of the gigantic size of the invading army. Before pronouncing the burial process complete, Israel will appoint search parties to scour the entire land for any remaining bodies or body parts that might have been overlooked (vv. 13–16). Only when the burials are complete can the land be declared ceremonially clean again (Numbers 19:11–22).

THE RUSSIAN APPLICATION

In Ezekiel 38–39, we find a compelling prophecy about the ultimate destruction of Russia, a nation that has long been antagonistic toward God and disruptive to the order of the world. In today's world events, we can see the historical character of that nation asserting itself once again as it seeks to expand its power and disruptive influence, especially in the Middle East. It is merely a matter of time before Russia stretches its malignant claws toward the rich and free nation of Israel.

In these same chapters, Ezekiel also told the story of another nation, a mere sliver of land surrounded by enemies, increasingly isolated by allies, and struggling to maintain its very existence. This, of course, is Israel—God's chosen nation that often, throughout its beleaguered history, has not chosen God. But God has promised Israel a glorious future, and as these two prophetic chapters show, He will keep that promise in a way that ends with a spectacular and satisfying twist. Ron Rhodes elaborates:

> What a turn of events all this will be. The invading troops come with the intention of killing, but they themselves are killed. They believe their power to be overwhelming, but they end up being overwhelmed by the greater power of God. They come to take over a new land (Israel) but instead end up being buried in the land. The whole world will surely marvel at this turn of events![38]

Yes, the whole world will indeed marvel at how God will accomplish two goals with one act. He will bring down a virulent and powerful enemy while preserving the existence of His people. When this happens, the world cannot help but stand in awe of the name and power of God: "Thus I will magnify Myself and sanctify Myself, and I will be known in the eyes of many nations. Then they shall know that I am the LORD" (Ezekiel 38:23).

Five times in Ezekiel 38–39, God repeats this desire to make His name known among the nations (38:16, 23; 39:6, 7). I have heard some characterize God's oft-repeated desire to be known and glorified as pride, arrogance, or megalomania. It is an empty charge that indicates a misunderstanding of God's glory. God wants us to recognize and adore Him not because He has any need for affirmation and recognition, but because we have no other life but in Him. As Paul said, "for in Him we live and move and have our being" (Acts 17:28). Knowing and adoring God is for our benefit, not His. He knows who He is, and He does not need our recognition or praise to affirm it. Yet we need to recognize Him and praise Him. We need to know who we belong to and to express our awe and praise for His love and care for us.

I can understand why people shudder at today's headlines. The daily news shows an alarming disintegration of world order and security—the hate and instability in the Middle East, the rising rumblings of Russia, and the inability of the United States to exercise its traditional power to keep these tensions in balance. We see growing disorder now and chaos ahead, and we wonder whether God has turned His face away from us.

A few years ago the late pastor and author Ray Stedman was scheduled to speak at a theological conference in England. The meetings were held in a Methodist chapel somewhere between Cambridge and London. Each session of the conference began with a song service, and the full chapel of Christians singing their hearts out fairly raised the rafters of the building. One night the leader led the worshippers in the popular chorus of "Our God Reigns." Stedman knew the song well enough that he had no need to look at the song sheet. But somewhere in the middle of the song, he glanced down at the sheet, which had been prepared by the church staff. What he saw caused him to stop singing and smile. Some apparently hurried secretary, intending to type the title as "Our God Reigns," had actually typed "Our God Resigns."[39]

Let me assure you that our God will never resign. We who trust Him have no reason to fear. As I have read Ezekiel 38–39 over and over, the one thing that stands out is the sovereignty of God. He is in control. He orchestrates this whole scenario in order to demonstrate to His people Israel that He is their God and worthy of their trust. Israel has no hope without God, and God wins the battle for the nation. Godless Russia is no match for the King of kings.

The God of Israel is also our God, which means whatever we fear is also no match for the King of kings. When it looks like there is no hope, hope is just waiting for the proper moment to show up. God can be trusted—that is the message of this chapter.

So as today's ominous headlines thrust themselves at you, remember that your God is the God of justice; evil will not prevail. He is the God of love; He will protect all His people as He does Israel. He is the God of truth; He keeps His promises no matter what. Finally, He is the God of the future. He is already there. He knows tomorrow better than you and I know yesterday. Though it may seem that things are spinning out of control, God has not abandoned us. It may seem, as it must have seemed to Israel, that the forces coming down on us are formidable and irresistible, and we have no hope. It is not so. The Lord is on our side; we need not fear.

Countless icebergs drift in the frigid waters around Greenland, some tiny and some gigantic. If you observe them carefully, you notice that sometimes the small bergs move in one direction while their massive counterparts flow in another. The explanation is simple. Surface winds drive the little ones, whereas the huge masses of ice are carried along by deep ocean currents.

When we face trials and tragedies, it's helpful to see our lives as being subject to two forces—surface winds and ocean currents. The winds represent everything changeable, unpredictable, and distressing. But operating simultaneously with these gusts and gales is another force even more powerful. It is the sure movement of God's wise and sovereign purposes, the deep flow of His unchanging love.

CHAPTER 9

THE RAPTURE OF THE REDEEMED

In 1970, Hal Lindsey coauthored the book *The Late Great Planet Earth*. This book brought the message of Bible prophecy into the everyday conversation of the people, and it became "the best-selling nonfiction book of the 1970s. The book has sold more than fifteen million copies . . . and has been translated into more than fifty languages." Some pundits have calculated that, altogether, Lindsey's book has sold more than 35 million copies.[1]

Lindsey graduated from Dallas Theological Seminary, the seminary from which I graduated in 1967. Both of us were privileged to sit under some of the greatest teachers of Bible prophecy in the modern era: J. Dwight Pentecost, John F. Walvoord, and Charles Ryrie, just to name a few. In his book, Lindsey took the theological truths of the prophetic Scriptures that he had learned in seminary and from his own personal study and connected them to the events of the present and future.

The co-author of Lindsey's book was a gifted and godly woman by the name of Carole C. Carlson. In the early eighties, I met Carole and her husband, Ward, at the Forest Home Bible Conference in California, where I was one of the speakers.

Sometime during that week, we had coffee together, and she suggested that she might be able to assist me in putting some of my prophetic sermons into print. Two books came out of that conversation. The first one, *The Handwriting on the Wall*, was released in 1992, and it captured the message of the Old Testament book of Daniel.

The second book—*Escape the Coming Night*, a contemporary commentary on the New Testament book of Revelation—was released on the first day of the Gulf War and became my all-time bestselling book.

I remember with great fondness the hours Carole and I spent together talking about prophecy and discussing how to make it come alive for our readers. Both Carole and Ward have graduated into the presence of the Lord. They live today, not only in heaven but also in the books they helped two authors to create.

In the late 1970s and early '80s, I developed a relationship with a California pastor by the name of Tim LaHaye. Shortly afterward, I was called to be his successor at what was then called Scott Memorial Baptist Church in San Diego, California. Today that church is Shadow Mountain Community Church, and I am still, after thirty-five years, its pastor. Most Sundays, until his death in July 2016, Dr. LaHaye and his wife, Beverly, were in attendance at one of our morning services. Consecutively, the two of us pastored the same church for almost sixty years.

Dr. LaHaye was flying home from a speaking engagement in the early nineties when God placed a burden on his heart. His study of the Scriptures had led him to a firm conviction that all believing Christians would be removed from the world prior to the Tribulation by means of an event known as the Rapture. As he flew home that day, he couldn't help but notice one of the plane's pilots flirting with a flight attendant. He also noticed that the pilot was wearing a wedding ring. *What if*, Dr. LaHaye thought to himself, *this were the moment*

God picked to remove the faithful from the earth, leaving behind only their clothes and a lot of bewildered unbelievers?[2]

It was at that moment that he decided to write a fictional account of what would happen when the Lord returned and suddenly took all Christians to heaven. Dr. "LaHaye teamed up with . . . experienced ghostwriter" Jerry Jenkins, and their first book, *Left Behind*, was published in 1995. In the opening chapter a distraught flight attendant interrupts an airline pilot in mid-flight to report that dozens of their passengers have suddenly disappeared. "Clothes, shoes, and gold fillings are all that remain where these passengers once sat."[3]

The book was a runaway bestseller, as were many of the sequels that followed, topping the charts in the *New York Times*, *USA Today*, *Wall Street Journal*, and *Publisher's Weekly*, and for the Christian Booksellers Association. The ninth volume, *Desecration*, hit the bookstores shortly after the terror attacks of September 11, 2001, and sold enough copies in three short months to become the bestselling novel that year. As of this writing, the sixteen-volume Left Behind series has sold more than sixty-five million copies.[4]

I had the honor of walking through some of the exciting days of this series of prophetic books with my friend Dr. LaHaye. On a number of occasions, he invited me to lunch to present me with a signed copy of the latest release. I owe a lot to Dr. LaHaye and the many others who have helped me understand the importance of teaching the prophetic scriptures, which, by the way, comprise more than 28 percent of the Bible.

I believe one of the reasons God blessed the Left Behind books is the fact that the Rapture is the central event throughout the series. As one theologian wrote, "The Rapture of the church is one of the most important practical prophecies in Scripture for believers today. It is an essential part of the many other prophecies in the Scriptures."[5]

WHAT IS THE RAPTURE?

The Rapture is the event in which all who have put their trust in Jesus Christ will be suddenly caught up from the earth and taken into heaven by Him. It is set to occur at an unspecified time in the future.

The word *rapture* is a translation of the Greek word *harpazo*. It occurs fourteen times in the New Testament, and at least four meanings are assigned to it. Each of these meanings helps us to understand the nature of the event that is the subject of this chapter.

The first meaning of *harpazo* is "to carry off by force." Satan and his demonic cohorts will do everything in their power to keep the saints here on earth. But Christ's angelic forces will overpower them and carry the believers away by force, delivering them to heaven by the omnipotent power at His command. The devil is mighty; the Lord is almighty.

The second meaning is "to claim for oneself eagerly." At the end of this present age of grace, our blessed Savior will come to claim us as His very own. He has redeemed us by His precious blood and purchased us for Himself, and He will surely come to take us to be with Him.

The third meaning is "to snatch away speedily." This definition emphasizes the sudden nature of the Rapture. In a split second the Lord will call all believers to Himself to share in His glory—not one will remain behind.

The fourth meaning is "to rescue from the danger of destruction." This meaning provides strong support for the belief that the church will be kept from the danger and destruction of the Tribulation.[6]

My study of Scripture convinces me that the two most important events in world history are the first and second comings of the Lord Jesus Christ. We give great attention to His first coming, as we should, but His second coming deserves no less. In fact, I could make a strong case for an even greater emphasis on the Second Coming than on the first. For every prophecy in the Bible about the birth of Christ—His first coming—there are eight about His second coming. The 260 chapters of the New Testament contain 318 references to the second coming of Christ.[7]

I believe there will be two stages to the second coming of Christ. First, He will come suddenly in the air to snatch up His own. This is the Rapture, the "catching up" of the church, which will occur at the beginning of the Tribulation that is coming upon the earth.

The Tribulation will be an extended time of horror, agony, and devastation like nothing ever before seen or imagined. The Rapture is God's provision for His saints to escape the Tribulation. Jesus will return immediately before this time of world judgment to remove completely all those who have put their trust in Him. As He told the church in Philadelphia, "Because you have kept My command to persevere, I also will keep you from the hour of trial which shall come upon the whole world" (Revelation 3:10).

The second stage of Christ's second coming will occur at the end of the Tribulation. Revelation 19 gives us a spectacular and detailed picture of this ultimate event that signals the end of this fallen world's history. It is also described by many other Bible writers. For example, the prophet Zechariah wrote:

> Behold, the day of the Lord is coming . . .
> Then the Lord will go forth
> And fight against those nations,
> As He fights in the day of battle.
> And in that day His feet will stand on the Mount of Olives,
> Which faces Jerusalem on the east.

And the Mount of Olives shall be split in two,

From east to west. . . .

Thus the LORD my God will come,

And all the saints with You. (Zechariah 14:1, 3–5)

The New Testament writer Jude, quoting a prophecy of Enoch, graphically summarized the purpose of the final stage of Christ's second coming:

"Behold, the Lord comes with ten thousands of His saints, to execute judgment on all, to convict all who are ungodly among them of all their ungodly deeds which they have committed in an ungodly way, and of all the harsh things which ungodly sinners have spoken against Him." (Jude 14–15)

The Old Testament prophets spoke almost exclusively about the second stage of the Second Coming. The primary reason for this is obvious: The second stage is the final, climactic event in the history of the present world, whereas the first stage, the Rapture, is essentially a preliminary event that sets the scene for the second. But there is also another reason: The prophets simply did not see the first stage clearly. Their perspective on the future was incomplete, denying them the clarity to see the seven-year period of Tribulation that separates the first and second stages of Christ's final appearance.

If it surprises you to learn that the prophets did not understand everything they wrote about, Peter explained that in addition to the Holy Spirit's inspiration, these men also applied their own intellects to search for understanding of what was specifically revealed:

The prophets have inquired and searched carefully, who prophe-sied of the grace that would come to you, searching what, or what manner of time, the Spirit of Christ who was in them was indicat-ing when He testified beforehand the sufferings of Christ and the glories that would follow. (1 Peter 1:10–11)

Some have likened the vision of the Old Testament prophets to that of seeing a range of mountains from a distance. If you have ever traveled west from Texas across the northern plains of New Mexico toward the Rocky Mountains of Colorado, you know that distance obliterates detail and flattens perspective. You may see, in the dis-tance before you, what seems to be a double-peaked mountain. But as you approach, you begin to see that the two peaks are actually the tops of two mountains, one slightly offset in front of the other.

From their time-distanced vantage point, the prophets saw the two peaks of the Second Coming as one mountain. They identified it as the second coming of Christ *with* His saints, but they failed to see there was another mountain—the second coming of Christ *for* His saints—separated from the more distant mountain by the valley of the Tribulation.

As you will discover as you study the chart that follows, there are many distinguishing differences between the two stages of our Lord's return. Some have described the difference between the Rapture and the Second Coming this way: "The Rapture is a movement from earth to heaven. The Second Coming is a movement from heaven to earth."[8]

The focus of this chapter is solely on the first stage of Christ's second coming—the Rapture. I present this discussion of the second stage only to show that the two events are not the same; they are sepa-rated in time by the seven-year Tribulation.

THE RAPTURE	THE RETURN (SECOND COMING)
Christ comes in the air (1 Thessalonians 4:16-17)	Christ comes to the earth (Zechariah 14:4)
Christ comes for His saints (1 Thessalonians 4:16-17)	Christ comes with His saints (1 Thessalonians 3:13; Jude 1:14)
Believers depart the earth (1 Thessalonians 4:16-17)	Unbelievers are taken away (Matthew 24:37-41)
Christ claims His bride	Christ comes with His bride
Christ gathers His own (1 Thessalonians 4:16-17)	Angels gather the elect (Matthew 24:31)
Christ comes to reward (1 Thessalonians 4:16-17)	Christ comes to judge (Matthew 25:31-46)
Not in the Old Testament (1 Corinthians 15:51)	Predicted often in the Old Testament
There are no signs. It is imminent.	Portended by many signs (Matthew 24:4-29)
It is a time of blessing and comfort (1 Thessalonians 4:17-18)	It is a time of destruction and judgment (2 Thessalonians 2:8-12)
Involves believers only (John 14:1-3; 1 Corinthians 15:51-55; 1 Thessalonians 4:13-18)	Involves Israel and the Gentile nations (Matthew 24:1-25:46)
Will occur in a moment, in the time it takes to blink. Only His own will see Him (1 Corinthians 15:51-52)	Will be visible to the entire world (Matthew 24:27; Revelation 1:7)
Tribulation begins	Millennium begins
Christ comes as the bright morning star (Revelation 22:16)	Christ comes as the Sun of Righteousness (Malachi 4:2)

UNDERSTANDING THE RAPTURE

The fact that the Old Testament prophets did not identify the Rapture by no means diminishes its importance. The New Testament makes up for the omission, giving us three central passages that record the details of this event. One of these passages records the words of our Lord to His disciples (John 14:1–3), and the other two record the words of Paul to the believers in Corinth and Thessalonica (1 Corinthians 15:50–57; 1 Thessalonians 4:13–18).

Of these three passages, it is Paul's letter to the Thessalonians that presents the most concise and logical truth about the Rapture:

> I do not want you to be ignorant, brethren, concerning those who have fallen asleep, lest you sorrow as others who have no hope. For if we believe that Jesus died and rose again, even so God will bring with Him those who sleep in Jesus. For this we say to you by the word of the Lord, that we who are alive and remain until the coming of the Lord will by no means precede those who are asleep. For the Lord Himself will descend from heaven with a shout, with the voice of an archangel, and with the trumpet of God. And the dead in Christ will rise first. Then we who are alive and remain shall be caught up together with them in the clouds to meet the Lord in the air. And thus we shall always be with the Lord. Therefore comfort one another with these words. (1 Thessalonians 4:13–18)

Before we unpack this passage, I want to share a couple of preliminary and important truths with you.

First, the Lord imparted the truth about the Rapture to the apostle Paul as a *special revelation*. In his letter to the Corinthians, Paul spoke of the Rapture as "a mystery" (1 Corinthians 15:51). He was not indicating that it belongs to the world of the cryptic, mystical, or esoteric, but rather that it was a truth that had not been previously revealed. The Rapture was completely new information to Paul's hearers—a mystery unveiled for the first time.

In the Thessalonian passage, Paul revealed the source of this special revelation: "This we say to you by the word of the Lord" (1 Thessalonians 4:15). Here Paul was saying that this newly revealed information is not to be taken lightly. It is, after all, a revelation received directly from almighty God.

Second, Paul delivered this special revelation about the Rapture as a *serious response* to questions raised by members of the church at Thessalonica. Paul and his companion Silas had spent time with this church earlier and had apparently instructed them about the second coming of Christ. But persecution forced Paul and Silas to flee Thessalonica after only a few weeks, leaving the new believers with troubling questions on a variety of subjects. One of those questions included the fate of loved ones who had died before the Lord's return (vv. 13–18).

It was in response to this question that Paul wrote his explanation of the Rapture in 1 Thessalonians 4. We will explore this important passage in the pages that follow, drawing additional information from 1 Corinthians 15 and John 14 in order to gain a clear understanding of the Rapture and its relationship to the end times.

THE RAPTURE IS A "SIGN-LESS" EVENT

Matthew 24–25 give us many signs that point to the second coming of the Lord. They include all the deception, war, famine, pestilences, and earthquakes of the Tribulation. But it is important to realize that none of these signs point to the first stage of His coming. No signs will be given to prepare us for the arrival of the Rapture. It can occur at any moment—possibly before you finish reading this chapter, or possibly years from now.

The "at-any-moment" timing of the return of Christ is called the doctrine of *imminency*. In his definitive book on the Rapture, Renald Showers gave us an in-depth exploration of the word *imminent*:

> The English word "imminent" comes from the Latin verb "immi-neo, imminere," which means to "overhang" or "project." In light of this, the English word "imminent" means "hanging over one's head, ready to befall or overtake one; close at hand in its incidence." Thus, an imminent event is one that is always hanging overhead, is con-stantly ready to befall or overtake a person, is always close at hand in the sense that it could happen at any moment. Other things *may* happen before the imminent event, but nothing else *must* take place before it happens. If something else must take place before an event can happen, that event is not imminent. The necessity of something else taking place first destroys the concept of imminency.
>
> When an event is truly imminent, we never know exactly when it will happen.[9]

Bible expositor A. T. Pierson wrote, "Imminence is the combina-tion of two conditions . . .: certainty and uncertainty. By an imminent event we mean one which is certain to occur at some time, uncertain at what time."[10]

Without any sign, without any warning, Jesus Christ will return to rapture His saints and take them to heaven. Paul understood the implications of this sign-less event. It means that we must be ready for the Lord's return at any time and at all times. Thus, he urged his protégé Titus to be always "looking for the blessed hope and glorious appearing of our great God and Savior Jesus Christ" (Titus 2:13).

THE RAPTURE IS A SURPRISE EVENT

Radio evangelist Harold Camping gained considerable notoriety for publicly predicting that the Rapture of the church would occur on May 21, 2011. It was his second of three similar predictions. He had earlier set the date at September 6, 1994. When his first 2011 prediction failed, he reset the date at October 21, 2011, at which time he said God would destroy the universe.

Since you are reading these words today, you know that his predictions were not correct. The Rapture has not occurred, and the world has not ended. Sadly, many people placed their hopes for the future in this man's erroneous predictions, investing time and resources in rearranging their earthly affairs—all for nothing.

Fortunately, before his death in 2013, Camping repented of his prophetic errors and agreed with his critics that Jesus' words in Matthew 24:36 should be taken literally: "But of that day and hour no one knows, not even the angels of heaven, but My Father only."

If you hear or read of someone who says he or she knows when Jesus is coming back, you should make it your purpose to stay away from that person both in thought and in deed. To claim knowledge of the exact time of our Lord's return is to know what even the angels do not know and what our Lord did not know while He was on this earth.

The Bible does not give us specific information on the date of the Lord's return for the very reason we noted above: Awareness that He could return at any time encourages us to be ready at all times.

As St. Augustine said, "The last day is hidden that every day may be regarded."

THE RAPTURE IS A SUDDEN EVENT

The apostle Paul emphasized the suddenness of the Rapture when he said it will happen "in a *moment*, in the twinkling of an eye" (1 Corinthians 15:52). Mark Hitchcock describes how suddenly this event will transpire: "The Greek word for *moment* is *atomos*, from which we get our English word *atom*. *Atomos* refers to something that is indivisible, that cannot be divided. When Paul wrote these words, no one could imagine splitting the *atomos*. Today, we would translate this 'in an instant,' 'in a split second,' or 'in a flash.'"[11]

Paul's reference to "the twinkling of an eye" naturally conjures up the image of an eye blinking, which is a reasonably good metaphor for suddenness. But Paul's "twinkling" probably does not mean "blinking"; rather, it likely refers to the amount of time it takes for light, traveling at 186,000 miles per second, to be reflected on the retina in one's eye. The whole idea is that this event will occur suddenly—at the speed of light. In less than a nanosecond, the Lord will call all believers to Himself to share His glory.

One night Earl Kelly, a pastor in Mississippi, was preaching about the Second Coming. He had just quoted Matthew 24:27—"For as the lightning comes from the east and flashes to the west, so also will the coming of the Son of Man be"—when a large light bulb suddenly dropped from the ceiling and burst on the floor in front of the pulpit, startling the worshippers. Without missing a beat, Kelly said, "His coming will be just as sudden and unexpected and devastating to the dreams that are not Christ-centered."[12]

In his book *The Rapture*, Dr. LaHaye vividly imagined what the unexpected suddenness of the Rapture will be like:

> When Christ calls His living saints to be with Him, millions of people will suddenly vanish from the earth. An unsaved person who happens to be in the company of a believer will know immediately that his friend has vanished. There will certainly be worldwide recognition of the fact, for when more than one-half of a billion people suddenly depart this earth, leaving their earthly belongings behind, pandemonium and confusion will certainly reign for a time.
>
> A million conversations will end midsentence.
>
> A million phones . . . will suddenly go dead.
>
> A woman will reach for a man's hand in the dark . . . and no one will be there.
>
> A man will turn with a laugh to slap a colleague on the back and his hand will move through empty air.
>
> A basketball player will make a length-of-the-floor pass to a teammate streaking down the court and find there is no one there to receive it.
>
> A mother will pull back the covers in a bassinet, smelling the sweet baby smell one moment but suddenly kissing empty space and looking into empty blankets.[13]

THE RAPTURE IS A SELECTIVE EVENT

All three of the major passages that teach the Rapture make it clear that it involves believers only.

In John 14:1–3, Jesus addressed His disciples as believers in God and in Him, indicating that what He was about to tell them was for believers only. He went on to say that He would soon leave to prepare for them a place in His Father's house—a place reserved for family members only. Then He said, "I will come again and receive you to Myself; that where I am, there you may be also" (v. 3). That coming again is the moment of the Rapture. The entire passage speaks of the Rapture as a family affair reserved solely for those who have put their faith in Jesus Christ.

Paul affirmed the selective nature of the Rapture in 1 Corinthians 15:23, where he described its participants as "those who are Christ's at His coming." Furthermore, in the first verse of that chapter, he identified his readers as "brethren," a term used in the New Testament almost exclusively to describe believers. As if intentionally removing all possibility of misunderstanding, Paul concluded this passage on the Rapture with encouragement directed specifically to the church: "Therefore, my beloved brethren, be steadfast, immovable, always abounding in the work of the Lord, knowing that your labor is not in vain in the Lord" (v. 58).

Finally, in 1 Thessalonians 4:13–18—Paul's main passage on the Rapture—he affirmed its selectivity in triplicate. First, he opened his description of the event by referring to his readers as "brethren." Second, he identified them in verse 14 as those who "believe that Jesus died and rose again." Third, in verse 16, he described the deceased family members of the Thessalonian church as dead "in Christ."

These passages leave no doubt that the Rapture is restricted exclusively to believers. Only those who are followers of Christ will be taken up into heaven when He returns. So here is my crucial question for you: Are you a follower of Christ?

THE RAPTURE IS A SPECTACULAR EVENT

No scene described in the Bible is more glorious, stunning, or sensational than the second coming of Christ. But it is usually the second stage of His coming at the end of the Tribulation that draws the spotlight. And for good reason. The apostle John's graphic description of the event is unrivaled by anything else recorded in the Bible. It staggers the most vivid imagination:

> Now I saw heaven opened, and behold, a white horse. And He who sat on him was called Faithful and True, and in righteousness He judges and makes war. His eyes were like a flame of fire, and on His head were many crowns. He had a name written that no one knew except Himself. He was clothed with a robe dipped in blood, and His name is called The Word of God. And the armies in heaven, clothed in fine linen, white and clean, followed Him on white horses. Now out of His mouth goes a sharp sword, that with it He should strike the nations. And He Himself will rule them with a rod of iron. He Himself treads the winepress of the fierceness and wrath of Almighty God. And He has on His robe and on His thigh a name written: KING OF KINGS AND LORD OF LORDS. (Revelation 19:11–16)

It is no wonder that the events surrounding the Rapture are left in the shadow. Not only is the final stage of the Second Coming a glorious spectacle, it is a worldwide event that will impact every person alive on the planet at the time. The Rapture, on the other hand, is a limited, family event that will affect only believers.

But I want to present to you my case for the spectacular nature of the Rapture. Take your seat in the jury box and judge whether I succeed. I call as my primary witness the great apostle Paul, who by the inspiration of the Holy Spirit recorded the preeminent description of the event in 1 Thessalonians 4. As exhibit A, I direct your attention to verse 16: "For the Lord Himself will descend from heaven with a shout, with the voice of an archangel, and with the trumpet of God."

Here Paul testified that the Rapture of the church would be initiated by the descent of Christ Himself. He did not describe Christ's appearance, but who can deny that the sight of Christ descending from the clouds of heaven will be spectacular? When Christ appears, three sensational and stirring sounds will reverberate through the heavens like rolling thunder—a great shout, the voice of an archangel, and the blast of a trumpet.

In my book *What in the World Is Going On?* I wrote this about those three spectacular sounds: "Some have claimed that the shout is for the church, the archangel's voice is for the Jews, and the trumpet is for all gentile believers. But these claims are mistaken. The three allusions to sounds are not to be taken as coordinate but rather as subordinate. Paul was not describing three separate sounds; he was describing only one sound in three different ways."[14]

While this is the view of many and has been my view for a number of years, as I have continued to explore the meaning of these three events, I cannot help but wonder if they will be three distinct moments that announce the Lord's coming for His people. Let's assume that these events are meant to be considered individually. What could they mean?

The Sound of the Lord's Command

The Greek word used to describe the Lord's shout "is that of a command of a military leader who comes out of his chief commander's tent and issues a command. One day the Chief Commander will come out of His heavenly tent and give *a shout*, a command for the resurrection and the translation to occur."[15]

When the Lord returns at the Rapture, the shout that believers hear will be His. Just as He stood outside the tomb of Lazarus and commanded him to come forth from the dead (John 11:43), He will command all believers whose bodies are in the grave to come forth! At the sound of that shout, Paul told us, "the dead in Christ will rise first" (1 Thessalonians 4:16).

The Sound of Michael's Voice

Ringing out along with the command of the Lord will be the thunderous voice of the archangel. We know from Scripture exactly who this archangel is. He is Michael, the only archangel named in the Bible and the chief of all the angels (Daniel 12:1; Jude 9). In the entire Bible, only two angels are identified by name: Gabriel, who told Mary that she would give birth to Jesus, is God's announcing angel. Michael is God's warring angel, a role that makes the sound of his voice at the Rapture significant:

> Angels are often used to put God's plan into motion. Michael the Archangel will be used in the case of the Rapture. The content of what the voice says is not stated. But if known military procedure can be applied to this situation, then this is simply the repetition by the sub-commander of the order (*shout*) of the chief commander. Jesus gives the *shout* or command for the program of the Rapture to begin, and it is Michael's task to set it into motion, so he repeats the command.[16]

Michael's shout at the Rapture may be his command to his legions upon legions of angelic warriors, calling them to defend believers from Satan's forces and escort them safely to heaven the moment Christ calls them from the grave.

The Sound of the Trumpet

The third sound heard at the Rapture will be "the trumpet of God." Paul referred to this blast as "the last trumpet" (1 Corinthians 15:52). Dr. John F. Walvoord explained the purpose of this trumpet using an analogy from the discipline of the ancient Roman army:

> The Rapture trumpet will call all Christians to rise from the earth to meet the Lord in the air and from there they will go to heaven, as Christ promised in John 14:3. The last trumpet for the church may be analogous to the last trumpet used in the Roman army. Soldiers were awakened by a first trumpet blast early in the morning, which served as their alarm clock. A second trumpet assembled them for instructions for the day. At the third and last trumpet they marched off to their assignments.
>
> Similarly, receiving salvation is like hearing a trumpet call. Then God's call to service is like hearing a second trumpet. And at the third or last trumpet believers will go to heaven.[17]

In summary, the first sound of the Rapture—the shout of Christ—is a call for believers to rise from the grave. The voice of the archangel is a sound of protection and safe passage. The blast of the trumpet is a call announcing the believers' reception into heaven.

All the evidence clearly shows that the Rapture of the saints will be a cosmic spectacle like nothing humans have ever seen or heard. I rest my case.

THE RAPTURE IS A SEQUENTIAL EVENT

In 1 Thessalonians 4, Paul identified five major aspects of the Rapture in their sequential order.

The Return

"At some point in the future, Jesus will come out of the Heaven of heavens and descend into the atmospheric heavens."[18] Paul specified this as the initiating event of the Rapture: "For the Lord Himself will descend from heaven with a shout, with the voice of an archangel, and with the trumpet of God" (1 Thessalonians 4:16).

In the Rapture, it is the Lord Himself who is coming. This is in keeping with the words of the two angels who spoke to the disciples at the time of Jesus' ascension: "Men of Galilee, why do you stand gazing up into heaven? This same Jesus, who was taken up from you into heaven, will so come in like manner as you saw Him go into heaven" (Acts 1:11).

If Jesus is to descend in the same manner in which He ascended, then we can certainly expect His coming to be personal and physical. It is not the Holy Spirit who is coming or even one of God's angels—it is the Lord Jesus Himself!

And when the Lord returns, He will bring with Him all of the souls of those who have died as believers. Here is what Paul wrote about that: "God will bring with Him those who sleep in Jesus" (1 Thessalonians 4:14).

The Resurrection

When Christ descends from heaven with a shout, He will begin by summoning to Himself "those who are asleep" (v. 15). Paul's terminology—"those who are asleep"—is New Testament language identifying Christians who have died. Bible writers never use the words *sleep* or *asleep* to describe the death of an unbeliever, but they use them often to describe the death of a believer. Consider these examples:

These things He said, and after that He said to them, "Our friend Lazarus *sleeps*, but I go that I may wake him up." (John 11:11)

Then [Stephen] knelt down and cried out with a loud voice, "Lord, do not charge them with this sin." And when he had said this, he fell *asleep*. (Acts 7:60)

For David, after he had served his own generation by the will of God, fell *asleep*, was buried with his fathers, and saw corruption. (13:36)

Now Christ is risen from the dead, and has become the firstfruits of those who have fallen *asleep*. (1 Corinthians 15:20)

Dr. Arnold G. Fruchtenbaum explains:

The Bible views the death of believers as a temporary suspension of physical activity until the believer awakens at the Rapture. Just as physical sleep is temporary (a temporary suspension of physical activity until one awakens, yet there is no suspension of mental activity), so is death: it is a temporary suspension of physical activity until one awakens at the resurrection. . . . There is no cessation of spirit-soul activity, only physical activity.[19]

You and I set our alarm clocks every night expecting to awaken in the morning. If we die before Christ's return, we know that one day our bodies will be awakened by the alarm clock of our Lord's coming in the clouds. At that resurrection moment, God will miraculously assemble the necessary molecules and reconstruct our physical bodies. As Paul wrote, all genetic flaws will be corrected, all illnesses healed, and all damage repaired to perfection:

The body is sown in corruption, it is raised in incorruption. It is sown in dishonor, it is raised in glory. It is sown in weakness, it is raised in power. It is sown a natural body, it is raised a spiritual body. . . . The trumpet will sound, and the dead will be raised incorruptible. (1 Corinthians 15:42–44, 52)

The Bible teaches that those who are sleeping in Jesus will not be left out of the Rapture. In fact, they will have the prominent place when Jesus comes in the skies: "We who are alive and remain until the coming of the Lord will by no means precede those who are asleep. . . . The dead in Christ will rise first" (1 Thessalonians 4:15–16).

In other words, if I am still alive when Jesus comes back, I will not ascend skyward until my parents go up. They will be "caught up" first. The Rapture is initially for those who have been saved and whose bodies are resting in the cemeteries.

The Redemption

Not only will those who have died as believers be changed as part of the resurrection, but Paul spoke of those "who are alive and remain" (v. 15). They will also be changed. That comes to us at the sure word of Paul, who wrote to his Corinthian friends: "We shall not all sleep, be we shall all be changed" (1 Corinthians 15:51).

In his letter to the Romans, Paul wrote of this change as "the redemption of our body" (Romans 8:23). In his letter to the Philippians, he described it as the moment when the Lord Jesus Christ will "transform our lowly body that it may be conformed to His glorious body" (Philippians 3:21). The apostle John said it this way: "We know that when He is revealed, we shall be like Him, for we shall see Him as He is" (1 John 3:2). What will those bodies be like? Dr. Fruchtenbaum wrote:

It is possible that information as to the nature of the new body may be gleaned from a study of the nature of the resurrected body of

Jesus. . . . We know that His voice was recognized as being the same as the one He had before His death and resurrection (Jn. 20:16). Also, His physical features were recognized, though not always immediately (Jn. 20:26–29; 21:7). It was a very real body of flesh and bone and not a mere phantom body, since it was embraceable (Jn. 20:17, 27). The resurrected Messiah was able to suddenly disappear (Lk. 24:31) and go through walls (Jn. 20:19). It was a body that was able to eat food (Lk. 24:41–43).[20]

In her book *Heaven: Your Real Home*, Joni Eareckson Tada—who, because of a diving accident, has been a quadriplegic since she was a teenager—wrote about her anticipation of this transformation:

Somewhere in my broken, paralyzed body is the seed of what I shall become. The paralysis makes what I am to become all the more grand when you contrast atrophied, useless legs against splendorous, resurrected legs. I'm convinced that if there are mirrors in heaven (and why not?), the image I'll see will be unmistakably "Joni," although a much better, brighter "Joni." So much so that it's not worth comparing. . . . I will bear the likeness of Jesus, the man from heaven.[21]

The Rapture

While raptures are extremely rare, they have happened before, and they will happen again. There are six raptures recorded and described in the Bible. Four of those raptures have already taken place, and two are yet to come.

Four Raptures that Have Already Occurred

THE RAPTURE OF ENOCH: By faith Enoch was *taken away* so that he did not see death, "and was not found, because God had *taken* him"; for before he was *taken* he had this testimony, that he pleased God. (Hebrews 11:5; see also Genesis 5:24)

THE RAPTURE OF ELIJAH: And it came to pass, when the LORD was about to *take up* Elijah into heaven by a whirlwind, that Elijah went with Elisha from Gilgal . . . [and] suddenly a chariot of fire appeared with horses of fire, and separated the two of them; and Elijah *went up* by a whirlwind into heaven. (2 Kings 2:1, 11)

THE RAPTURE OF JESUS CHRIST: And while they looked steadfastly toward heaven as He *went up*, behold, two men stood by them in white apparel, who also said, "Men of Galilee, why do you stand gazing up into heaven? This same Jesus, who was *taken up* from you into heaven, will so come in like manner as you saw Him go into heaven." (Acts 1:10–11)

She [Mary] bore a male Child who was to rule all nations with a rod of iron. And her Child was *caught up* to God and His throne. (Revelation 12:5)

THE RAPTURE OF THE APOSTLE PAUL: I know a man in Christ who fourteen years ago—whether in the body I do not know, or whether out of the body I do not know, God knows—such a one was *caught up* to the third heaven. And I know such a man—whether in the body or out of the body I do not know, God knows—how he was *caught up* into Paradise and heard inexpressible words, which it is not lawful for a man to utter. (2 Corinthians 12:2–4)

While Paul described this event in the third person, the context and other clues lead most scholars to conclude that the experience he related here was his own.

Two Raptures that Are Yet to Happen

THE RAPTURE OF THE CHURCH *(the discussion of this chapter)*: We who are alive and remain shall be *caught up* together with them in the clouds to meet the Lord in the air. And thus we shall always be with the Lord. (1 Thessalonians 4:17)

THE RAPTURE OF THE TWO WITNESSES: And they heard a loud voice from heaven saying to them, "*Come up* here." And they ascended to heaven in a cloud, and their enemies saw them. (Revelation 11:12)

So here is a summary of what happens: The Lord Jesus Christ returns from heaven, bringing the souls of those who have already died with Him. The bodies of those dead saints are resurrected and changed, and then the bodies of those Christians who are alive and remain at His coming are also changed.

When this happens, God is going to hover over this universe, and all who have accepted Jesus Christ as Savior, those who have been resurrected and those who have never died, are going to be snatched up like particles of iron drawn upward by a magnet, pulled right out of the population, suctioned off the planet. It is going to happen instantly. No time to get ready. No prelude. No preliminaries. As the old hymn says,

> *Caught up! caught up! no wing required,*
> *Caught up to Him by love inspired,*
> > *To meet Him in the air.*
> *Spurning the earth, with upward bound,*
> *Nor casting a single glance around,*
> *Nor listing a single earth-born sound,*
> > *Caught up in the radiant air.*

Caught up, with rapture and surprise,
Caught up, our fond affections rise
    Our coming Lord to meet;
Hearing the trumpet's glorious sound,
Soaring to join the rushing crowd,
Glazing beyond the parted cloud,
    Beneath His pierced feet![22]

The Reunion

The Rapture sets up a delightful series of meetings or reunions. Paul wrote, "Then we who are alive and remain shall be caught up together with them in the clouds to meet the Lord in the air. And thus we shall always be with the Lord" (1 Thessalonians 4:17).

The word *then*, which begins this passage, is an adverb of sequence. The bodies of the dead have been raised, and *then*, Paul said, here's what happens next. And what happens next is a series of three reunions:

- First, the souls that descend with Christ will be reunited with their resurrected bodies, which will ascend in the Rapture.
- Second, resurrected believers will meet living believers. It will be a reunion of saints from the church age, uniting finally as the one universal church.
- Third, these groups together will experience the joy of reunion with their Lord. They met Him first at their conversion; now they meet Him face to face.

Our reunion with Christ reflects the diplomatic protocol of antiquity. When a city welcomed a visiting dignitary, the magistrate and the visiting guest met outside the walls of the city and then returned through its gates to continue the formalities. Christ will honor us with this same kind of welcome. He will come out of heaven to greet us before taking us with Him into heaven. At that moment, our reunion will be complete. There will be no subsequent parting. We will spend eternity in uninterrupted union and communion with our Lord.

THE RAPTURE IS A STRENGTHENING EVENT

Studying the Rapture has much more purpose than just being an academic exercise to increase our Bible knowledge. It can change our lives. It gives a reason for our hope and substance to our desire. This is not merely theological jargon; it is solidly biblical and supported by many scriptures. How does our certainty of the coming of Christ affect how we live now? Let me suggest four words that summarize the answer.

Consolation

Paul explicitly communicated the truth of the Rapture to the Thessalonians so that they would not "sorrow as others who have no hope. For if we believe that Jesus died and rose again, even so God will bring with Him those who sleep in Jesus" (vv. 13–14).

Paul was telling these grieving Thessalonians that death is not final. All who die in Christ will be restored to bodily life and taken up to be with Him when He returns. The certainty of the Rapture is a great comfort to those whose loved ones have died.

What comfort do we get from our awareness of the coming Rapture? The same comfort the Jewish leader Jairus felt after Jesus raised his daughter from death. The same comfort Mary and Martha felt after He raised their brother, Lazarus, from the grave. As we lose loved ones to death, the Rapture comforts us with the same assurance of ultimate resurrection and reunion. "O death, where is your victory? O death, where is your sting?" (1 Corinthians 15:55 NLT). The promise of resurrection in the Rapture draws the poison fang from the jaw of death.

On the night before His death, Jesus told His disciples not to be troubled by his His impending absence, because He would return and take them to live with Him forever (John 14:1–3). The Rapture signals the fulfillment of His promise, which encourages us to endure as we wait and gives us strength to face whatever trials may assail us in the interim.

Paul urged us to use our knowledge of the Rapture to "comfort one another " (1 Thessalonians 4:18). He added this sentence at the end of his explanation of the Rapture. Notice that he began it with the word *therefore*, which introduces an independent result clause. In other words, "In light of what I have just told you, here is what you should do: Comfort one another." The word for *comfort* is the Greek *parakaleo*, which is written in a form that indicates continuous action.[23] We are instructed to comfort one another continually with the assurance of the Resurrection. Make it a habitual practice until the Lord returns.

Expectation

Charles Haddon Spurgeon, the great English pastor of Metropolitan Tabernacle in London, believed that the Lord could return at any time. He repeatedly urged his people to cultivate an attitude of continual expectancy. Listen to this man preach:

Oh, Beloved, let us try every morning, to get up as if that were the morning in which Christ would come! And when we go to bed at night, may we lie down with this thought, "Perhaps I shall be awakened by the ringing out of the silver trumpets heralding His Coming. Before the sun arises, I may be startled from my dreams

by the greatest of all cries, 'The Lord is come! The Lord is come!'"
What a check, what an incentive, what a bridle, what a spur such
thoughts as these would be to us! Take this for the guide of your
whole life—act as if Jesus would come in the act in which you are
engaged—and if you would not wish to be caught in that act by the
Coming of the Lord, let it not be your act.[24]

It sounds as if Spurgeon had been reading Paul's mail—particularly
his letter to the young preacher Titus:

> For the grace of God that brings salvation has appeared to all men,
> teaching us that, denying ungodliness and worldly lusts, we should
> live soberly, righteously, and godly in the present age, looking for
> the blessed hope and glorious appearing of our great God and
> Savior Jesus Christ, who gave Himself for us, that He might redeem
> us from every lawless deed and purify for Himself His own special
> people, zealous for good works. (Titus 2:11–14)

I have heard it said that when first-century Christians traveled from
city to city, they would stop at every crossroads and look in all directions, always anticipating the possibility that they might see Christ
returning. The ensuing centuries seem to have dulled that imminent
expectation, but they should not. We must ever be aware that the
Rapture could occur at any moment.

Consecration

Robert Murray M'Cheyne was a brilliant, highly influential
pastor and poet in nineteenth-century Scotland. He died of typhus
shortly before his thirtieth birthday, causing some to think his enormous potential was wasted. Yet in those brief thirty years, God used

M'Cheyne to accomplish more than most of us would ever dream in a lifetime. He wrote several books, conducted highly successful evangelistic campaigns, and set up a missionary program to reach Jews in Israel. I am told that M'Cheyne wore a special wristwatch on which he had engraved "The Night Cometh." Every time he checked his watch, he was reminded that a time was coming when he would no longer be able to spread the news of God's love. This reminder motivated him to be fervent in his witness.

The hands of time are still moving steadily toward the moment when "the night cometh." Are you working for your Lord while it is still day, or are you simply waiting passively to be rescued? Our objective as Christians is not merely to be included in the Rapture but to take as many people with us as we can.

Many New Testament passages use the impending return of the Lord to motivate us toward greater consecration and service to Him. The apostle John wrote, "Little children, abide in Him, that when He appears, we may have confidence and not be ashamed before Him at His coming" (1 John 2:28); and "Beloved, now we are children of God; and it has not yet been revealed what we shall be, but we know that when He is revealed, we shall be like Him, for we shall see Him as He is. And everyone who has this hope in Him purifies himself, just as He is pure" (3:2–3).

Dr. Walvoord amplified John's exhortation:

> The rapture not only confronts people with the challenge to receive Christ before it is too late; it also challenges Christians to live with eternal values in view. Since the Rapture can occur at any moment and believers' lives on earth will thus be cut short, we need to maximize our commitment to Christ, doing all we can for the Lord in upright living and service to Him and others.[25]

Dr. Showers concludes his book on the Rapture with these words: "The fact that the glorified, holy Son of God could step through the door of heaven at any moment is intended by God to be the most pressing, incessant motivation for holy living and aggressive ministry (including missions, evangelism, and Bible teaching) and the greatest cure for lethargy and apathy. It should make a difference in every Christian's values, actions, priorities, and goals."[26]

Examination

Suppose that the Lord Jesus chose this very moment to return. Would you be ready? Jesus warned us that He is coming quickly (Revelation 22:12). When that moment strikes, there will be no time for you to get ready for heaven. So the question you must ask is this: Have I committed myself to Jesus Christ and submitted to Him as my Lord and Savior? Everything you need to know in order to make that decision lies before you in the Bible.

After Jesus promised His disciples that He would leave to prepare a place for them and return to take them there, He added, "And where I go you know, and the way you know" (John 14:4). Immediately, His analytical "show-me" disciple, Thomas, asked, "Lord, we do not know where You are going, and how can we know the way?" (v. 5). Jesus answered with one of the most important statements in the Bible. It is heaven's answer to anyone seeking salvation from eternal death. He said, "I am the way, the truth, and the life. No one comes to the Father except through Me" (v. 6).

I will now come full circle and end this chapter where I began it, speaking of Dr. LaHaye's blockbuster, bestselling book series, Left Behind. That is not a comforting title, nor was it meant to be. In fact, it expresses the ultimate tragedy. The series tells the stories of unbelievers who have been left behind after the church has been raptured to heaven. Dr. LaHaye's intent was to show the world the seriousness of failing to be ready for the Lord's inevitable return. I urge you not to be among those who are left behind when He comes. Make today the day of your salvation! Today is your opportunity to be sure you are ready when the Rapture occurs. It could happen at any moment.

CHAPTER 10

TRANSLATED BEFORE
THE TRIBULATION

Johannes Stöffler was a highly respected scientist and religious figure in sixteenth-century Germany. He was the professor of astronomy and mathematics at the University of Tübingen and later became the university's rector. In 1499, Stöffler plotted the movements of the planets and found that in twenty-five years they would form an alignment within the constellation Pisces. Since Pisces is the sign of the fish, Stöffler concluded that the planetary conjunction within that particular astrological sign signaled the coming of a great deluge that would inundate the entire earth. He announced that the flood would begin on February 20, 1524.

Because of Stöffler's high status as a scientist, religionist, and adviser to royalty, many people in Germany and other European nations took his prediction seriously. As the predicted catastrophe drew near, pamphlets were distributed, warning people and urging them to prepare. Many people living in low areas sold their property at a loss to opportunistic skeptics. Boats were bought or built and stocked with provisions. Many abandoned their properties and camped on mountaintops.

Among the boat-builders was the German Count von Iggleheim, who constructed a three-story ark large enough for his family and the families of several friends. Before sunrise on the predicted date, Iggleheim and his entourage entered the ark as servants loaded it with survival supplies. Soon a large crowd gathered outside. It was composed mostly of curiosity seekers and flood-skeptics, some of whom mocked and jeered at the families peering out of the ark.

But the jeering turned to panic as raindrops began to fall. The crowd surged toward the craft, trampling several to death in the stampede. They pounded on the ark, demanding that Iggleheim take them on board. When he refused, mob mentality took over, and they stormed the boat, dragging the count from it and stoning him to death. Shortly afterward, the rain shower ended, and the day passed into history without another drop falling.[1]

Predictions of impending catastrophes have terrified people throughout history. Most of them, like Stöffler's, have been false. Many of us remember the Y2K scare as the year 2000 approached. Experts predicted that all computers would cease to function at midnight, December 31, 1999, because they were not programmed to handle the changeover to the number sequence of the next millennium.

On the other hand, many events have come to pass exactly as predicted. In 1783, Ezra Stiles, president of Yale University, analyzed the population growth patterns of Europe to predict that the US population would reach three hundred million by 1983.[2] He was right. In 1840, Alexis de Tocqueville accurately predicted the Cold War of the second half of the twentieth century.[3] How can we tell the false predictions from the real?

One sound measure of prophetic accuracy is the predictor's track record. By this measure, the Bible has no competitor. Every event prophesied in the Bible has occurred except those remaining to be fulfilled in the end times. The Flood of Noah, the famine in Egypt, the captivity of the Jews, their return to their homeland, the sequence of rising and falling nations from Babylon to Rome, and the destruction of Jerusalem come immediately to mind. The Bible's record of 100 percent accuracy in prophesying events of the past gives us absolute confidence in the fulfillment of those it prophesies to occur in the future.

One of the most persistent prophecies of catastrophe yet to come concerns what Bible scholars call "the Tribulation"—a period filled with unprecedented horrors, upheavals, persecutions, natural disasters, massive slaughter, and political turmoil in the years immediately prior to Christ's second coming. All who accept the authority of the Bible believe the Tribulation will occur. And the spiraling chaos of today's world leads many to fear that it may be upon us and that they might soon be trapped in that horrific period with no way of escape.

Is that a realistic possibility? In this chapter, I will give you a biblical answer to that question.

THE PICTURE OF THE TRIBULATION

I have found that many people wonder just what the Tribulation is, or even what the word means. Their perplexity gives us a good place to start. The word is little used in ordinary conversation today. Most of us are aware of it only because of its use in the Bible. *Tribulation* is translated from the Greek *thlipsis*, a term designating the giant weight used to crush grain into flour.[4] So the idea behind *tribulation* is utterly crushing, pulverizing, or grinding a substance into powder.

Many of the modern Bible translations no longer use the term, choosing alternatives more common in today's language such as *affliction, persecution, trouble, suffering, misery, distress,* or *oppression.* Its most common use today is as a technical term to designate a specific traumatic event prophesied in the Bible to occur at an unspecified time in the future. That event—the Tribulation—is one of the prominent features of the prophetic end times.

Let's explore what the Bible tells us about this terrible time.

The Surprise of the Tribulation

In his first letter to the church in Thessalonica, the apostle Paul described the event that will signal the beginning of the Tribulation Period (1 Thessalonians 4:13–18). We have come to call this initiating event "the Rapture of the church"—the moment when Christ appears, raises the godly dead, and draws living Christians from the earth to be with Him. The next natural question for Paul's readers would have been, "When will this happen?" Paul anticipated the question and began chapter 5 with these words: "But concerning the times and the seasons, brethren, you have no need that I should write to you. For you yourselves know perfectly that the day of the Lord so comes as a thief in the night" (vv. 1–2).

"The day of the Lord includes everything that happens from the Rapture all the way through the Tribulation and the Millennium."[5] Paul was saying that you cannot know when the Rapture will occur any more than you can know when a thief is planning to ransack your house. No thief sends a letter announcing that he will arrive tomorrow night at 2:00 a.m. We are not given the ETA of the Rapture. It will come upon us unexpectedly, and the Tribulation will follow immediately in its wake.

The Severity of the Tribulation

Nowhere in all Scripture will you find one word or description that says anything good about the Tribulation Period (unless it is the promise that it will end after seven years). Moses called it "the day of their calamity" (Deuteronomy 32:35). Zephaniah said it was "the day of the LORD's anger" (Zephaniah 2:2). Paul referred to it as "the wrath to come" (1 Thessalonians 1:10). John called it "the hour of trial" (Revelation 3:10) and "the hour of His judgment" (14:7). Daniel described it as "a time of trouble, such as never was since there was a nation" (Daniel 12:1). According to the prophet Zephaniah,

> That day is a day of wrath,
> A day of trouble and distress,
> A day of devastation and desolation,
> A day of darkness and gloominess,
> A day of clouds and thick darkness,
> A day of trumpet and alarm
> Against the fortified cities
> And against the high towers. (Zephaniah 1:15–16)

Jesus told us that the Tribulation will be a time of terror and horror without precedent: "For then there will be great tribulation, such as has not been since the beginning of the world until this time, no, nor ever shall be. And unless those days were shortened, no flesh would be saved; but for the elect's sake those days will be shortened" (Matthew 24:21–22).

The central chapters of Revelation give us a vivid description of the horrors of the Tribulation Period. Great wars will ravage the world as nations rise up, lusting for conquest. All peace will end, and rampant slaughter will bloody the earth. Hail and fire will burn up the earth's grass and destroy a third of all trees. Intense famine will dry up food supplies. Rivers and seas will become too polluted to sustain life. Many rivers will dry up entirely. The sun will scorch the earth and its inhabitants like fire. A quarter of the world's population will die from war, starvation, and beastly predators. Giant earthquakes, accompanied by thunder and lightning, will destroy cities. Mountains will crash into the seas, killing a third of the fish. Tidal waves from the cataclysm will sink a third of all the world's ships. A massive meteor shower will strike the earth. Ashes and smoke rising from its devastation will hide the sun and moon. Swarms of demonic insects will darken the sun and inflict painful stings. Rampant, epidemic plagues will kill one-third of all mankind. Everyone, from national leaders to servants and slaves, will flee the cities to hide in caves and under rocks (Revelation 6:2–17; 8:8–13; 9:1–20; 16:1–21).

To make matters even worse, a maniacal despot known as the Antichrist will rise to power. He will be multiple times more demonic than Antiochus IV, Nero, Stalin, and Hitler combined. He will demand total allegiance to his satanically inspired program, and those who resist will be barred from buying or selling food or any other product. His lust for power will not cease until the entire civilized world chokes in his tyrannical grasp (13:1–18).

It is not an overstatement to say that the Tribulation will be hell on earth, from which Dr. J. Dwight Pentecost tells us there will be no escape and no relief: "No passage can be found to alleviate to any degree whatsoever the severity of this time that shall come upon the earth."[6]

When people today see the order and stability they have known begin to crumble, they naturally become anxious. Does this mean the end times are upon us? Does the rise of Russia, the isolation of Israel, the terror of ISIS, the chaos of immigration, and the rising persecution of Christians mean the Tribulation Period is imminent? Does it mean that we who know and love Jesus Christ are destined to endure this time? Or is there some way we can be delivered from it? Let's begin to uncover the answers to these questions.

THE PURPOSE OF THE TRIBULATION

The Tribulation will be brought on the earth by man's increasing rebellion and rampant sin. But God's hand will be heavily involved, just as it was when He brought the plagues on the rebellious nation of Egypt. The Tribulation is a planned program designed to accomplish two important goals.

The Tribulation Will Purify Israel

The Jewish nation exists as a result of God's promise to Abraham that his seed would be as numerous as the stars in heaven and would endure throughout all eternity (Genesis 12:1–3; 15:5). The Jewish nation has tested God's patience throughout the many centuries of its existence, turning away from Him time and time again. But despite Israel's persistent rebellion, God will keep His promise, not only because He is God and does not break His promises but also because of His deep love for Israel.

One of the last phases of His promise to Israel was fulfilled in 1948, when the nation was reestablished on its originally promised land. Yet after all God's care to preserve the scattered Jews through the centuries, enabling them to remain intact so they could inherit their land, they remain rebellious even today. The first purpose of the Tribulation is to purge out the Jewish rebels and bring about the final conversion of the nation. The Tribulation will be the fire that purifies Israel by burning out all the dross and impurities. As the prophet Ezekiel recorded, "I will make you pass under the rod. . . . I will purge the rebels from among you, and those who transgress against Me" (Ezekiel 20:37–38).

Moses also wrote of Israel's purging in the last days and urged the nation to respond by turning back to God:

When you are in distress, and all these things come upon you in the latter days, when you turn to the LORD your God and obey His voice (for the LORD your God is a merciful God), He will not forsake you nor destroy you, nor forget the covenant of your fathers which He swore to them. (Deuteronomy 4:30–31)

The apostle Paul left no ambiguity as to whether this purging prophesied by Moses and Ezekiel would be effective:

And so all Israel will be saved, as it is written:

"The Deliverer will come out of Zion,
And He will turn away ungodliness from Jacob;
For this is My covenant with them,
When I take away their sins." (Romans 11:26–27)

The Tribulation Will Punish Sinners

The overall purpose of the Tribulation will be to execute God's wrath upon those who oppose Him—first upon the Jews who have rebelled, as we have already shown, and then upon the rebellious Gentiles. As Paul wrote, "For the wrath of God is revealed from heaven against all ungodliness and unrighteousness of men, who suppress the truth in unrighteousness" (Romans 1:18).

We like to think and speak about the love of God, but not so much about His wrath. But wrath goes hand in hand with judgment, and it is as much an expression of His goodness as His love. In fact, love and wrath are two sides of the same coin. One who is infinitely good, as God is, rightly abhors evil because evil is the enemy of goodness. Evil is, in fact, like a parasite, a blight, or a cancer on goodness. It feeds on and, thus, destroys good. Therefore, God rightly directs His wrath at evil:

The biblical doctrine of God's wrath is rooted in the doctrine of God as the good, wise and loving creator, who hates—yes, hates, and hates implacably—anything that spoils, defaces, distorts, or damages his beautiful creation, and in particular anything that does that to his image-bearing creatures. If God does not hate racial prejudice, he is neither good nor loving. If God is not wrathful at child abuse, he is neither good nor loving. If God is not utterly determined to root out from his creation, in an act of proper wrath and judgment, the arrogance that allows people to exploit, bomb, bully and enslave one another, he is neither loving, nor good, nor wise.[7]

The prophet Nahum explained the nature of God's wrath in this way:

> The LORD avenges and is furious.
> The LORD will take vengeance on His adversaries,
> And He reserves wrath for His enemies;
> The LORD is slow to anger and great in power,
> And will not at all acquit the wicked. (Nahum 1:2–3)

To sum it up, the overall purpose of the seven-year Tribulation Period is to expose unregenerate people, both Jews and Gentiles, to the wrath of God. Just as the sun hardens clay and softens butter, God's wrath will harden some hearts and soften others. This shows us that the purpose of the Tribulation includes both conversion and punishment, depending essentially on how the objects of God's wrath respond to it.

THE PERSPECTIVES ON THE TRIBULATION

How will the Tribulation affect the church? Scholars of biblical prophecy answer this question in different ways. There are three basic viewpoints, each of which places the tribulation at a different point in time.

Posttribulationism, as the word itself indicates, teaches that the Rapture of the church will occur *after* the seven-year Tribulation Period. This means Christians will be left on earth to endure all the terrors of the Tribulation along with the unbelievers. They will be taken up to be with Christ when the Tribulation ends at His second coming.

Midtribulationism teaches that the church will be raptured at the halfway point of the seven-year Tribulation period. In this view, Christians escape the last three-and-a-half years of it, which is when the very worst of the Tribulation disasters will occur.

Pretribulationism teaches that the Rapture will take place before the Tribulation. This means the church will be removed from the earth before the Tribulation begins, sparing Christians from enduring any part of the seven-year barrage of God's wrath to be poured out upon the earth.

THE PROTECTION FROM THE TRIBULATION

I firmly believe that pretribulationism is the accurate perspective on the timing of end-time events. This means the church will not suffer any of the terrible miseries of the Tribulation. The Bible gives us at least five reasons why believers can be assured of God's protection from this coming onslaught of His wrath.

Our Protection Is Affirmed by Christ's Promise

The clearest teaching on the believers' deliverance from the Tribulation comes to us from Christ's letter to the church in the Asia Minor city of Philadelphia: "Because you have kept My command to persevere, I also will keep you from the hour of trial which shall come upon the whole world, to test those who dwell on the earth" (Revelation 3:10).

Let's delve a little deeper into this clear promise of Christ to show what it means to us today.

The Promise Is Comprehensive

This promise goes much farther than merely protecting believers from the devastation and misery going on around them. Daniel 3 shows us an example of that kind of protection. The three Hebrew captives—Shadrach, Meshach, and Abed-Nego—were cast into a fiery furnace for upholding their faith, but God kept them safe from the flames roaring about them. Although the fire did not harm them, we read that they were *in* the fire and that they walked *through* the fire. But Jesus' promise goes further: Believers will not even be *in* the Tribulation, nor will they have to go *through* it. He told us that the church will be kept "*from* the hour of trial."

The Promise Is Clear

The fact that Christ promised to keep the church from "the hour of trial" is highly significant. Prophetic scholar Mark Hitchcock explains: "The Lord promises to keep his people not just from the testing but from 'the hour of testing.' God's people are exempt not just from the trials during the Tribulation but from the very Tribulation itself. We are removed from the whole period of time, not just the trials of it."[8]

Charles Ryrie, who was one of my professors at Dallas Theological Seminary, has given us a vivid illustration of this truth from a teacher's viewpoint:

> As a teacher, I frequently give exams. Let's suppose that I announce an exam will occur on such and such a day at the regular class time.

Then suppose I say, "I want to make a promise to students whose grade average for the semester so far is A. The promise is: I will keep you from the exam."

Now I could keep my promise to those A students this way: I would tell them to come to the exam, pass out the exam to everyone, and give the A students a sheet containing the answers. They would take the exam and yet in reality be kept from the exam. They would live through the time but not suffer the trial. This is posttribulationism: protection while enduring.

But if I said to the class, "I am giving an exam next week. I want to make a promise to all the A students. I will keep you from the hour of the exam." They would understand clearly that to be kept from the hour of the test exempts them from being present during that hour. This is pretribulationism, and this is the meaning of the promise of Revelation 3:10. And the promise came from the risen Savior who Himself is the deliverer of the wrath to come (1 Thessalonians 1:10).[9]

God knows that if He left His church on earth, even though He would protect us from actual harm, we would be deeply grieved by the suffering and devastation around us. Therefore, in His mercy and love, He will remove us from the scene entirely when the Tribulation comes.

Our Protection Is in Accord with Biblical Precedent

Throughout all Scripture we see God protecting His people by removing them prior to His judgment against the evil surrounding them.

- Enoch was transferred to heaven before the judgment of the Flood.
- Noah and his family were safely enclosed within the ark before the judgment of the Flood.

- Lot and his family were taken out of Sodom before judgment destroyed Sodom and Gomorrah.
- The firstborn among the Hebrews in Egypt were sheltered by the blood of the Paschal Lamb before judgment decimated the firstborn of the Egyptians.
- The Israelite spies were safely out of Jericho before judgment fell on that city.

The apostle Peter held up these incidents of God's protection as assurance that what He did for those heroes, He will also do for us:

> If God . . . did not spare the ancient world, but saved Noah . . . and turning the cities of Sodom and Gomorrah into ashes . . . delivered righteous Lot . . . then the Lord knows how to deliver the godly out of temptations and to reserve the unjust under punishment for the day of judgment. (2 Peter 2:4–7, 9)

It is easy to see the consistent pattern presented in these examples: God rescues the righteous before punishing the wicked. He allows the righteous and the wicked to live together in the world prior to judgment, as Jesus explained in the parable of the farmer allowing weeds to grow together with his wheat. But when harvest time comes, the wheat will be separated out before the weeds are cast into the fire (Matthew 13:24–30).

After Paul explained the Rapture in 1 Thessalonians 4, he added this significant phrase: "Therefore comfort one another with these words" (v. 18). There would be no comfort whatsoever in Paul's words if the church was not to be removed until after it had endured the misery of the Tribulation. The only way the term *comfort* makes sense is for the Rapture to occur before the Tribulation. The pretribulation perspective validates the logical purpose of the Rapture.

Our Protection Is Apparent in the Book of Revelation

Several passages throughout the Bible describe the events that will occur during the Tribulation Period. These descriptions occur in the writings of various Old Testament prophets, in the words of Christ Himself in Matthew 24, and in brief references here and there in other books of the Bible. But it is the book of Revelation that describes the Tribulation events in the greatest detail.

You have probably heard all your life that the book of Revelation is the most difficult and confusing book in the entire Bible. I am going to turn that claim on its head and tell you that Revelation is one of the easiest books to understand. We tend to make it complex because we bring to it so much interpretive baggage based on the many theories, doctrines, and distortions thrown at us by various interpreters.

But the book becomes much simpler if you just let it interpret itself. It's like the backwoods man who purchased his first chainsaw. After one day of woodcutting, he took it back to the store, complaining it was too hard to use and would barely cut wood.

"What happened when you started the engine?" asked the salesman.

"Started the engine? What do you mean?" responded the customer.

"You mean you never turned the saw on? No wonder it was so hard to use!" exclaimed the salesman. "If you turn the engine on, you don't have to work to cut wood. The saw will do it for you."

If you let it, Revelation will do the interpreting for you because it is, in fact, a self-interpreting book. The first chapter gives us an outline of its entire structure. At the outset, John the apostle saw the vision of Christ, who told him to "Write the things which you have seen, and the things which are, and the things which will take place after this" (1:19). Here we have the outline—the headings of the three major sections of the book: the things you have seen, the things which are, and the things that are to come.

1. **"The things which you have seen."**

   This short section covers Revelation 1:1–20. Here we have the record of the vision John saw while on the isle of Patmos. He told of worshipping on the Lord's Day when he heard the blast of a trumpet and turned to see the glorious figure of Christ, which he described in magnificent detail. Christ spoke and explained the meaning of the symbols surrounding Him.

2. **"The things which are."**

   This section includes the next two chapters, Revelation 2–3, which contain seven letters to the seven churches of Asia Minor. John served as the primary leader of these churches before his exile to Patmos. These chapters deal with the "things which are." Each letter describes the spiritual health of a given church, accompanied by commendations, reprimands, warnings, and rebukes.

3. **"The things which will take place after this."**

   This section begins with Revelation 4 and continues through the end of the book. These chapters detail events that will take place in the future. Almost everything in Revelation 4–19 has to do with the Tribulation, describing in great detail the pouring out of God's wrath upon the earth. Most of this description occurs in the three "judgment" accounts—the "Seal Judgments," which include the infamous four horsemen of the Apocalypse; the "Trumpet Judgments"; and the "Bowl Judgments." These sequences project horrifying pictures of the Tribulation using a sort of split-screen technique, showing the inception of the judgments in heaven and their devastating results on earth. Included in this third and final futuristic section are the final victory of Christ over Satan, the reuniting of heaven and earth, and the glory of the thousand-year reign of Christ.

Do you know what is conspicuously absent from these Tribulation chapters? The church. The word *church* appears nineteen times in Revelation 1–3, but it is not mentioned once in Revelation 4–19. Why? Because the church is not there. It is no longer on the earth. Believers have been removed from the Tribulation and taken into heaven.

Masters Seminary professor Richard Mayhue has observed:

> It is remarkable and totally unexpected that John would shift from detailed instructions for the church to absolute silence about the church . . . if, in fact, the church continued into the tribulation. If the church will experience the tribulation . . . then surely the most detailed study of tribulation events would include an account of the church's role. But it doesn't![10]

There is no account of the church's role during the Tribulation because the church has no role in the Tribulation. As we noted earlier, the Tribulation Period marks the final application of God's wrath upon Israel's transgressions (Ezekiel 20:37–38). God's wrath is reserved for apostate Israel—those He nurtured and cherished, yet they departed from Him. The Tribulation is essentially a family matter between Israel and God, and the faithful church need not endure the fallout. According to Hitchcock, "The whole Tribulation period is the outpouring of God's wrath; this requires that Christ's bride be exempt from this entire time of trouble, not just some part of it." He adds, "What is it about the Tribulation that necessitates our absence from this time? The Tribulation is the product of God's wrath upon wickedness. The book of Revelation clearly refers to God's wrath at least seven times (6:17–18; 14:8–10; 14:19; 15:7; 16:1, 19; 19:15). The wrath of God commences with the first seal (Revelation 6:1) and continues all the way until the Second Coming (Revelation 19:11–21)."[11]

In none of this are we saying that the church, God's people on earth, are exempt from suffering and persecution. As I have noted in chapter 3 of this book, persecution of Christians has been pervasive throughout history and is increasing in our time. Much of the New Testament is comprised of warnings of suffering and encouragement for those going through it. Paul summed up this fact in his second letter to Timothy: "All who desire to live godly in Christ Jesus will suffer persecution" (3:12). Jesus told His disciples, "Here on earth you will have many trials and sorrows. But take heart, because I have overcome the world" (John 16:33 NLT).

Yet in all the New Testament, there is not one single statement to warn Christians of the coming Great Tribulation or to help them prepare for it. If it were our lot to endure the wrath that will devastate the earth during those seven years, isn't it strange that God never gave us one tidbit of information, encouragement, warning, or instruction on our preparation for it? The reason for that omission is clear: The church will not be present at all when the Tribulation comes.

Our Protection Is Assured by God's Love

Paul assured his readers that once they become Christians, they have no more need to fear God's judgment: "There is therefore now no condemnation to those who are in Christ Jesus" (Romans 8:1). We have learned already that part of the purpose of the Tribulation is to execute God's wrath on those who reject Him. By simple logic, then, we can see why believers are to be spared the Tribulation. What would be the point of having them endure it? By turning to God, they render themselves exempt from the whole purpose of those horrific seven years. Their rebellion has been forgiven, and they have no need to be purged of it or punished for it.

The Bible is filled with scriptures telling us that God's wrath is strictly reserved for those who do not follow Him.

> We all once conducted ourselves in the lusts of our flesh, fulfilling the desires of the flesh and of the mind, and were by nature children of wrath, just as the others. But God, who is rich in mercy, because of His great love with which He loved us, even when we were dead in trespasses, made us alive together with Christ (by grace you have been saved). (Ephesians 2:3–5)

> Much more then, having now been justified by His blood, we shall be saved from wrath through Him. (Romans 5:9)

When God put Jesus on the cross, He exacted from Him the full penalty due for our sin. We have nothing left to pay. But if we who have been cleansed by the blood of Christ are put through the Tribulation, which is a time of punitive judgment from God, it would mean that the price that Christ paid on the cross was not enough—that we still need the additional penalty of God's punitive wrath. The whole idea negates the efficacy of Christ's sacrifice for our sins. Did the cross save us from wrath or not? Did it save us from condemnation or not? Did it save us from the judgment of God or not? Certainly it did! J. F Strombeck wrote:

> One is forced to ask, how could the Lamb of God die and rise again to save the Church from wrath and then allow her to pass through the wrath that He shall pour upon those who reject Him? Such inconsistency might be possible in the thinking of men, but not in the acts of the Son of God.[12]

The Tribulation is for those who are in darkness, not for those in the light. As Paul put it, "God did not appoint us to wrath, but to obtain salvation through our Lord Jesus Christ" (1 Thessalonians 5:9). The salvation Paul spoke of in this particular passage is not salvation from our sin, but salvation or deliverance from the Tribulation Period by translation into heaven.

Dr. John F. Walvoord adds, "Paul is expressly saying that our appointment is to be caught up to be with Christ; the appointment of the world is for the Day of the Lord, the day of wrath. One cannot keep both of these appointments."[13]

The unsaved will keep the appointment with the day of wrath—the Tribulation. The saved will keep the appointment with Christ when we are drawn from the earth in the pretribulation Rapture.

Our Protection Is Accomplished by Christ's Sacrifice

What qualifies us to be spared the traumas of the Tribulation? We can say that being a Christian, following Christ, submitting our lives to Him, or trusting Him as our Savior qualifies us. All of these answers are true, but they do not tell the whole story. To see the complete picture, we need to look behind these truths, where we will find a central truth that is much deeper and more profound. If trusting Christ as our Savior qualifies us for the Rapture, we must know what it means to call Christ our Savior. What did He do to earn that title? What is there about His being our Savior that exempts us from the Tribulation?

Christ is our Savior because He paid an enormous price to save us from the eternal doom we deserved because of our sin. We accept that gift by putting our trust in Him, and when we make that commitment, He accepts us as His own. That is what it means to be His church—to be those He will exempt from the wrath of the Tribulation and bring into heaven with Him.

The following story helps us to understand what it means to call Christ our Savior. It is adapted from a story frequently told by Dr. R. G. Lee, former president of the Southern Baptist Convention and longtime pastor of a large and influential church in Memphis, Tennessee.

A century ago in a backwater village deep in the mountains of Virginia, there was a community school consisting of a single room. Students of all grades attended the school, mostly the children of mining or logging families. The older boys, raised to survive the hardscrabble life of the mountains, were tough and mean-spirited. No teacher at the school had lasted more than two months—some only a few days—because these boys took great pride in their ability to run off every teacher daring or naïve enough to take the job.

Shortly after yet another teacher had left, a young man fresh out of teachers' college applied for the job. The moment he walked into the office for an interview, the director took pity on him. He did not want this young, green teacher to face impossible odds and end his first teaching assignment in discouragement.

"I frankly advise you not to take this job," said the director. "You have no idea what you'll be up against. We've never had a teacher last more than two months—not even the most experienced. You will likely take an awful beating because you are so young."

"I do appreciate the warning, sir," replied the teacher, "but I need the job, and I'm willing to take the risk."

The director sighed deeply and hired him.

The next morning, the young teacher sat at his desk watching the students as they came into the classroom. Several of the boys gathered at the back before they took their seats. It was clear to the teacher that their leader was the biggest and obviously the oldest boy. Big Tom, they called him: the bully of the class. The boys were talking in low tones among themselves, looking often toward the teacher. Finally, Big Tom said—deliberately loud enough for the teacher to overhear—"I don't need no help on this one. When I get done with him, he won't dare set foot in this classroom again."

When all the students were seated, the teacher rose and said, "Good morning. I'm Mr. Wilson, your new teacher. I can't teach without order, and we can't have order without rules. So I want you to help me make the rules. Tell me what rules you think we ought to have, and I will list them on the blackboard."

The class had never been asked to participate in establishing order, and Big Tom didn't know what to make of it. He decided to wait and see how it all came out before he put the screws on the new teacher.

"No stealin'," called out a student.

Mr. Wilson wrote the rule on the board.

"No bein' late," cried another.

"No lyin'," rang out a third voice.

The students began to get into the swing of things, and soon Mr. Wilson had ten rules on the board. "This looks like a good set of rules," he said. "They are your own rules, so do all of you agree to them?"

"Sure, we agree to them," the class replied, snickering and looking slyly at one another.

"Okay," continued Mr. Wilson, "Rules can't be enforced without penalties for breaking them. What penalty should we impose if a rule is broken?"

Big Tom spoke up: "Whoever breaks a rule gets ten licks across his bare back." Making a tough rule bolstered his pugnacious reputation.

Mr. Wilson thought the penalty was too severe. "Does everyone agree to this penalty?" he asked. No one dared counter Big Tom, and since the teacher had put the rule-making process into the students' hands, he felt he had to let the penalty stand. "Very well. Ten licks it will be."

Big Tom's involvement in the process made him feel big enough that he didn't bother Mr. Wilson that day. Class resumed the next morning and went smoothly until the noon bell was about to ring. Big Tom's voice boomed out, "Somebody stole my lunch!"

"Keep your seats, class," said the teacher. "No one eats until we find out who stole Tom's lunch." He questioned each member of the class, one by one, and all denied committing the theft. But finally, a little ten-year-old boy wearing a worn-out coat wailed, "I done it. It was me. I was so hungry I couldn't help myself. I'm sorry!"

Mr. Wilson's heart sank. "Jimmy, you know the rule. I have to give you ten licks across the back. Take off your coat."

"Oh, teacher, please!" Jimmy begged. "Do whatever you got to do, but don't make me take off my coat."

But the teacher was firm, and the boy slowly began to unbutton his coat as tears streamed down his cheeks. He was wearing no shirt. There was nothing on his thin upper body but the suspenders holding up his pants.

Mr. Wilson faced a hard dilemma. *How can I possibly whip this poor child?* he thought. *But if I don't, I will forever lose control of this class.* He stalled and asked, "Jimmy, why didn't you wear a shirt today?"

"It's 'cause Mom's been real poor since Dad got killed in the mine. I only got one shirt. On washday Mom washes it, and I have to wear my brother's coat. I'll get my shirt back tomorrow."

It was all Mr. Wilson could do to make himself pick up the paddle. He turned Jimmy's scrawny back to him, lifted the paddle, and hesitated, trying to work up the courage to administer the punishment.

Suddenly Big Tom jumped up and cried, "Don't do it, Mr. Wilson.

I wanna take Jimmy's lickin' for him." He walked quickly to the front of the classroom, stripping off his shirt as he went.

The teacher nodded, handed Jimmy his coat, and stood Big Tom in his place. As he administered the strokes, he realized that every child in the room was crying—little Jimmy most of all. Suddenly the boy ran to Big Tom, threw his thin arms around his neck and clung to him.

"Oh, Tom," Jimmy cried, "I'm so sorry I stole your lunch. I hate that I done this to you. But I want you to know that I'll love you till my dyin' day for takin' the lickin' I should've got."

The hearts of those hardened boys were broken forever. Big Tom had become little Jimmy's savior.

This story is a picture of what it means to call Jesus our Savior. All of us have broken the rules, and we deserve the prescribed punishment, which, in our case, is death. But Jesus looked on us frail, fallen creatures and could not stand to see us destroyed. He loved us so much that He could not bear the thought of spending eternity without us. So He took off His coat—the one His executioners gambled for—stretched His arms over the wooden bar of the cross, and suffered the punishment of death that you and I deserve. He is our Savior.[14]

You may be reading this chapter as an unbeliever, perhaps out of simple curiosity. You have never recognized Christ as your Lord or submitted your life to Him. You may or may not have grasped everything you have read here, but I hope you can at least see that God will bring about an end to the chaos of this sin-damaged world and restore His perfect rule over it. He wants you to be a part of that new beginning. He has delayed His return for centuries to give you, and others like you, the opportunity to come to Him before the door closes, which will inevitably happen either at His return or at your own death.

Pastor Steven Cole tells the story of Joe, who, by his own admission, was not a religious man. He drank too much, gambled, swore like a sailor, and lied and cheated to get what he wanted. God was not a part of his thoughts or life.

Joe finally retired. He relished the prospect of spending his days on the lake fishing. But a persistent pain in his stomach drove him to the doctor. His greatest fear was that he would be forced to stop drinking, but the doctor's report was even worse: It was cancer, and it had spread beyond control. The doctor gave Joe less than six months to live.

While Joe was in the hospital, a pastor dropped by and talked with him about eternity. For the first time in his life, Joe listened. A long-suppressed truth awoke in Joe's heart, convicting him of squandering his entire life in utterly selfish pursuits. He trembled, knowing he would soon face God's judgment. But the pastor explained how Christ had paid the penalty for Joe's sin, and on that basis, He offered forgiveness and eternal life if Joe would only receive it. Joe gladly accepted the gift and died in peace shortly afterward.[15]

Joe's case was what we commonly call "deathbed repentance." It is neither the most noble nor the safest way to come to Christ. But God, in His infinite love and desire to have us with Him throughout eternity, accepts even those who come in at the last minute. Jesus promised salvation even to the thief who was dying on the cross next to Him (Luke 23:39–43). In His parable of the workers in the vineyard, the master paid the workers who had come in at the last hour of the day as much as those who came in at the first hour (Matthew 20:1–16). Our God gives us better than we deserve. He is a merciful God who is "longsuffering toward us, not willing that any should perish but that all should come to repentance" (2 Peter 3:9). But He never forces us to come to Him; the choice is always ours.

The important thing to note is that Joe came to Christ because he saw the signs that his end was near. Deathbed repentance though it was, he did the wise thing: He acted on what he knew and took the right step in the face of it. It was late, but not too late.

The time is coming and now looms on the horizon when it will be too late. When the Tribulation arrives and God's people are taken into heaven, the door will close on those who have heard and rejected the gospel. I urge you to take the step that Joe took today, while the Tribulation is still just an approaching shadow and not the dooming finality of God's wrath. God's grace is available to rescue you from that wrath, so there is no need to despair. But there is a sense of urgency to His offer. Act now, and you need have no concern about being caught in the Tribulation.

ACKNOWLEDGMENTS

This book is the most challenging writing project I have ever undertaken, and were it not for the people I am about to mention, there is no way it could ever have been accomplished. When I set about to research and write about ten of the most significant issues facing our culture, I actually took on ten projects instead of one. Thanks to my wife, Donna, I did not give up hope. For fifty-three years we have been believing in each other, and together we have continued to believe God for the impossible.

When a book like this is conceived and has to be completed in a few short months, there can be no detours, no delays. Diane Sutherland helps me stay on mission as she manages the many pieces of my busy life so that writing can continue to be a top priority. Diane, all of us who get to work with you agree: you are amazing!

Barbara Boucher keeps everything running smoothly in my office at Shadow Mountain Community Church. After twenty-two years of service, she has decided to retire so she can spend more time with her grandchildren. Barbara, I am so grateful to you for all you have done behind the scenes to enable me to fulfill my calling as a pastor and writer. You will be greatly missed.

My annual book project has its home in the ministry of Turning Point radio and television. My son, David Michael, is vice president and director of operations at Turning Point, and he is vitally involved with each book that I write. Besides managing day-to-day operations, David also plans and directs our arena events which feature each new book we release. Working with my son is one of the great blessings of my life.

The Creative Department of Turning Point has made the release of this book the main focus of their collective efforts for the six months that precede its release. I never cease to be amazed at the ideas God gives to Paul Joiner and his team and their ability to bring those ideas to life.

If you examine the notes section at the end of this book, you will get a pretty clear picture of the amount of research that has gone into this project. For the last several years Beau Sager has been my research assistant. Beau, your commitment to excellence is evident to us all, and we are so thankful for your sacrificial investment in *Is This the End?*

Rob Morgan and William Kruidenier have to be two of the most well-read men in America. Thanks to both of you for your investment in this book. Tom Williams always makes our books his number one priority, and without him I am certain we could not have made our deadline. Tom, you are far more than an editor and a gifted wordsmith; you are a valued member of our publishing team.

As the publishing world continues to grow more complex and challenging, I am blessed to have the counsel and direction that come from the firm of Yates and Yates. For more than thirty years Sealy Yates has been my literary agent and my good friend.

I also want to express my gratitude to the people at Thomas Nelson. From our very first meeting in Nashville to discuss this book, publisher Matt Baugher and his team have demonstrated their deep commitment to get this book into the hands and hearts of as many people as possible.

Finally, whatever glory comes from this endeavor belongs exclusively to Jesus Christ. He alone is worthy!

NOTES

Introduction

1. Elizabeth Thom, "New Survey Reveals an Anxious and Nostalgic America Going into the 2016 Election," Brookings, November 18, 2015, http://www .brookings.edu/blogs/fixgov/posts/2015/11/18-american-values-survey -release-thom.

Chapter 1: The Age of Anything Goes

1. Erin Strecker, "Tony Bennett Says Another Lady Gaga Collaboration Album Is Coming," *Billboard*, October 22, 2015, billboard.com/articles/columns /pop-shop/6738127/tony-bennett-lady-gaga-collaboration-album-cole -porter.

2. "Amazon Music Q&A: Lady Gaga & Tony Bennett Talk 'Magical' Duets Album, 'Cheek to Cheek,'" accessed March 11, 2016, www.amazonfrontrow .com/post/100776560575/amazon-music-qa-lady-gaga-tony-bennett-talk.

3. William McBrien, *Cole Porter* (New York: Vintage Books, 1998), 394–95. See also Dan Barker, "Cole Porter out of Both Closets?," *Freedom from Religion Foundation*, October 2004, ffrf.org/faq/feeds/item/18440-cole-porter-out -of-both-closets.

4. Sheila Johnston, "How Cole Porter Got His Kicks," *The Telegraph*, September 24, 2004, telegraph.co.uk/culture/film/3624393/How-Cole- Porter-got-his-kicks.html.

5. Cy Feuer with Ken Gross, *I Got the Show Right Here: The Amazing, True Story of How an Obscure Brooklyn Horn Player Became the Last Great Broadway Showman* (New York: Applause Theatre and Cinema Books, 2003), 159–60.

6. McBrien, 394.

7. Ibid., 395.

8. George Eells, *The Life That Late He Led: A Biography of Cole Porter* (New York: G. P. Putnam's Sons, 1967), 312.

9. Jeff Kinley, *As It Was in the Days of Noah: Warnings from Bible Prophecy About the Coming Global Storm* (Eugene: Harvest House, 2014), 15–16.

10. David Jeremiah, *I Never Thought I'd See the Day!: Culture at the Crossroads* (New York: Faith Words, 2011), 126–27.

11. Charles R. Swindoll, *Growing Deep in the Christian Life: Essential Truths for Becoming Strong in the Faith* (Grand Rapids: Zondervan, 1995), 204.

12. J. Dwight Pentecost, *Things Which Become Sound Doctrine: Doctrinal Studies of Fourteen Crucial Words of Faith* (Grand Rapids: Kregel, Inc., 1965), 10.

13. Jonathon van Maren, "I Thought the Porn Industry Couldn't Shock Me Any More. Then PornHub Released Their 2015 Stats," January 13, 2016, www.lifesitenews.com/blogs/pornhub-just-released-their-2015 -statistics.-and-its-sickening.

14. Cited by Harry Leibowitz, World of Children Award Co-Founder and Board Chairman, in "The Numbers: Child Sexual Imposition in the United States," *Huffpost Impact*, February 12, 2016, www.huffingtonpost .com/harry-leibowitz/the-numbers-child-sexual-_b_9101508.html.

15. Leif Coorlim, "Injured U.S. Vets Now Hunting Child Predators," CNN, February 29, 2016, updated April 4, 2016, www.cnn.com/2016/02/29/us /freedom-project-hero-corps/index.html?eref=rss_topstories.

16. Leibowitz, "The Numbers."

17. Ibid.

18. David Kinnaman, "The Porn Phenomenon," Barna.org, accessed March 11, 2016, www.barna.org/blog/culture-media/david-kinnaman/the-porn -phenomenon#.Vti-A1KVe2o.

19. Ibid.

20. Ben Shapiro, *Porn Generation: How Social Liberalism Is Corrupting Our Future* (Washington, DC: Regnery Publishing, Inc., 2013), excerpted from chapter 1; locations 66, 73–74, and 77 in Kindle edition.

21. Adam Liptak, "Supreme Court Ruling Makes Same-Sex Marriage a Right Nationwide," *New York Times*, June 26, 2015, www.nytimes.com/2015 /06/27/us/supreme-court-same-sex-marriage.html?_r=0.

22. Todd Starnes, "Bible Removed from POW/MIA Display Inside VA Clinic,"

FoxNews.com, February 29, 2016, http://www.foxnews.com/opinion /2016/02/29/bible-removed-from-powmia-display-outside-va-clinic.html.

23. John J. Murray, "Moral and Spiritual Erosion in Two Generations," *The Aquila Report*, July 26, 2015, http://theaquilareport.com/moral-and -spiritual-erosion-in-two-generations/.

24. Jack Minor, "Doc Faces Boot for Citing 'Gay' Health Dangers," WND. com, June 27, 2015, http://www.wnd.com/2015/06/doc-faces-boot-for -citing-gay-health-dangers/.

25. "Abortion Statistics: United States Data and Trends," *National Right to Life Educational Foundation*, accessed June 22, 2016, http://www.nrlc.org /uploads/factsheets/FS01AbortionintheUS.pdf.

26. Philip Yancey, *Vanishing Grace: What Ever Happened to the Good News?* (Grand Rapids: Zondervan, 2014), 154.

27. Marie-Jean-Antoine-Nicolas de Caritat, qtd. in Frank E. Manuel and Fritzie P. Manuel, *Utopian Thought in the Western World* (Cambridge: Belknap Press, 1979), 491.

28. Dave Breese, *Seven Men Who Rule the World from the Grave* (Chicago: Moody, 1990), 153.

29. Ibid., 170.

30. Ibid., 175.

31. Ravi Zacharias, *Deliver Us from Evil* (Nashville: Word Publishing, 1997), 23.

32. Os Guinness, qtd. in Zacharias, 24.

33. Albert Mohler, "Everything That Is Solid Melts into Air—the New Secular Worldview," March 3, 2016, http://www.albertmohler.com/2016/03/03 /everything-that-is-solid-melts-into-air-the-new-secular-worldview/#_ftn1.

34. Breese, 48.

35. Andrew Fraknoi, "How Fast Are You Moving When You Are Sitting Still?" *The Universe in the Classroom*, Spring 2007, https://astrosociety.org/edu /publications/tnl/71/howfast.html. Since the velocities of Earth are heading in different directions, it is possible to find a variety of ways of explaining the speed of Earth. The unquestioned fact, however, is that Earth is moving at an enormous speed in several different trajectories simultaneously.

36. Carl Pettit, "10 Amazing Facts About the Universe You Won't Believe," The FW, accessed March 11, 2016, http://thefw.com/facts-about-the-universe/.

37. D. M. Baillie, *God Was in Christ* (New York: Scribner's, 1948), 52.

38. David Jeremiah, *The Jeremiah Study Bible* (Nashville: Worthy Publishing, 2013), 1543.

39. Donald Grey Barnhouse, *Man's Ruin, God's Wrath: Romans Vol. I* (Grand Rapids: Eerdmans, 1959), 271.

40. D. Martyn Lloyd-Jones, *Romans: Exposition of Chapter 1, The Gospel of God* (Grand Rapids: Zondervan, 1985), 392.

41. Cornelius Plantinga Jr., *Not the Way It's Supposed to Be: A Breviary of Sin* (Grand Rapids: Eerdmans, 1995), 199.

42. Ibid., xiii.

43. D. Martyn Lloyd-Jones, *Romans: An Exposition of Chapters 3:20-4:25, Atonement and Justification* (Grand Rapids, MI: Zondervan, 1970), 57.

44. "Ichabod's Mother," BibleGateway.com, accessed June 3, 2016, https://www.biblegateway.com/resources/all-women-bible/Ichabod-8217-s-Mother.

45. Yancey, 158.

Chapter 2: The Bleeding of Our Borders

1. Adapted from Victor Davis Hanson, "Do We Want Mexifornia?" *City Journal*, Spring 2002, accessed March 25, 2016, http://www.city-journal.org/html/do-we-want-mexifornia-12236.html.

2. Emma Lazarus, "The New Colossus," 1883, *Poetry Foundation*, accessed June 20, 2016, http://www.poetryfoundation.org/poems-and-poets/poems/detail/46550.

3. "US Immigration History Statistics," accessed March 25, 2016, http://m.emmigration.info/us-immigration-history-statistics.htm.

4. Jens Manuel Krogstad and Jeffrey S. Passel, "5 facts about illegal immigration in the U.S." *Pew Research Center*, November 19, 2015, http://www.pewresearch.org/fact-tank/2015/11/19/5-facts-about-illegal-immigration-in-the-u-s/.

5. "Bringing Vitality to Main Street—How Immigrant Small Businesses Help Local Economies Grow," Fiscal Policy Institute and Americas Society/Council of the Americas, January 2015, http://www.as-coa.org/sites/default/files/ImmigrantBusinessReport.pdf.

6. *A Day Without a Mexican*, directed by Sergio Arau, Altavista Films, 2004.

7. "*A Day Without a Mexican*," Films, The Loft Cinema, accessed June 21, 2016, https://loftcinema.com/film/a-day-without-a-mexican/.

8. Joseph Castleberry, Ed.D., *The New Pilgrims: How Immigrants Are Renewing America's Faith and Values* (Nashville, TN: Worthy Publishing, 2015), back cover.

9. Ibid., 270.

10. Ibid., 4.

11. Marco Rubio, qtd. in "Go-Getters, Gone?", Ian Tuttle, *National Review*, March 17, 2016, http://www.nationalreview.com/article/432928/americas -pioneer-spirit-dead-gone.

12. See *Bureau of Labor Statistics*, accessed June 3, 2016, http://www.bls.gov /news.release/empsit.t15.htm.

13. Victor Davis Hanson, "Do We Want Mexifornia?" *City Journal*.

14. Samuel P. Huntington, *Who Are We?: The Challenges to America's National Identity* (New York: Simon and Schuster, 2004), as summarized by M. Daniel Carroll R., *Christians at the Border: Immigration, the Church, and the Bible* (Grand Rapids: Brazos Press, 2013), 18–19.

15. "Immigrants making no effort to assimilate into U.S. culture," *The Citizen*, March 6, 2012, http://thecitizen.com/articles/03-06-2012 / immigrants-making-no-effort-assimilate-us-culture.

16. Alex Swoyer, "Concerns of Muslim Immigration Surge in Western World Come into Focus," *Breitbart*, May 7, 2015, http://www.breitbart.com /big-government/2015/05/07/concerns-of-muslim-immigration-surge -into-western-world-come-into-focus/.

17. Ibid.

18. Ian Tuttle, "The Troubling Math of Muslim Migration," *National Review*, January 13, 2015, http://www.nationalreview.com/article/396262/troubling -math-muslim-migration-ian-tuttle.

19. Mary Brophy Marcus, "Injuries from Paris attacks will take long to heal," CBS News, November 19, 2015, http://www.cbsnews.com/news/injuries -from-paris-attacks-will-take-long-to-heal/ and "Paris attacks: Who were the victims?" BBC.com, November 27, 2015, http://www.bbc.com/news /world-europe-34821813.

20. Erik Kirschbaum, "Germany pledges to act after mass sexual attacks on women on New Year's Eve," *Los Angeles Times*, January 5, 2016, http://www .latimes.com/world/europe/la-fg-germany-assaults-20160106-story.html.

21. "Brussels attacks: Airport, metro rocked by explosions killing at least 34; Islamic State claims attack," ABC, March 22, 2016, http://www.abc.net .au/news/2016-03-22/brussels-airport-metro-rocked-by-explosions/7268106.

22. Pete Hoekstra, qtd. in Swoyer, "Concerns of Muslim Immigration Surge in Western World Come into Focus."

23. Summarized from Jim Kouri, "Illegal aliens linked to rise in crime statistics," *Renew America*, June 22, 2006, http://www.renewamerica.com/columns /kouri/060622. Based on statistics from the Government Accounting Office, US Department of Justice, and National Security Institute.

24. Summarized from a circulating e-mail confirmed to be accurate by Snopes.com, August 2015: http://www.snopes.com/politics/immigration /parkland.asp.

25. Bill Costello, "The Fiscal Burden of Educating Children of Illegal Aliens," *American Thinker*, August 13, 2010, http://www.americanthinker.com /blog/2010/08/the_fiscal_burden_of_educating.html#ixzz43YxJn2lp.

26. "Immigration Facts: Public Opinion Polls on Immigration" *Federation for American Immigration Reform*, accessed March 21, 2016, http://www .fairus.org/facts/public-opinion. See also Howard Foster, "Democrats Benefit from Illegal Immigrant Voting," *Huffpost Politics*, April 13, 2012, http://www.huffingtonpost.com/howard-foster/democrats-benefit-from -illegal-immigrants-voting_b_1418523.html.

27. John Ankerberg, John Weldon, Dave Breese, and Dave Hunt, *One World: Bible Prophecy and the New World Order* (Chicago: Moody, 1991), 17.

28. Castleberry, *The New Pilgrims*, 46.

29. John F. Walvoord, *The Millennial Kingdom* (Findlay: Dunham Publishing, 1963), 319.

30. Russell Moore, "Immigration and the Gospel," accessed April 14, 2016, http://www.russellmoore.com/2011/06/17/immigration-and-the-gospel/.

31. Samuel Rodríguez, qtd. in M. Daniel Carroll R., *Christians at the Border*, xii.

32. James Kessler, "New Dimensions in Mission America," *Pentecostal Evangel* (August 4, 1985), 26.

33. Rodríguez, qtd. in M. Daniel Carroll R., ix.

Chapter 3: The Increase of Intolerance

1. David French, "How the Atlanta Fire Chief's Christian Views Cost Him His Job," *National Review*, February 25, 2016, http://www.nationalreview .com/article/431859/kelvin-cochrans-christian-views-cost-atlanta-fire -chief-his-job.

2. Catherine E. Shoichet and Halimah Abdullah, "Arizona Gov. Jan Brewer

Vetoes Controversial Anti-Gay Bill, SB 1062," CNN.com, February 26, 2014, http://www.cnn.com/2014/02/26/politics/arizona-brewer-bill/. See also Al Jazeera, "Arizona Gov. Vetoes Controversial 'Religious Freedom' Bill," Aljazeera America, February 26, 2014, http://america.aljazeera.com /articles/2014/2/26/brewer-gay-law.html.

3. Todd Starnes, "Fired for Preaching: Georgia Dumps Doctor over Church Sermons" *Fox News Opinion*, April 20, 2016, http://www.foxnews.com /opinion/2016/04/20/fired-for-preaching-georgia-dumps-doctor-over -church-sermons.html.

4. Joshua Rhett Miller, "eHarmony to Provide Gay Dating Service After Lawsuit," FoxNews.com, November 20, 2008, http://www.foxnews.com /story/2008/11/20/eharmony-to-provide-gay-dating-service-after-lawsuit .html.

5. "The Declaration of Independence," UShistory.org, accessed June 14, 2016, http://www.ushistory.org/declaration/document/.

6. J. Paul Nyquist, *Prepare: Living Your Faith in an Increasingly Hostile Culture* (Chicago: Moody Publishers, 2015), 14.

7. "America's Changing Religious Landscape," *Pew Research Center*, May 12, 2015, http://www.pewforum.org/2015/05/12/americas-changing-religious -landscape/.

8. Kelly Shattuck, "7 Startling Facts: An Up Close Look at Church Attendance in America," *Church Leaders*, http://www.churchleaders.com/pastors/pastor -articles/139575-7-startling-facts-an-up-close-look-at-church-attendance-in -america.html.

9. Nyquist, 14.

10. Ibid., 16.

11. Geoffrey W. Bromiley, "Persecute; Persecution," in *The International Standard Bible Encyclopedia*, ed. Geoffrey W. Bromiley, vol. 3 (Grand Rapids: Eerdmans, 1986), 771.

12. "Inside the Persecution Numbers," *Christianity Today*, 58, no. 2 (March 2014): p. 14.

13. Fay Voshell, "Persecution of Christians in America: It's Not Just 'Over There,'" *American Thinker*, May 10, 2015, http://www.americanthinker .com/articles/2015/05/persecution_of_christians_in_america_its_not _just_over_there.html.

14. Ibid.

15. Grace Chen, "Christmas Carols: Banned on Public School Campuses," *Public School Review,* May 30, 2016, http://www.publicschoolreview.com /blog/christmas-carols-banned-on-public-school-campuses.

16. Thomas M. Messner, "Same-Sex Marriage and the Threat to Religious Liberty," *The Heritage Foundation,* October 30, 2008, http://www.heritage .org/research/reports/2008/10/same-sex-marriage-and-the-threat-to -religious-liberty.

17. "Christian Fired for Sharing God," WND.com, March 28, 2007, http://www .wnd.com/2007/03/40820/.

18. Eric Rich, "Bible-Reading Student Gets Lesson in Litigation," *Washington Post,* October 3, 2006, http://www.washingtonpost.com/wp-dyn/content /article/2006/10/02/AR2006100201238.html.

19. "Christian Fired for Sharing God."

20. Sarah McBride, "Mozilla CEO Resigns, Opposition to Gay Marriage Drew Fire," *Reuters,* April 3, 2014, http://www.reuters.com/article/us-mozilla -ceo-resignation-idUSBREA321Y320140403.

21. "Ninth Circuit Decision Denies Parents' Rights," *Education Reporter,* December 2005, http://www.eagleforum.org/educate/2005/dec05 /9th-circuit.html.

22. "ACLU vs. Civil Liberties," *National Review,* December 10, 2013, http:// www.nationalreview.com/article/365947/aclu-vs-civil-liberties-editors.

23. Nyquist, *Prepare,* 13.

24. Qtd. in Andrew T. Walker, "California's Culture War Against Religious Liberty," *National Review,* June 9, 2016, http://www.nationalreview.com /article/436380/religious-liberty-threatened-california-new-law-gender -identity.

25. "Elane Photography v. Willock," *Alliance Defending Freedom,* April 7, 2014, http://www.adfmedia.org/news/prdetail/5537.

26. Todd Starnes, "Christian Bakers Fined $135,000 for Refusing to Make Wedding Cake for Lesbians," *Fox News Opinion,* July 3, 2015, http://www .foxnews.com/opinion/2015/07/03/christian-bakers-fined-135000-for -refusing-to-make-wedding-cake-for-lesbians.html.

27. "Principal Cleared of Criminal Count over Meal Blessing," WND.com, September 18, 2009, http://www.wnd.com/2009/09/110207/#wAdZPFAQe 4EVY3i9.99.

28. Bob Unruh, "Graduating Students Defy ACLU," WND.com, June 5, 2009, http://www.wnd.com/2009/06/100274/.

29. Voshell, "Persecution of Christians in America."

30. Eugene H. Peterson, *Christ Plays in Ten Thousand Places: A Conversation in Spiritual Theology* (Grand Rapids: Eerdmans, 2005), 288.

31. William Ernest Henley, "Invictus," accessed June 22, 2016, http://www.poetryfoundation.org/poems-and-poets/poems/detail/51642.

32. Gordon Franz, "The King and I: The Apostle John and Emperor Domitian," Part 1, *Associates for Biblical Research*, January 18, 2010, http://www.biblearchaeology.org/post/2010/01/18/The-King-and-I-The-Apostle-John-and-Emperor-Domitian-Part-1.aspx.

33. Darryl Eberhart, "The Bloody History of Papal Rome," AmazingDiscoveries.org, June 26, 2009, http://amazingdiscoveries.org/R-Reformation_Rome_crusade_slaughter.

34. "English Dissenters," Exlibris.org, accessed June 20, 2016, http://www.exlibris.org/nonconform/engdis/lollards.html.

35. Scott M. Manetsch, "St. Bartholomew's Day Massacre," *Christianity Today*, accessed June 22, 2016, http://www.christianitytoday.com/history/issues/issue-71/saint-bartholomews-day-massacre.html.

36. Gemma Betros, "The French Revolution and the Catholic Church," HistoryToday.com, December 2010, http://www.historytoday.com/gemma-betros/french-revolution-and-catholic-church.

37. Rev. Archimandrite Nektarios Serfes, "In Memory of the 50 Million Victims of the Orthodox Christian Holocaust," Serfes.org, October 1999, http://www.serfes.org/orthodox/memoryof.htm.

38. James M. Nelson, *Psychology, Religion, and Spirituality* (New York: Springer Science and Business Media, 2009), 427.

39. "Bishops Ridley and Latimer Burned," Christianity.com, July 2007, http://www.christianity.com/church/church-history/timeline/1501-1600/bishops-ridley-and-latimer-burned-11629990.html.

40. "Christian Persecution," *Open Doors*, accessed June 18, 2016, https://www.opendoorsusa.org/christian-persecution/.

41. "World Watch List," *Open Doors*, accessed June 22, 2016, https://www.opendoorsusa.org/christian-persecution/world-watch-list/.

42. John Ortberg, "Don't Waste a Crisis," *Christianity Today*, accessed

June 22, 2016, http://www.christianitytoday.com/le/2011/winter /dontwastecrisis.html?share=l0HlsPIanX8yIehpv%2fUKjdpWoSF01TBb.

43. C. S. Lewis, *The Problem of Pain* (New York: MacMillan, 1962), 93.

44. Adapted from Alson Jesse Smith, *Live All Your Life*, qtd. in Gerald Kennedy, *A Second Reader's Notebook* (New York: Harper & Brothers, 1959), 88.

45. A. W. Tozer, *Man: The Dwelling Place of God* (Seattle, WA: Amazon Digital Services, 2010), Kindle edition, location, 1404.

46. D. Martyn Lloyd-Jones, *Romans: An Exposition of Chapter 8:5–17, The Sons of God* (Grand Rapids: Zondervan, 1974), 433.

47. John Stott, *Romans: God's Good News for the World* (Downer's Grove: Inter-Varsity Press, 1994), 237.

48. Nyquist, *Prepare*, 90.

49. Sabina Wurmbrand, "The Authentic Pastor Richard Wurmbrand Biography," accessed June 22, 2016, http://richardwurmbrandbio.info/.

50. Richard Wurmbrand, qtd. in John Piper, *Let the Nations Be Glad!* (Grand Rapids, MI: Baker Publishing Group, 2010), 101.

51. Alexandr Solzhenitsyn, "A World Split Apart" (commencement address, Harvard University, Cambridge, MA, June 8, 1978).

52. Lauren Effron, Eric Johnson, and Ashley Louszko, "Benham Brothers Say HGTV Knew About Controversial Comments Over a Year Ago," ABC News, May 9, 2014, http://abcnews.go.com/Entertainment/benham-brothers -hgtv-knew-controversial-comments-year-ago/story?id=23663928.

53. Joni B. Hannigan, "Cultural 'Resistance' Not 'Relevance' Is Biblical Approach to Reach Millennials, Benham Says," *Christian Examiner*, November 11, 2014, http://www.christianexaminer.com/article/cultural-resistance-not-relevance -is-biblical-in-teaching-millennials-benham-says/47593.htm.

54. Katrina Fernandez, "How the Nine Days of Prayers Comforted Me While I Fought Demons," *Patheos*, January 19, 2013, http://www.patheos.com /blogs/thecrescat/2013/01/how-the-nine-days-of-prayers-comforted-me -while-i-fought-demons.html.

55. Piper, *Let the Nations Be Glad!*, 75.

56. Ian Tuttle, "The Indiana Governor's Critics Use Silly Means to Protest a Serious Law," *National Review*, April 8, 2016, http://www.nationalreview .com/article/433879/mike-pence-abortion-law.

57. Adapted from "John Chrysostom," *Christianity Today*, accessed June 15, 2016, http://www.christianitytoday.com/history/people/pastorsand

preachers/john-chrysostom.html; and "Chrysostom: Nothing You Can Do to Harm Me," *The Gospel Coalition*, August 10, 2009, https://blogs. thegospelcoalition.org/justintaylor/2009/08/10/chrysostom-nothing-you -can-do-to-harm/.

Chapter 4: The Apathy of America

1. Commonly attributed to Alexander Tytler, a Scottish lord and history professor at the University of Edinburgh in the late eighteenth century. See "Democracy: And the Fall of the Athenian Republic," TheRoadtoEmmaus .org, accessed May 30, 2016, http://theroadtoemmaus.org/RdLb/21PbAr /Hst/US/DmocAthnsUS.htm.

2. "Apathy," *Merriam-Webster*, accessed May 31, 2016, http://www.merriam -webster.com/dictionary/apathy.

3. Howard Steven Friedman, "The United States of Apathy's Motto Is 'We Don't Care,'" *Huffpost Politics*, October 5, 2010, http://www.huffingtonpost .com/howard-steven-friedman/the-united-states-of-apat_b_751296.html.

4. "George Washington's Inaugural Address," *National Archives*, accessed June 22, 2016, https://www.archives.gov/legislative/features/gw-inauguration/.

5. John Phillips, *Exploring Romans (The John Phillips Commentary Series)* (Grand Rapids, MI: Kregel Publications, 2002), 213.

6. "Coats Asks NBC for Explanation of Why 'Under God' Omitted from Pledge During U.S. Open Broadcast," June 21, 2011, https://www.coats .senate.gov/newsroom/press/release/coats-asks-nbc-for-explanation-of -why-under-god-omitted-from-pledge-during-us-open-broadcast.

7. Todd Starnes, "NBC Omits 'God' from Pledge of Allegiance . . . Again," FoxNews.com, January 8, 2015, http://www.foxnews.com/opinion /2015/01/08/nbc-omits-god-from-pledge-allegiance-again.html.

8. James Madison, in *The Statutes at Large and Treaties of the United States of America*, vol. 11 (Boston: C.C. Little and J. Brown, 1859), 764.

9. Herbert Hoover, *Addresses Upon the American Road* (Stanford, CA: Stanford University Press, 1955), 154.

10. Erik Sherman, "America Is the Richest, and Most Unequal, Country," *Fortune*, September 30, 2015, http://fortune.com/2015/09/30/america -wealth-inequality/; and Kerry A. Dolan and Luisa Kroll, "Forbes 2016 World's Billionaires: Meet the Richest People on the Planet," *Forbes*,

March 1, 2016, http://www.forbes.com/sites/luisakroll/2016/03/01
/forbes-2016-worlds-billionaires-meet-the-richest-people-on-the-planet/.

11. OECD.org, Official Development Assistance, http://www.oecd.org/dac
/stats/documentupload/ODA%202014%20Tables%20and%20Charts.pdf.

12. "The 100 Best Universities in the World Today," *The Best Schools*, accessed
June 22, 2016, http://www.thebestschools.org/features/100-best
-universities-in-world-today/.

13. Larry Gordon, "The World's Top Research University? It's Caltech—
Again," *Los Angeles Times*, September 30, 2015, http://www.latimes.com
/local/education/la-me-ln-caltech-ranking-20150930-story.html.

14. "America's Changing Religious Landscape," Pew Research Center, May 12,
2015, http://www.pewforum.org/2015/05/12/americas-changing-religious
-landscape/.

15. Ibid.

16. Joel C. Rosenberg, *Implosion: Can America Recover from Its Economic and
Spiritual Challenges in Time?* (Carol Stream: Tyndale House, 2012), 8–10.

17. Ibid., 125.

18. David Jeremiah, *What in the World Is Going On?: 10 Prophetic Clues You
Cannot Afford to Ignore* (Nashville: Thomas Nelson, 2008), 130.

19. Adapted from David Jeremiah, *What in the World Is Going On?*, 130.

20. "The World Factbook," Central Intelligence Agency, accessed June 16,
2016, https://www.cia.gov/library/publications/the-world-factbook
/rankorder/2079rank.html.

21. Tom Coburn, "A Deficit of Debt Discussion," *USA Today*, July 22, 2015,
http://www.usatoday.com/story/opinion/2015/07/22/tom-coburn-deficit
-debt-discussion/30417819/.

22. Erwin W. Lutzer, *Is God on America's Side?: The Surprising Answer and
How It Affects Our Future* (Chicago: Moody Publishers, 2008), 11–12, 16.

23. "America's Changing Religious Landscape," *Pew Research Center*.

24. Retold from various sources, including Dr. Harold J. Sala, "The Divine
'A,'" CBN Asia, accessed June 27, 2016, http://cbnasia.org/home/2013/11
/the-divine-a/.

25. William Barclay, "William Barclay's Daily Study Bible," Studylight.org,
accessed June 22, 2016, https://www.studylight.org/commentaries/dsb
/1-peter-1.html.

26. Rev. Walter Baxendale, *Anecdote, Incident, Illustrative Fact, Selected and*

Arranged for the Pulpit and the Platform (New York: Thomas Wittaker, 2 and 3 Bible House, 1988), 592.

27. Qtd. in William Barclay, *The Letters of James and Peter (The New Daily Study Bible)* (Louisville: Westminster John Knox Press, 2003), 194–95.

28. Qtd. in *The Westminster Collection of Christian Quotations*, ed. Martin H. Manser (Louisville: Westminster John Knox Press, 2001), 351.

29. David Jeremiah, *The Jeremiah Study Bible* (Franklin, TN: Worthy Publishing, 2013), 1705.

30. Justin Martyr, "The First Apology of Justin, the Martyr," *Christian Classics Ethereal Library*, accessed June 22, 2016, http://www.ccel.org/ccel /richardson/fathers.x.ii.iii.html.

31. See *My Faith Votes*, accessed June 22, 2016, http://www.myfaithvotes.com/.

32. Qtd. in Warren W. Wiersbe, *The Bible Exposition Commentary: The Prophets* (Colorado Springs: David C. Cook, 2002), 435.

33. Tom Murse, "Can One Vote Make a Difference?" *About News*, accessed June 22, 2016, http://uspolitics.about.com/od/CampaignsElections/a/Can -One-Vote-Make-A-Difference.htm.

34. Martin Niemoller, qtd. in "The Holocaust," *The National Holocaust Memorial*, accessed June 22, 2016, http://www.nehm.org/the-holocaust/.

35. Harry Thurston Peck, *Harpers Dictionary of Classical Antiquities*, "Lampadedromia," accessed June 22, 2016, http://www.perseus.tufts.edu /hopper/text?doc=Perseus:text:1999.04.0063:id=lampadedromia-cn.

36. Randy Alcorn, "A Life of Endurance," *Eternal Perspective Ministries*, September 16, 2008, http://www.epm.org/resources/2008/Sep/16/life -endurance/.

Chapter 5: The Remedy of Revival

1. Mike Yorkey and Jesse Florea, *Linspired: The Jeremy Lin Story* (Zondervan, 2012), adapted from chapters 4 and 5.

2. Jesus Gomez, "It's not Linsanity, but Jeremy Lin Is Experiencing a Revival in Charlotte," *SB Nation*, December 18, 2015, www.sbnation.com/nba /2015/12/18/10575088/jeremy-lin-highlights-stats-hornets-helping.

3. Jared Allen, "Linsanity Revived in Charlotte, for at Least One Night," *Niner Times*, December 19, 2015, http://ninertimes.com/2015/12/linsanity -revived-in-charlotte-for-at-least-one-night/.

4. "The Quiet Revival of Linsanity," *Hoop Files*, January 28, 2015, http://hoopfiles.com/nba/2015/01/the-quiet-revival-of-linsanity/.

5. Barry Rascovar, "Baltimore Needs a Comprehensive Revival Plan," *Maryland Reporter*, March 21, 2016, http://marylandreporter.com/2016/03/21/rascovar-baltimore-needs-a-comprehensive-revival-plan/.

6. Czarina Ong, "Jeremy Lin Tells Fans to Pray for 'Global Christian Revival,' Particularly in China," *Christian Today*, March 13, 2016, www.christiantoday.com/article/jeremy.lin.tells.fans.to.pray.for.global.christian.revival/81725.htm.

7. Duncan Campbell, "Notes of an Address Given at a Meeting for Ministers at Oxford and Manchester," *Revival in the Hebrides* (Self-published, 2015), 57.

8. J. Stephen Lang and Mark A. Noll, "Colonial New England: An Old Order, New Awakening," *Christianity Today*, accessed June 21, 2016, http://www.christianitytoday.com/history/issues/issue-8/colonial-new-england-old-order-new-awakening.html.

9. Cassandra Niemczyk, "The American Puritans: Did You Know?," Christian History, *Christianity Today*, accessed June 21, 2016, www.christianitytoday.com/history/issues/issue-41/american-puritans-did-you-know.html.

10. Paraphrased from Increase Mather's sermon, "Ichabod, Or, The Glory Departing from New England," 24–25, 32, 67–69, accessed June 21, 2016, http://quod.lib.umich.edu/e/evans/N00897.0001.001/1:4?rgn=div1;view=fulltext.

11. Samuel Torrey, qtd. in *The Christian History, Containing Accounts of the Revival and Propagation of Religion in Great Britain and America* (Boston: Kneeland and T. Green, 1744), 98.

12. Jonathan Edwards, "Sinners in the Hands of an Angry God," *Jonathan Edwards Center at Yale University*, accessed June 4, 2016, http://edwards.yale.edu/archive?path=aHR0cDovL2Vkd2FyZHMueWFsZS5lZHUvY2dpLWJpbi9uZXdwaGlsby9nZXRRvYmplY3QucGw/Yy4yMTo0Ny53amVv.

13. Ibid.

14. Adapted from Robert J. Morgan, *On This Day* (Nashville: Thomas Nelson, 1997), entry for July 8.

15. "Spiritual Awakenings in North America: Did You Know?," *Christian History*, 8:3 (issue 23) (1989), p. 4.

16. Benjamin Rice Lacy Jr., *Revivals in the Midst of the Years* (Hopewell: Royal Publishing Company, 1943), 32.

17. Mark A. Noll, *A History of Christianity in the United States and Canada* (Grand Rapids: Eerdmans, 1992), 163.

18. W. W. Sweet, *The Story of Religion in America* (New York: Harper and Brothers, 1939), 224.

19. Roberta Buckingham Mouheb, *Yale Under God: Roots and Fruits* (self-published, 2012), 84.

20. Thomas Paine and Jean-Jacques Rousseau, *The Theological Works of Thomas Paine: To Which Are Added the Profession of Faith of a Savoyard Vicar* (Boston: The Advocates of Common Sense, 1832), 149.

21. J. Edwin Orr, *Campus Aflame: A History of Evangelical Awakenings in Collegiate Communities* (Glendale: G/L Publications, 1971), 19.

22. Ibid., 25.

23. Robert Christy Galbraith, *The History of the Chillicothe Presbytery: From Its Organization in 1799 to 1889* (Chillicothe: H. W. Guthrie, Hugh Bell, and Peter Platter, 1889), 11–13.

24. The prayer meeting on Fulton Street was just a stone's throw from the later site of the Twin Towers of the World Trade Center.

25. "The Time for Prayer: The Third Great Awakening," *Christian History*, 8:3 (issue 23) (1987), p. 33.

26. "Did You Know?: Little Known or Remarkable Facts About Christianity During the American Civil War," *Christian History*, 11:1 (issue 33) (1992), p. 2.

27. J. William Jones, *Christ in the Camp* (Atlanta: The Martin and Hoyt Co., 1904), 255.

28. Robert J. Morgan, *On This Day in Christian History: 365 Amazing and Inspiring Stories About Saints, Martyrs, and Heroes* (Nashville: Thomas Nelson, 1997), entry for March 29.

29. Wesley Duewel, *Revival Fire* (Grand Rapids: Zondervan, 1995), 182.

30. Ibid., 206.

31. Ibid., 207.

32. Ibid., 209.

33. Ibid., 323.

34. Ibid., 331–32.

35. Orr, *Campus Aflame*, 111.

36. Ibid., 110.

37. Duewel, 210.

38. Ibid., 211.

39. Ibid., 346-47, 364.

40. Timothy Leary, "Turn On, Tune In, Drop Out," accessed June 4, 2016, http://www.allmusic.com/album/turn-on-tune-in-drop-out-mw0000096275.

41. Richard A. Bustraan, *The Jesus People Movement: A Story of Spiritual Revolution Among the Hippies* (Eugene, OR: Pickwick Publications, 2014), 8–9.

42. "A Brief History of the Jesus Movement," *The Hollywood Free Paper*, accessed June 4, 2016, http://www.hollywoodfreepaper.org/portal.php?id=2.

43. Billy Graham, *The Jesus Generation* (Grand Rapids, MI: Zondervan, 1975).

44. Brian Vachon, "The Jesus Movement Is Upon Us," *Look*, February 9, 1971, 15–21.

45. "The Alternative Jesus: The Psychedelic Christ," *Time*, June 21, 1971, accessed June 22, 2016, http://content.time.com/time/magazine/article/0,9171,905202,00.html.

46. Portions of the preceding paragraphs of this chapter appeared in my article, "The Return of the Jesus People," *Turning Points Magazine*, August 2013.

47. Vance Havner, *The Secret of Christian Joy* (Old Tappan: Fleming H. Revell Co., 1938), 24.

48. F. B. McKinney, "Send a Great Revival," Hymnary.org, accessed May 19, 2016, http://www.hymnary.org/text/coming_now_to_thee_o_christ_my_lord.

Chapter 6: The Isolation of Israel

1. "American-Israeli Richard Lakin dies two weeks after terrorist attack on Jerusalem bus," *The Jerusalem Post*, accessed June 4, 2016, http://www.jpost.com/Arab-Israeli-Conflict/American-Israeli-victim-dies-two-weeks-after-brutal-attack-on-Jerusalem-bus-430168.

2. Lela Gilbert, "Jerusalem Notebook: Shattered Hopes and Dreams on Bus No. 78," *Philos Project*, November 4, 2015, https://philosproject.org/israel-jerusalem-attack-terror/.

3. Eli, "Everywhere in Israel We Can Feel the Terror Tension, by Rockets, Stones, Riots or Molotov Cocktails," July 9, 2014, http://www.livinginisrael.info/everywhere-israel-can-feel-terror-tension-rockets-stones-riots-molotov-cocktails/.

4. Mark Silverberg, "Slitting Throats is 'Natural,'" *Gatestone Institute*, April 4, 2011, http://www.gatestoneinstitute.org/2010/slitting-throats-is-natural.

5. Ramon Bennett, *When Day and Night Cease: A Prophetic Study of World Events and How Prophecy Concerning Israel Affects the Nations, the Church and You* (Jerusalem: Arm of Salvation, 1996), 193.

6. Marvin Olasky, "Israel at Age 67: Slammed If You Do, Dead If You Don't," *World*, April 21, 2015, http://www.worldmag.com/2015/04/israel_at_age_67_slammed_if_you_do_dead_if_you_dont.

7. Sam Harris, "Why Don't I Criticize Israel?" July 27, 2014, https://www.samharris.org/podcast/item/why-dont-i-criticize-israel.

8. See *Holocaust: A Call to Conscience*, accessed June 4, 2016, http://www.projetaladin.org/holocaust/en/40-questions-40-answers/basic-questions-about-the-holocaust.html.

9. David Jeremiah, *The Jeremiah Study Bible* (Franklin, TN: Worthy Publishing, 2013), 23.

10. Paul R. Wilkinson, *Understanding Christian Zionism: Israel's Place in the Purposes of God* (Bend, OR: The Berean Call, 2013), 21.

11. Amnon Rubinstein, "Peace Won't Be Instant, but Dream Can't Be Dropped," *JWeekly*, May 9, 2003, http://www.jweekly.com/article/full/19844/peace-won-t-be-instant-but-dream-can-t-be-dropped/.

12. J. F. Walvoord, "Will Israel Possess the Promised Land?" in *Jesus the King Is Coming*, ed. Charles Lee Feinberg (Chicago: Moody, 1975), 128.

13. Wilkinson, 17.

14. John F. Walvoord, *Israel in Prophecy* (Grand Rapids: Zondervan, 1962), 72.

15. Wilkinson, 23.

16. 2 Maccabees 9, Apocrypha (London: Oxford University Press, 1953), 408.

17. See "The Six Day War," accessed June 4, 2016, http://www.sixdaywar.org/content/israel.asp.

18. "Six-Day War," *Encyclopedia Britannica*, accessed March 4, 2016, http://www.britannica.com/event/Six-Day-War.

19. "Full Transcript of Netanyahu's Address to UN General Assembly," Haaretz, October 2, 2015, http://www.haaretz.com/israel-news/1.678524.

20. Tim LaHaye and Ed Hindson, *Target Israel: Caught in the Crosshairs of the End Times* (Eugene: Harvest House, 2015), 9–10.

21. Mark Hitchcock, *The End* (Carol Steam, IL: Tyndale House, 2012), 54.

22. Sam Sokol, "WIN/Gallup International: Israel One of Least Religious Countries," *The Jerusalem Post*, April 21, 2015, http://www.jpost.com/Israel-News/Gallup-Israel-one-of-least-religious-countries-398823.

23. Yaron Druckman, "Christian in Israel: Strong in Education," YNetNews.com, December 23, 2012, http://www.ynetnews.com/articles/0,7340,L-4323529,00.html.

24. See *Bible Hub*, accessed June 4, 2016, http://biblehub.com/hebrew/7307.htm.

25. See *Bible Hub*, accessed June 4, 2016, http://biblehub.com/greek/4151.htm.

26. Matti Friedman, qtd. in Marvin Olasky, "Israel: The Pool into Which the World Spits," *World*, September 11, 2014, http://www.worldmag.com/2014/09/israel_the_pool_into_which_the_world_spits.

Chapter 7: The Insurgency of ISIS

1. Jared Malsin, "Christians Mourn Their Relatives Beheaded by ISIS," *Time*, February 23, 2015, http://time.com/3718470/isis-copts-egypt/.

2. Ibid.

3. Ibid.

4. Jonathan Rashad, "'Christian Martyrs Change the World': We Meet the Families of the Egyptian Christians Beheaded by the Islamic State," *Vice News*, February 26, 2015, https://news.vice.com/article/christian-martyrs-change-the-world-we-meet-the-families-of-the-egyptian-christians-beheaded-by-the-islamic-state.

5. Ibid.

6. Ibid.

7. Fareed Zakaria, "Fareed Zakaria: Let's Be Honest, Islam Has a Problem Right Now," *Washington Post*, October 9, 2014, https://www.washingtonpost.com/opinions/fareed-zakaria-islam-has-a-problem-right-now-but-heres-why-bill-maher-is-wrong/2014/10/09/b6302a14-4fe6-11e4-aa5e-7153e466a02d_story.html.

8. Rabbi Shalom Lewis, "'Ehr Daw'—They're Here," *Frontpage Mag*, October 6, 2014, http://www.frontpagemag.com/fpm/242514/ehr-daw-theyre-here-rabbi-shalom-lewis?.

9. "The Islamic State," *Vice News*, August 13, 2014, https://news.vice.com/video/the-islamic-state-part-1.

10. Nabeel Qureshi, *Answering Jihad: A Better Way Forward* (Grand Rapids: Zondervan, 2016), 85.

11. Charles Dyer and Mark Tobey, *The ISIS Crisis: What You Really Need to Know* (Chicago: Moody Publishers, 2015), 32–44.

12. "Hadith," *Encyclopedia Britannica*, accessed June 16, 2016, http://www
.britannica.com/topic/Hadith.

13. Ashley Killough, "Strong Reaction to Obama Statement: 'ISIL Is Not Islamic,'"
CNN Politics, September 11, 2014, http://www.cnn.com/2014/09/10/politics
/obama-isil-not-islamic/.

14. Graeme Wood, "What ISIS Really Wants," *The Atlantic*, March 2015,
http://www.theatlantic.com/magazine/archive/2015/03/what-isis-really
-wants/384980/.

15. Qureshi, *Answering Jihad*, 31.

16. Ibid., 30.

17. Ibid., 31.

18. Summarized from Feras Hanoush, "ISIS Is Training an Army of Child
Soldiers," *Newsweek*, November 21, 2015, http://www.newsweek.com
/isis-training-army-child-soldiers-396392; and Cassandra Vinograd,
Ghazi Balkiz, and Ammar Cheikh Omar, "ISIS Trains Child Soldiers at
Camps for 'Cubs of the Islamic State,'" NBC News, November 7, 2014,
http://www.nbcnews.com/storyline/isis-uncovered/isis-trains-child
-soldiers-camps-cubs-islamic-state-n241821.

19. "San Bernardino Shooting," CNN.com, accessed June 21, 2016, http://
www.cnn.com/specials/san-bernardino-shooting.

20. See "In Depth: Orlando Nightclub Massacre," CBS News, accessed
June 21, 2016, http://www.cbsnews.com/orlando-shooting/.

21. Elliot Friedland, "The Muslim Brotherhood: Special Report," *Clarion
Project*, June 2015, https://www.clarionproject.org/sites/default/files/Muslim
-Brotherhood-Special-Report.pdf.

22. Ibid.

23. Ryan Mauro, "The Islamists Multi-Staged Strategy for Victory Over the
West," *Clarion Project*, January 21, 2013, http://www.clarionproject.org
/analysis/gradualism-islamist-strategy-victory#.

24. Valentina Colombo, "The Muslim Brotherhood's 'Peaceful Conquest,'"
Gatestone Institute International Policy Council, May 28, 2014, http://www
.gatestoneinstitute.org/4299/muslim-brotherhood-peaceful-conquest.

25. Friedland, "The Muslim Brotherhood."

26. Georges Sada, *Saddam's Secrets: How an Iraqi General Defied and Survived
Saddam Hussein* (Brentwood: Integrity Publishers, 2006), 285–90.

27. Tom Wyke and Imogen Calderwood, "Russian Tanks Roll into Ancient

Syrian City of Palmyra as Bodies of 42 Men, Women and Children Butchered by ISIS Are Found in Mass Grave," DailyMail.com, April 2, 2016, http://www.dailymail.co.uk/news/article-3520370/Life-ISIS-New-photos -Palmyra-reveal-Assad-regime-controlling-archaeological-site-mass-grave -containing-dozens-bodies-uncovered.html.

28. Qtd. in Dyer and Tobey, 73–74.
29. "Special Specifications of Imam al-Mahdi," Islam.org, accessed June 16, 2016, https://www.al-islam.org/shiite-encyclopedia-ahlul-bayt-dilp-team /special-specifications-imam-al-mahdi.
30. James T. Johnson, "Just War," *Encyclopedia Britannica*, accessed June 16, 2016, http://www.britannica.com/topic/just-war.
31. John Stuart Mill, "The Contest in America," *Dissertations and Discussions*, 1 (1868), 26. First published in *Fraser's Magazine*, February 1862, accessed June 16, 2016, http://www.bartleby.com/73/1934.html.
32. David Platt, *Radical: Taking Back Your Faith from the American Dream* (Colorado Springs: Multnomah Books, 2010), 3.

Chapter 8: The Resurrection of Russia

1. Sarah Rainsford, "Ukraine Crisis: Putin Shows Who Is Boss in Crimea," BBC. com, August 19, 2015, http://www.bbc.com/news/world-europe-33985325.
2. Ian Bremmer, "These 5 Facts Explain Putin's War in Syria," *Time*, October 1, 2015, http://time.com/4058216/these-5-facts-explain-putins-war-in-syria/.
3. Oren Dorell, "Russian President Putin Pays a Visit to Iran Bearing Gifts," *USA Today*, November 23, 2015, http://www.usatoday.com/story/news /world/2015/11/23/russian-president-putin-pays-visit-iran-bearing -gifts/76251032/.
4. Neil MacFarquhar, "Putin Lifts Ban on Missile Sales to Iran," *New York Times*, April 13, 2015, http://www.nytimes.com/2015/04/14/world /europe/putin-lifts-ban-on-russian-missile-sales-to-iran.html?_r=0.
5. Bremmer, "These 5 Facts Explain Putin's War in Syria."
6. John F. Walvoord, *The Nations in Prophecy* (Grand Rapids: Zondervan, 1978), 108.
7. H. W. F. Gesenius, *Gesenius' Hebrew-Chaldee Lexicon*, trans. S. P. Tregelles (Grand Rapids: Eerdmans, 1957), 752.
8. Charles Lee Feinberg, *The Prophecy of Ezekiel: The Glory of the Lord* (Chicago: Moody, 1969), 223.

9. Qtd. in Charles Lee Feinberg, *The Prophecy of Ezekiel*, 223.

10. Walvoord, 106.

11. Mark Hitchcock, *The Complete Book of Bible Prophecy* (Wheaton, IL: Tyndale House, 1999), 128.

12. Matthew Henry, *Matthew Henry's Commentary on the Bible*, accessed February 18, 2016, https://www.biblegateway.com/resources/matthew -henry/Ezek.38.1-Ezek.38.13.

13. David Jeremiah, *The Jeremiah Study Bible* (Franklin, TN: Worthy Publishing, 2013), 1100.

14. Mark Hitchcock, *The Coming Islamic Invasion of Israel* (Sisters: Multnomah, 2002), 31–32.

15. C. I. Scofield, *The Scofield Study Bible* (New York: Oxford University Press, 1909), 883.

16. Jackie Northam, "Lifting Sanctions Will Release $100 Billion to Iran. Then What?" NPR.org, July 16, 2015, http://www.npr.org/sections /parallels/2015/07/16/423562391/lifting-sanctions-will-release-100-billion -to-iran-then-what.

17. Adam Kredo, "Iran 'Shouts Hatred' for Israel, Backs Palestinian Terror," *Washington Free Beacon*, July 8, 2015, http://freebeacon.com/national -security/iran-shouts-hatred-for-israel-backs-palestinian-terror/.

18. Editorial Board, "Obama's Iran Deal Falls Far Short of His Own Goals," *Washington Post*, April 2, 2015, https://www.washingtonpost.com /opinions/obamas-iran-deal-falls-well-short-of-his-own-goals/2015 /04/02/7974413c-d95c-11e4-b3f2-607bd612aeac_story.html.

19. Lee Smith, "The Iranian Nuclear Deal, Explained," *The Weekly Standard*, April 7, 2015, http://www.weeklystandard.com/the-iranian-nuclear-deal -explained/article/912097.

20. Mustafa Fetouri, "Libya Looks to Russia for Arms," *Al-Monitor*, April 20, 2015, http://www.al-monitor.com/pulse/originals/2015/04/libya-us-uk -france-russia-uneast-west-armament-deal-morocco.html#.

21. John Phillips, *Exploring the Future: A Comprehensive Guide to Bible Prophecy* (Grand Rapids: Kregel, 1983), 327.

22. Henry M. Morris, *The Genesis Record: A Scientific and Devotional Commentary on the Book of Beginnings* (Grand Rapids: Baker Book House, 1976), 247.

23. Dr. David Jeremiah, *What in the World Is Going On?* (Nashville, TN: Thomas Nelson Inc., 2008), 174.

24. *Jewish Virtual Library*, accessed June 6, 2016, http://www.jewishvirtual library.org/jsource/Society_&_Culture/newpop.html.

25. Ibid.

26. Mark Hitchcock, *The End: A Complete Overview of Bible Prophecy and the End of Days* (Wheaton: Tyndale House, 2012), 310.

27. Adapted from Schumpeter columnist, "Beyond the Start-Up Nation," *The Economist*, December 29, 2010, http://www.economist.com/node /17796932.

28. Gary Shapiro, "What Are the Secrets Behind Israel's Growing Innovative Edge?" *Forbes*, November 7, 2013, http://www.forbes.com/sites/realspin /2013/11/07/what-are-the-secrets-behind-israels-growing-innovative -edge/#3546fa821172.

29. Maureen Farrell, "Israel as Incubator," *Forbes*, November 10, 2009, http:// www.forbes.com/2009/11/10/israel-innovation-entrepreneurs-opinions -book-review-contributors-start-up-nation.html.

30. Paul Muggeridge, "These Are the Most Innovative Countries in the World," *World Economic Forum*, July 9, 2015, https://www.weforum.org /agenda/2015/07/these-are-the-most-innovative-countries-in-the-world/.

31. David Horovitz, "They Tried to Kill Us, We Won, Now We're Changing the World," *The Jerusalem Post*, April 1, 2011, http://www.jpost.com /Opinion/Columnists/They-tried-to-kill-us-we-won-now-were-changing -the-world.

32. Roee Bergman, "Israel in 2015: 17 Billionaires, Over 88,000 Millionaires," YNetNews.com, October 14, 2015, http://www.ynetnews.com/articles /0,7340,L-4711244,00.html.

33. See "9 Israelis Break Forbes 500 Rich List," YNetNews.com, March 4, 2015, http://www.ynetnews.com/articles/0,7340,L-4632901,00.html; and Gabe Friedman, "10 Jews in Forbes Top 50 Billionaires," *The Times of Israel*, March 3, 2015, http://www.timesofisrael.com/10-jews-in-forbes -top-50-billionaires/.

34. J. Dwight Pentecost, "Where Do the Events of Ezekiel 38–39 Fit into the Prophetic Picture?," accessed June 22, 2016, http://arielcanada.com/en /wp-content/uploads/2013/07/J.Dwight-Pentecost-Where-do-the-Events -of-Ez.-38-39-Fit-into-the-Prophetic-Picture.pdf.

35. John F. Walvoord and Roy B. Zuck, eds., *The Bible Knowledge Commentary* (Wheaton: Victor, 1985), Logos Bible Software.

36. Phillips, *Exploring the Future*, 353.

37. Jeremiah, *What in the World Is Going On?*, 183.

38. Ron Rhodes, *Northern Storm Rising: Russia, Iran, and the Emerging End-Times Military Coalition Against Israel* (Eugene: Harvest House, 2008), 151.

39. Adapted from Ray C. Stedman, *God's Final Word: Understanding Revelation* (Grand Rapids: RBC Ministries, 1991), 123.

Chapter 9: The Rapture of the Redeemed

1. David Brog, *Standing with Israel: Why Christians Support the Jewish State* (Lake Murray: FrontLine, 2006), 58–59.

2. Ibid., 59.

3. Ibid., 59–60.

4. Ibid.

5. John F. Walvoord, *End Times: Understanding Today's World Events in Biblical Prophecy*, gen. ed. Charles R. Swindoll (Nashville: Word Publishing, 1998), 17.

6. See "harpazo," *Bible Hub*, accessed June 6, 2016, http://biblehub.com/greek/726.htm.

7. Mark Hitchcock, *The Complete Book of Bible Prophecy* (Wheaton, IL: Tyndale House, 1991), 70.

8. John F. Walvoord, *The Final Drama: 14 Keys to Understanding the Prophetic Scriptures* (Grand Rapids, MI: Kregel Publications, 1993), 121.

9. Renald Showers, *Maranatha—Our Lord, Come!: A Definitive Study of the Rapture of the Church* (Bellmawr: Thee Friends of Israel Ministry, 1995), 127.

10. A. T. Pierson, qtd. in Showers, *Maranatha—Our Lord, Come!*, 127.

11. Mark Hitchcock, *The End: A Complete Overview of Bible Prophecy and the End of Days* (Wheaton: Tyndale House, 2012), 129.

12. Paul Lee Tan, *Encyclopedia of 7,700 Illustrations: Signs of the Times* (Rockville: Assurance Publishers, 1979), 1239–40.

13. Tim LaHaye, *The Rapture: Who Will Face the Tribulation* (Eugene, OR: Harvest House Publishers, 2002), 39.

14. Jeremiah, *What in the World Is Going On?*, 107.

15. Dr. Arnold G. Fruchtenbaum, *The Footsteps of the Messiah: A Study of the Sequence of Prophetic Events* (San Antonio: Ariel Press, 2004), 144.

16. Ibid.

17. Walvoord, *End Times*, 28–29.

18. Fruchtenbaum, 144.

19. Ibid.

20. Ibid., 149.

21. Joni Eareckson Tada, *Heaven: Your Real Home* (Grand Rapids: Zondervan, 1995), 39.

22. "The Rapture of the Church," in A. J. Gordon and Arthur T. Pierson, *The Coronation Hymnal* (Philadelphia: American Baptist Publication Society, 1894).

23. See "Parakaleo," *Bible Hub*, accessed June 13, 2016, http://biblehub.com /greek/3870.htm.

24. Charles Haddon Spurgeon, "Watching for Christ's Coming," April 2, 1893, http://www.spurgeongems.org/vols37-39/chs2302.pdf.

25. Walvoord, *End Times*, 38.

26. Showers, *Maranatha—Our Lord, Come!*, 256.

Chapter 10: Translated Before the Tribulation

1. Radu Alexander, "Ten Embarrassing Mistakes Historical Figures Want You to Forget," *Listverse*, March 28, 2015. http://listverse.com/2015/03/28/10 -embarrassing-mistakes-historical-figures-want-you-to-forget/.

2. "Amazing Predictions that Became Reality of Today," *Before It's News*, December 16, 2015, http://beforeitsnews.com/strange/2015/12/amazing -predictions-that-became-reality-of-today-very-strange-but-true-2462438 .html.

3. "Alexis de Tocqueville, Quotes," *Goodreads*, accessed June 6, 2016, http:// www.goodreads.com/quotes/1265628-there-are-at-the-present-time-two -great-nations-in.

4. A. T. Robertson, *Word Pictures in the New Testament*, accessed June 6, 2016, http://www.ccel.org/ccel/robertson_at/word.iv.xii.html?highlight=tribulation #highlight.

5. David Jeremiah, *The Jeremiah Study Bible*, 1688.

6. J. Dwight Pentecost, qtd. in Mark Hitchcock, *The End*, 235.

7. N. T. Wright, qtd. in "The Necessity of God's Wrath," *Preaching Today*, accessed June 13, 2016, http://www.preachingtoday.com/illustrations/2009 /september/6092809.html.

8. Hitchcock, *The End*, 158.

9. Charles C. Ryrie, *Come Quickly, Lord Jesus: What You Need to Know About the Rapture* (Eugene: Harvest House, 1996), 137–38.

10. Richard Mayhue, *Christ's Prophetic Plans: A Futuristic Premillennial Primer* (Chicago: Moody, 2012), 89.

11. Hitchcock, *The End*, 154–155.

12. J. F Strombeck, *First the Rapture: The Church's Blessed Hope* (Grand Rapids: Kregel, 1992), 133.

13. John F. Walvoord, *The Thessalonian Epistles* (Grand Rapids: Zondervan, 1974), 54.

14. Adapted from a story commonly attributed to R. G. Lee. Original source unknown.

15. Adapted from Steven J. Cole, "Lesson 110: A Deathbed Conversion (Luke 23:39–43)," Bible.org, June 21, 2013, https://bible.org/seriespage/lesson-110-deathbed-conversion-luke-2339-43.

ABOUT THE AUTHOR

Dr. David Jeremiah is the founder of Turning Point, an international ministry committed to providing Christians with sound Bible teaching through radio and television, the Internet, live events, and resource materials and books. He is the author of more than fifty books, including *Captured by Grace*; *Angels: Who They Are and How They Help*; *What in the World Is Going On?*; and *Agents of the Apocalypse*.

Dr. Jeremiah serves as the senior pastor of Shadow Mountain Community Church in San Diego, California, where he resides with his wife, Donna. They have four grown children and twelve grandchildren.

stay connected to the teaching series of

DR. DAVID JEREMIAH

· · · · · · · ·

Publishing | Radio | Television | Online

FURTHER YOUR STUDY OF THIS BOOK

• • • • • • • •

People Are Asking...Is This the End? Resource Materials

To enhance your study on this important topic, we recommend the correlating audio message album, study guide, and DVD messages from the *People Are Asking...Is This the End?* series.

Audio Message Album

The material found in this book originated from messages presented by Dr. David Jeremiah at the Shadow Mountain Community Church where he serves as Senior Pastor. These ten messages are conveniently packaged in an accessible audio album.

Study Guide

This 128-page study guide correlates with the *People are Asking...Is This the End?* messages by Dr. Jeremiah. Each lesson provides an outline, an overview, and application questions for each topic.

DVD Message Presentations

Watch Dr. Jeremiah deliver the *People are Asking...Is This the End?* original messages in this special DVD collection.

To order these products, call us at 1-800-947-1993
or visit us online at www.DavidJeremiah.org.

ALSO AVAILABLE FROM
DAVID JEREMIAH

· · · · · · · ·

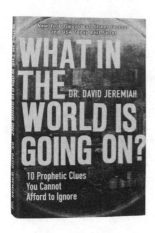

New York Times Bestseller
What in the World Is Going On?
by Dr. David Jeremiah

The Bible has plenty to say about the end times. But until now, there has been no other book that—in straightforward prose that's easy to understand—gathers ten spiritual prophecies, lays out a chronological checklist, and offers a guideline for sorting it all out.

In *What in the World Is Going On?* Dr. David Jeremiah answers the hard questions, including these: "How is prophecy playing out in modern Europe?" "Why does Israel matter?" "How are oil reserves and Islamic terrorism related?" "Does the United States play a role in prophecy?" "How should we live in the end times?"

Events unfolding in today's world are certainly unsettling, but they need not be confusing or frightening. Now you can know the meaning behind what you see in the daily news—and understand what is going on!

To order this book, call us at 1-800-947-1993
or visit us online at www.DavidJeremiah.org.

New York Times Bestseller
Living with Confidence in a Chaotic World
by Dr. David Jeremiah

"Let not your heart be troubled..."

Confidence can be hard to come by these days. People are losing their jobs, their houses, and their life savings at an unprecedented rate. Violence, natural disasters, and moral depravity seem to be skyrocketing. In the midst of all this chaos, we need to know...what on earth should we do now?

In the follow-up to the *New York Times* bestseller *What in the World is Going On?* Dr. David Jeremiah brings a message of hope and confidence from the priceless counsel of the Word of God. He answers our most urgent questions, including:

- How can we weather this storm with a calm heart?
- What does it truly mean to "wait on the Lord?"
- What is Jesus saying to our chaotic world today?
- How on earth did we get into this mess?
- Can we take a broken world and rebuild it into something fruitful?

Living with Confidence in a Chaotic World shows us all that with the power and love of Almighty God, we can live with confidence in this age of turmoil.

To order this book, call us at 1-800-947-1993
or visit us online at www.DavidJeremiah.org.

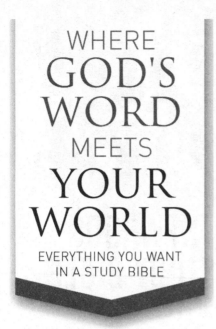
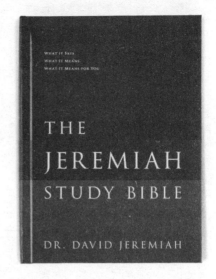

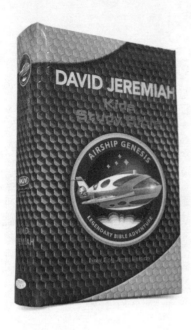

NEW KIDS STUDY BIBLE
FROM DAVID JEREMIAH

Special Features Include:

66 Mission Overviews: Individual book introductions provide background for discovering the main theme and purpose for each book in the Bible.

100 Rupert Reports: Short informational notes include interesting descriptions and explanations about the items in the Bible such as: cubit, shekel, the covenant, etc.

66 LOGOS Discovery: These exciting stories take kids on a journey through the Bible.

75 Power Force: These action steps present biblical truths and practical Christian living kids can apply in their own lives.

51 Bible Heroes: Character studies on main Bible heroes to develop a deeper understanding of each hero.

For more information visit AirshipGenesis.com

STAY CONNECTED

· · · · · · · ·

Take advantage of two great ways to let
Dr. David Jeremiah give you spiritual direction every day!
Both are absolutely free!

① *Turning Points* Magazine and Devotional

each magazine features:

- A monthly study focus
- 48 pages of life-changing reading
- Relevant articles
- Special features
- Devotional readings for
  each day of the month
- Bible study resource offers
- Live event schedule
- Radio & television information

② Your Daily Turning Point E-Devotional

Start your day off right!
Receive a daily e-devotional
from Dr. Jeremiah that will
strengthen your walk with God
and encourage you to live the
authentic Christian life.

Request your devotions today:

CALL: (800) 947-1993
CLICK: DavidJeremiah.org/Magazine

Books Written By David Jeremiah

· · · · · · · · ·

Escape the Coming Night

Count It All Joy

The Handwriting on the Wall

Invasion of Other Gods

Angels—Who They Are and How They Help…What the Bible Reveals

The Joy of Encouragement

Prayer—The Great Adventure

God in You

Until Christ Returns

Stories of Hope

Slaying the Giants in Your Life

My Heart's Desire

Sanctuary

The Things That Matter

The Prayer Matrix

31 Days to Happiness—Searching for Heaven on Earth

When Your World Falls Apart

Turning Points

Discover Paradise

Captured by Grace

Grace Givers

Why the Nativity?

Signs of Life

Life-Changing Moments with God

Hopeful Parenting

1 Minute a Day—Instant Inspiration for the Busy Life

Grandparenting—Faith That Survives Generations

In the Words of David Jeremiah

What in the World Is Going On?

The Sovereign and the Suffering
The 12 Ways of Christmas
What to Do When You Don't Know What to Do
Living with Confidence in a Chaotic World
The Prophecy Answer Book
The Coming Economic Armageddon
Pathways, Your Daily Walk with God
What the Bible Says About Love, Marriage, and Sex
I Never Thought I'd See the Day
Journey, Your Daily Adventure with God
The Unchanging Word of God
God Loves You: He Always Has—He Always Will
Discovery, Experiencing God's Word Day by Day
What Are You Afraid Of?
Destination, Your Journey with God
Answers to Questions About Heaven
Answers to Questions About Spiritual Warfare
Answers to Questions About Adversity
Quest—Seeking God Daily
The Upward Call
Ten Questions Christians are Asking
Understanding the 66 Books of the Bible
A.D.—The Revolution That Changed the World
Agents of the Apocalypse
Agents of Babylon

To order these books, call us at 1-800-947-1993 or
visit us online at www.DavidJeremiah.org.